MARGATE CITY PUBLIC LIBRARY

8100 ATLANTIC AVENUE

MARGATE CITY, NJ 08402

(609) 822-4700

www.margatelibrary.org

1. Most items may be checked out for two weeks and renewed for the same period. Additional restrictions may apply to high-demand items.

2. A fine is charged for each day material is not returned according to the above rule. No material will be issued to any person incurring such a fine until it has been paid.

3. All damage to material beyond reasonable wear and all losses shall be paid for.

4. Each borrower is responsible for all items checked out on his/her library card and for all fines accruing on the same.

AUG   2012

DEMCO

The Food and Feasts of Jesus

Religion in the Modern World

Series Advisors
Kwok Pui-lan, Episcopal Divinity School
Joerg Rieger, Southern Methodist University

This series explores how various religious traditions wrestle with the dynamic and changing role of religion in the modern world and examines how past changes reflect on today's critical issues. Accessibly and engagingly written, books in this series will look at secularization, global society, gender, race, class, sexuality and their relation to religious life and religious movements.

Titles in Series:

The Food and Feasts of Jesus

Inside the World of First-Century Fare
With Menus and Recipes

Douglas E. Neel
Joel A. Pugh

ROWMAN & LITTLEFIELD PUBLISHERS, INC.
Lanham • Boulder • New York • Toronto • Plymouth, UK

Published by Rowman & Littlefield Publishers, Inc.
A wholly owned subsidary of The Rowman & Littlefield Publishing Group, Inc.
4501 Forbes Boulevard, Suite 200, Lanham, Maryland 20706
www.rowman.com

10 Thornbury Road, Plymouth PL6 7PP, United Kingdom

Copyright © 2012 by Rowman & Littlefield Publishers, Inc.

All rights reserved. No part of this book may be reproduced in any form or by any
electronic or mechanical means, including information storage and retrieval systems,
without written permission from the publisher, except by a reviewer who may quote
passages in a review.

British Library Cataloguing in Publication Information Available

Library of Congress Cataloging-in-Publication Data

Neel, Douglas E., 1954–
   The food and feasts of Jesus : inside the world of first-century fare, with menus and
recipes / Douglas E. Neel, Joel A. Pugh.
      p. cm.
   Includes bibliographical references and index.
   ISBN 978-1-4422-1290-9 (cloth : alk. paper) — ISBN 978-1-4422-1292-3 (electronic)
   1. Food in the Bible. 2. Food habits—Palestine—History. 3. Bible. N.T.—Criticism,
interpretation, etc. 4. Jews—Palestine—Social life and customs. 5. Judaism—History—
Post-exilic period, 586 B.C.–210 A.D. 6. Jewish cooking—History. 7. Food—Religious
aspects—Christianity. 8. Fasts and feasts in the Bible. I. Pugh, Joel A., 1949– II. Title.
   BS680.F6N44 2012
   225.9'5—dc23   2012005319

∞™ The paper used in this publication meets the minimum requirements of
American National Standard for Information Sciences—Permanence of Paper
for Printed Library Materials, ANSI/NISO Z39.48-1992.

Printed in the United States of America

Contents

Acknowledgments

This book would not have been possible without the support and assistance of a number of people. We would be remiss if we did not begin by thanking our wives, Sally and Lisa. They were patient and tolerant as we spent years researching, writing, and cooking. During that time, they ate a lot of lentils and bulgur wheat. We are grateful to a number of family and friends who read various chapters and provided us with good constructive criticism. Susan Barwick was an excellent proofreader and was indispensible while we were preparing the text. Doug's good friend Peter Schindler worked with him for several years with his catering company and prepared many of the recipes, some of which were still just lists of ingredients. A number of people attended our first-century meals, giving us the opportunity to describe what we were learning and providing valuable feedback, all while eating lamb stew.

The staff at the Bridwell Library at SMU in Dallas must be thanked. They opened the stacks to us for over a year, allowing us access to one of the best theological libraries in the Southwest and providing us with their valuable expertise. We owe a debt of gratitude to Jeoerg Rieger, Wendland-Cook Professor of Constructive Theology at Perkins. After reading three of our completed chapters and discussing the book with us, he strongly recommended that we contact a publisher and introduced us to Rowman & Littlefield. His faith in our project was both inspiring and gratifying.

An original set of drawings for the book were made by our friend Janet Brown, and they motivated us. She was well-loved by us and we were saddened by her death. The set of drawings included here are by Chris Torres, a very talented Dallas artist who took Joel's lifeless sketches and made the characters come to life.

Finally, we thank Sarah Stanton and Jin Yu from Rowman & Littlefield for shepherding us through the process of finishing and formatting a manuscript and publishing a book.

To encounter such wonderful and talented people along this journey has truly been a blessing.

Menus and Recipes

CHAPTER ONE

Why Eat the Food of
Jesus and His Followers?

The people came to Jesus and said to him, "Why do John's disciples and the disciples of the Pharisees fast, but your disciples do not fast?" Jesus said to them, "The wedding-guests cannot fast while the bridegroom is with them can they? As long as they have the bridegroom with them, they cannot fast." (Mark 2:18–19)

This is a book for those who want to study, taste, and experience the culture of the first-century Holy Land. What was it like when Jesus and his disciples shared a meal? What did they eat? How did they eat? When Jesus told a parable about a wedding feast, was he referring to a party with a three-tiered cake, champagne, and sherbet punch, with cashews and mints served in small sterling silver bowls? Jesus ate in the homes of Pharisees and other religious leaders. What was it about these settings that prompted Jesus to teach in the way he did? We have the ability to learn about the people who lived in a certain culture at a given time in history by studying the way food was produced and eaten. This is definitely true of first-century Palestine.

By studying the food and feasts described in this book and using the recipes, the reader will begin to answer these questions and discover the Palestine that was home to Jesus and the setting for most of his ministry. Our hope is that the reader will experience the food, feasts, and culture of Jesus in a variety of ways. The chapters in this book are built around the kind of meals that Jesus ate. Most of them are dinners and feasts mentioned in the New Testament. Others are ordinary meals that were shared by everyone who lived in the Holy Land. Food production and storage are also explored. Readers will also learn what foods and ingredients were available in the first century and how they were prepared. Finally, menus, recipes, and dining suggestions are provided so you can enjoy your own first-century culinary experience.

This book is designed for groups as well as individuals. Certainly individuals can read this book and learn from the cultural and culinary information that is presented. But we hope that it will also be used by all kinds of groups: prayer groups, study groups, women's groups, men's groups, neighborhood groups, book clubs, supper clubs, groups of friends, and extended families. We also hope that many of these gatherings will discuss the ideas and information we present in this book while enjoying a meal prepared using the recipes.

For thousands of years, topics great and small have been thoroughly discussed during banquets and special meals. Food and fellowship have been paired with philosophy, religion, politics, sports, and a myriad of other subjects. We hope that this book will promote this time-honored tradition and that it will generate the kinds of insights that can be reached by sharing good food.

Understanding the Foods of Jesus

History is important because it shows us who we are. First-century history is important to many of us because it shows us who we are in light of a Jewish rabbi named Jesus and his first followers.

Try to imagine what it was like to eat a meal with Jesus. The gospels are full of stories about banquets and dinners with Jesus. He must have eaten often with his disciples. We suspect that most of his meals were with the common people of Galilee. Most of those meals were plain and uneventful, though we cannot possibly imagine any meal with Jesus being uneventful. Picture Jesus sitting on a bench or squatting on the ground with friends and disciples around a small common table, tearing a piece bread and dipping it into a common pot of stewed lentils, or eating fresh and dried fruit from pottery bowls. This is quite different than our experience of eating in a dining room or breakfast nook, while sitting in well-constructed chairs around a special table. A typical first-century household included three or four generations of family: grandparents; parents; sons and their wives; grandchildren; as well as servants, hired hands, and guests. An average dinner was a community experience in and of itself! Jesus also ate at banquets and special dinners with religious leaders and the wealthier members of the communities where he visited and taught. Many of these meals were part of religious celebrations. Those dinners were especially important, much like our feasts on Thanksgiving Day when we remember both our shared history as citizens of this country and give thanks to God for blessings of family and prosperity. By learning about the foods Jesus likely ate, as well as the people he likely ate with and settings he ate in, we can enrich our understanding of the life of Jesus and how it relates to our lives today

Even a cursory glance at the gospels tells us that meals were important to first-century Jews and Christians. Feasts and celebrations that included special meals are often mentioned in the gospels. The reality is that, during this challenging economic time, many families did not have enough to eat. Psychologist Abraham Maslow believed that when people truly need it to live, the food they eat can lose cultural and religious meaning. They eat simply to stay alive. Wars and poverty were common during the first century. Excessive taxation caused many farmers to lose their land and livelihood. Social systems that guaranteed food for the poor began to fall apart. Eventually these changes resulted in a revolution against Rome. Especially among the ordinary people, the meaning of food shifted very easily and quickly from being an exalted symbol of life to being simply life sustaining. On many occasions, however, food and feasts still transcended the mundane purpose of fueling the body for work and keeping a person alive. Wedding, harvest, and religious feasts were occasions for fellowship and worship and provided the participants with symbols of life and community.

Food and Community

Can we not create communities and celebrate life while eating meat loaf and green beans? So why attempt to reproduce meals from two thousand years ago? Or why try twenty-first century food from any of a myriad of cultures with which we come into contact? Most likely Jesus would have answered the question with a story. Here is one he might have used: after Jesus told an inquisitive lawyer to go and love his neighbors as himself, a lawyer asked, "Who is my neighbor?" Who indeed? And this is how he answered:

A man was going down from Jerusalem to Jericho, and fell into the hands of robbers, who stripped him, beat him, and went away, leaving him half dead. Now by chance a priest was going down that road; and when he saw him, he passed by on the other side. So likewise a Levite when he came to the place and saw him, passed by on the other side. But a Samaritan while traveling came near him; and when he saw him, he was moved with pity. He went to him and bandaged his wounds, having poured oil and wine on them. Then he put him on his own animal, brought him to an inn, and took care of him. The next day he took out two denarii, gave them to the innkeeper, and said, 'Take care of him; and when I come back, I will repay you whatever more you spend.' Which of these three, do you think, was a neighbor to the man who fell into the hands of the robbers? (Luke 10:30–37)

The very clever lawyer answered, "The one who showed him mercy." That is how we are supposed to be neighbors, by showing mercy to the very people we like or understand the least. The truth be told, first-century Hebrews despised Samaritans. Samaritans were considered even worse than regular gentiles because they claimed to have the same faith as the Jews, except they claimed they "had it right." They were the ones who had the right version of the scriptures and worshiped in the right places and in the right ways. This made first-century Jews furious. After all, they reasoned, those Samaritans could not truly be of Jewish descent. Their bloodline seemed more of Assyria than of Moses. It was the Samaritans that had the wrong scriptures. Plus, they followed the practices of the Northern Hebrew tribes from almost one thousand years earlier and worshiped on Mount Gerizim instead of at the temple in Jerusalem. The good people of Jerusalem had been taught for hundreds of years that the people of the Northern Tribes were just a bunch of idolaters. It was common knowledge in all the best Jewish neighborhoods. And since the Samaritans claimed to be the descendents of the Northern Tribes, the same must be true of them.

Sometimes we look back on this first-century squabbling with wonder and amusement and think, "how could they fail to see and embrace their common ground?" Other times we are amazed at the parallels between those times and our times: how can *we* fail to see and embrace our common ground?

So Jesus told the lawyer that everyone was his neighbor, and especially those people he disliked the most, and that he was to have mercy on them. The reality is that, with globalization, the definition of *neighbor* is even broader today. We often have a difficult time understanding these new neighbors. Their cultures and beliefs can seem unusual. The worldview of Arabs in Saudi Arabia may mystify us. The religion of Zen Buddhists may be a puzzle. If the lifestyles of farmers in Southern Mexico with communal lands and subsistence livelihood can represent radically different values, we can only imagine trying to understand the Pygmies of Sub-Saharan Africa. Yet all these people are our neighbors, and we are to show them mercy.

The first step to being a good neighbor is to make an attempt to understand the beliefs and cultures of those who are different. Food and the traditions of eating and feasting give us a window into other cultures and help us understand them. This is as true of the past as it is of the present. One of the ways we can better understand the people of the first century is to better understand their culture. Eating their food and studying their customs and traditions is certainly a good way to help us accomplish that goal. The New Testament Gospels are full of stories about Jesus attending banquets. The epistles are saturated with discussions and arguments over food. Clearly cuisine and feasting were important to the Jews, Christians, Romans, Greeks, and everyone else of the first century, so perhaps we will gain historical, cultural, and theological insight by studying and dining on the food Jesus ate.

Food and Theology

Banquets, feasts, and other meals provide the setting for a significant amount of Jesus' teaching. A number of his parables use banquets and feasts as themes. The format and theme of many of the feasts and banquets even found their way into Christian theology and worship. Like the Jews and like the people of many other religions at that time, the early Christians literally worshiped while eating. Unless we know something about those meals, then we are certainly missing some of the meaning of the message.

The gospels tell us that Jesus was invited to dinners and banquets with a wide assortment of people, including farmers, fishermen, Pharisees, friends, tax collectors, and others. Many of these people were very common; some were quite wealthy and powerful. Likewise, some of the menus in this book are designed with the households of common people in mind and some with the image of banquets hosted by wealthy and powerful hosts. During every age there is a stark contrast between the diets of the very rich and the very poor. The first century was no different. Many of the feasts described in this book were beyond the reach of most common people. Others were enjoyed only occasionally.

Imagine the first-century home of a carpenter or fisherman and ask your guests to arrive wearing their cleanest gardening clothes. Use everyday dishes and rustic serving platters. Offer wine from jugs. Then consider the feasts Jesus shared with wealthy merchants or religious leaders. Maybe your guests should wear suits and dresses. Pull out the china and the silver if you want. Emphasize the contrast between the menus and lifestyles and realize that Jesus enjoyed the hospitality of both poor and rich alike. The difference between food for the poor and for the rich will also be explored in this book.

Food and Symbol

If we read the Bible, or for that matter other literature from the first century, we begin to realize that many things, such as numbers, climate, and clothing had symbolic meanings. If we are unaware of the meaning of the symbols, then we are missing something. With food, we actually *eat* the symbol and experience its meaning firsthand. As we describe the various feasts and present recipes, we will discuss the symbolic importance of food and of the meal itself.

For a number of years, Doug, one of the authors, served at a church in a small town outside Dallas. Each fall, a dozen or so adults met with him once a week for confirmation classes. Over a ten-week period, they studied scripture, church history, prayer, ministry, and worship, and he answered questions they had about Christianity or the Episcopal Church. He did the same thing in the spring with the youth of the church. At the end of the ten classes, students had the option to affirm their faith by being baptized or confirmed.

Confirmation services were held on a Saturday morning several times a year at the cathedral near downtown Dallas. The service was always special. People were present from all over the diocese. The bishop was there. Talented church musicians forced themselves out of bed and provided glorious music. And the adults and youth who chose to be confirmed were there, accompanied by their friends and families.

One of the great highlights of the day was lunch. Doug would announce, "Now that you are confirmed, we must eat the food that Jesus ate." Around the corner from the cathedral was an excellent Middle Eastern restaurant. The participants would pile into cars and flood into this great little restaurant. Waiters pushed together half the tables and started bringing platters of great food. They ate mahnoosh b'zaatar (flat bread topped with a paste of thyme, roasted sesame seeds, and olive oil), hummus (a dip made with chickpeas), baba ghanoush (a dip made with roasted eggplant), and stacks of warm pita bread. Next came orders of roasted lamb, plates of basmati rice topped with grilled vegetables, falafel (meatless meatballs made of fava beans and chickpeas), tabbouleh, shish kebab, and even more pita. After the feast, adults and teens alike pulled their chairs back from the table, refilled their glasses, and talked for another hour.

For everyone who experienced those feasts, the meal was an integral aspect of the entire Saturday morning event. Something important happened when they pulled those tables together, passed around platters of food, and shared the meal and good conversation. Not only did they celebrate the faith commitment made by those who were confirmed, but they also celebrated the existence of a small community that was created by the common experience of attending class week after week. But something else happened as well. The exotic tastes and textures of the food, combined with the table community, transported them to a different time and place. They could almost imagine Jesus dipping into a bowl of hummus. They could almost feel the fellowship of his small band of disciples as they shared food at the table. This might have been the setting for the story of the king's wedding feast for his son, or maybe Jesus stopped with a piece of bread halfway to his mouth and then told his friends that he was the vine and they were the branches. Was the food they ate in that restaurant really the food Jesus ate? Was the experience really that similar to a first-century feast or banquet? These are questions we hope to answer as our readers explore the contents of this book.

Using the Book and Recipes

This is not a book written for scholars and historians. It is designed for ordinary people who want to study and create the experience of first-century meals and feasts. A significant amount of research was required to write the sections on food and culture and to develop the recipes. We studied ancient treatises, food histories, documents like King Herod's will, and an ancient cookbook attributed to the Roman Apicius. We decided, however, not to fill our book with a large number of citations and footnotes. Scholars might be disappointed. For them and for anyone else who wants to know more about the topics covered, we include a bibliography in the back of the book. For everyone else, we have resorted to footnotes only for those occasions when we have directly quoted from another book or felt that additional information was absolutely necessary. We have used the New Revised Standard Version when quoting the Bible, with the exception of the psalms in the supplement to chapter 8, where we used the Episcopal Book of Common Prayer, which includes a translation of the psalms intended to be read orally. In all cases, the book, chapter, and verses are noted in parentheses after the reference or at the end of the sentence.

Almost all of the chapters focus on one type of meal or feast. Each chapter begins with historical and cultural information followed by a detailed discussion of one or more types of food. The chapter ends with suggestions for hosting the feast and recipes for a first-century meal. Menu items that have recipes in the book are marked with an asterisk (*). Of course the menus and recipes are only recommendations. Readers may use these recipes in any way desired. Some may even become family favorites. We suggest that the diners read the relevant chapter before the meal and spend at least part of the occasion discussing its contents.

When we began our research, we were hoping to discover that the Church in Corinth had published its own cookbook as a fund-raiser. Envision a first-century spiral-bound cookbook with recipes submitted by all the members of the women's guild: Aunt Prisca's recipe for Chickpea and Sesame Paste Dip on page 14. Unfortunately this cookbook does not exist. In fact, there are very few ancient cookbooks, no first-century eastern Mediterranean church cookbooks, and, for that matter, no Jewish chicken soup cookbooks either. We did find descriptions of food and drink in a number of historical documents, including the scriptures of the Old and New Testaments. Greek and Roman writers like Cato and Columella wrote treatises on agriculture and added an occasional recipe. We have also studied what historians call "secondary sources," that is, books and recipes that other writers believe were authentic to the first century. In addition, we have learned what ingredients were available to the biblical cook and have studied the cooking methods used in the first century. Based on all this information, and our own experimentation in the kitchen, we offer the recipes in this book that we have tried to make as authentic as possible.

Two thousand years ago there were good cooks, bad cooks, professional cooks, and amateur cooks just like there are today. All had access to the same cooking techniques and basic ingredients. Some had a better command of the techniques; others had a better understanding of how ingredients are combined to produce the best and most interesting flavors. Family and friends taught each other. One first-century cook might have used salt and pepper to flavor her stew of chickpeas, garlic, and onions. Another might have added a cinnamon stick or bay leaves and used lamb or chicken stock instead of water. Still another might have added chopped parsley or endive to the finished product before serving it to her family and guests. By using herbs, spices, vinegar, wine, and other flavorings available to the first-century cook, basic dishes became truly special. The reader should note that the poorest members of society, especially those who lived in larger cities, did not have access to the same variety of flavorings and seasonings. One of our goals is to help you reproduce the experience of these "good" first-century cooks.

A word of warning, except for a short primer on baking bread, this book does not teach basic cooking techniques. It assumes some level of competence, for example, that you know the difference between chopping, dicing, slicing and mincing an onion. Many good cookbooks and web pages are available that describe basic and advanced cooking techniques. We will describe methods only when we think it is necessary to help the average cook understand the recipe and prepare their own first-century meals.

Remember that the measurements and ingredients are only recommendations. If you like garlic, use more garlic. If you dislike cilantro, use parsley or another herb instead. Feel free to alter the recipes according to your taste. It was certainly the way of first-century cooks. The bread recipes are an exception. Unless you are an experienced baker, we strongly recommend that you use the ingredients and measurements in the recipes.

Chapter 2 provides a fairly complete list of foods and ingredients available in the first century. Try to use only ingredients that would have been available to the first-century cook, though you can cheat and add a pinch of sugar instead of using honey if you must. You can even add tomatoes to the bulgur and parsley salad and make a quite fine modern tabbouleh if you want. After all, it is your feast. We do suggest that you try these recipes at least once using only period ingredients so that you actually taste foods the way Jesus and his friends tasted them and save experimentation for later.

Be as authentic as you want in preparing these recipes. A friend of Doug's offered to build a bread oven for him in his back yard. He passed, at least for now. Our indoor ovens work just fine, thank you very much. You may wish to pound your garlic and chickpeas to a paste using a large wooden or stone mortar and pestle. We have used that method, but more often use our Cuisanarts. The book provides a recipe for making yogurt and cheese at home; the products at the grocery store will work as well. Though, surely everyone should make his or her own yogurt and pound garlic and chickpeas into a paste using a mortar and pestle at least once, don't you think?

Our Philosophy of Food and Dining

Food and feasts can create communities. One of the odd realities of the last century is that, as the population of our country has grown, its people have felt more and more isolated. We think back fondly to a time when our backyards were not separated by privacy fences and when our children were free to roam the neighborhood. We remember when our parents could ask several neighbors over for dinner and quickly fill the house with food and fellowship. The people of the first century instinctively understood something about the experience of dining that we seem to have forgotten. Common meals forge community. The act of dining together creates a bond between those at the meal. Everyone is equal at the table. All are served the same food. All have the opportunity to take a spoonful of mashed potatoes or add a little extra gravy to the roast beef. Each person gets a glass of tea. Equally important, everyone also has the opportunity to share.

Food is passed around the table. Host and hostess are attentive to everyone's needs. But most important, there is the opportunity for conversation and for self-revelation. It is one time when our lives should not be invaded

by televisions, computers, and cell phones. The meal may begin with compliments to those who prepared the feast. But as second helpings are passed
around the table or as dishes are cleared and dessert is being served, chairs
are pushed back and conversation becomes meaningful or, at least, more fun.
Questions about the future are asked and stories about the past are told. Lives
begin to intermingle and individual guests become a community.

Many of our actions and attitudes confirm that food and dining are important to us. We spend more money on expensive kitchen appliances and
gadgets than any people in history. Many of us have kitchens that rival small
restaurants. Bookstores dedicate entire sections to cookbooks. Restaurant
chefs have their own television network and some are international celeb-
rities. Our grocery stores are a cornucopia of fruits, vegetables, meats, and
exotic ingredients from around the world. The overarching message is clear:
cook! Cook for family and friends. Cook with fresh ingredients and make
your meals from scratch. Yet we eat at restaurants more and more frequently.
Fast food flourishes. When we do visit the grocery store, we tend to buy
prepared foods that are absolutely crammed with salt, sugar, chemicals and
preservatives. Is anyone surprised that so many more of us are overweight?
Our advice is to use that gas range, keep that convection oven busy, and
fill that refrigerator with homemade stock, fresh fruit, and vegetables. Use a
wide variety of herbs and spices to flavor your food. Keep your pantry stocked
with an assortment of cereals and grains instead of chips and candy. And for
heaven's sake, cook for your friends.

If the thought of a formal dinner party is terrifying, then do not host a formal dinner party. Simply choose a date and start calling friends. Use plastic
cups and everyday plates that can be washed in the dishwasher. If the idea of
cooking for eight adults and their children sounds daunting, then share the
responsibilities. Have one friend bring a salad, another prepare dessert or a
vegetable dish, and someone bring wine or a loaf of bread. The idea first and
foremost is to enjoy dinner for and with others. Even more, the idea is to
make community and celebrate the gift of friends and life!

The Authors

The authors share several common interests. They both love to cook and
they enjoy preparing feasts for friends and family. They are also both quite
fond of Mediterranean and Middle Eastern food. Joel Pugh has a background
in business and economics. He is especially fascinated by historical economics and the impact of food production and distribution on historical events.
Douglas Neel is an Episcopal priest who enjoys studying the relationship

between ancient culture and biblical theology. Doug owned a catering company for a number of years that specialized in preparing biblical period feasts. Both authors believe that there is much to be gained by studying the connections between food, culture, and history. Writing this book required years of studying, analyzing, cooking, tasting, writing, and editing. We hope you will enjoy our efforts.

The following chapters discuss a number of meals and feasts. We hope you use the recipes in this book to create a window to a different time and place. Our desire is that you will host one or all of these feasts for your family and friends. As part of the process of preparing this book, we did exactly that. Our banquets resulted in a common experience: a fusion of food, traditions, and teaching that transported our guests to a distant way of living and eating. We hope and pray that you have the same quality of experience.

A common kitchen contained oil lamps, storage jars, and table for food preparation and eating indoors. Families ate outdoors in good weather.

CHAPTER TWO

The Bounty of the
First-Century Kitchen

[They] brought beds, basins, and earthen vessels, wheat, barley, meal, parched grain, beans and lentils, honey and curds, sheep, and cheese from the herd for David and the people with him to eat. (2 Sam. 17:28–29)

The authors of this book both love Middle Eastern Food. We frequent the Middle Eastern restaurants in Dallas. We search out and visit Middle Eastern and Mediterranean markets. We keep on hand and use ingredients that are characteristic of Middle Eastern and Mediterranean cooking. So when we began the research for this book, both of us were quite surprised to discover that many of the ingredients that we think of as being essential to the Mediterranean diet were not available to friends and followers of Jesus.

Two thousand years ago, vegetables like corn and tomatoes may have been quite popular in the Americas, but they were not available in Europe or Palestine until the voyages of Columbus. Can you imagine tabbouleh, the popular salad made with parsley and bulgur, without the tangy acidity of diced tomatoes? Those delicious tomatoes that are enjoyed in sauces and salads around the world were still found only in the Americas. Rice, which is also an ingredient in a large number of Middle Eastern and Mediterranean recipes, had moved east from India to China and Japan and was beginning to make its way west. But it had not quite arrived in the land of Abraham, Isaac, and Jacob by the first century and certainly not in Athens and Rome by the time of Christ.

This chapter provides a summary of the different foods and ingredients available in the first century. It also gives hints on how to prepare or use certain foods. Many are discussed in more detail elsewhere in the book.

Grains and Legumes

Grains and legumes provided the largest component of the first-century diet. Grains are nutritious and can be stored for long periods. Their cultivation by prehistoric peoples was a major step in the development of civilization. Farmers in Galilee and Samaria had extensive fields of barley, wheat, and other grains, some of which was exported to cities like Jerusalem and even as far away as Rome.

These grains were mostly used for making bread, but they were also used in a wide variety of other foods. Bread was eaten at every meal, and making and baking bread was a major task in most households. The common people ate bread made from barley flour, while the more affluent ate bread that was made with wheat flour. The more refined the flour, the more it cost, and only the wealthiest could afford the white flour that was most like what we have in our grocery stores.

Today, cooks add pasta noodles or rice to give body to a soup, but first-century cooks used wheat or barley. Ground wheat and barley flours were used as thickening agents in the same way a modern cook uses a slurry of flour and water to thicken sauces and stews. Wheat berries and pearl barley were added to slow cooking stews and soups and to give substance and nutrition to a meal that had very little meat. Grains were also boiled and steamed in much the same way that we cook rice. Once cooked, they were served in a number of ways, sometimes hot as a side dish or in a salad similar to tabbouleh. Small, sweet cakes and porridge were also made with grain. Roasting freshly harvested grains over an open fire was an ancient practice long before the time of Jesus, as was the use of barley to brew beer. Beer was a common drink in Mesopotamia, Egypt, Greece, and Rome.

Legumes, like grains, were used in a variety of ways. Chickpeas (also called garbanzo beans), fava beans, and lentils were the most common. The dried beans were usually soaked and then boiled in water. The flavor could be enhanced with the addition of garlic, onions, or leeks. Sometimes they were boiled in stock, with different herbs and spices added to the pot. Cooks used legumes to make soups and stews, and they were even ground like grains and used for fried cakes or mixed with wheat or barley flour for bread. Salt and crushed pepper enhanced the flavor of both legumes and grains.

Special attention should be given to preparing fava beans. Even though favas are the most cooked bean in the world, most of us in this country are unfamiliar with them and have never prepared or eaten them. Begin, as with other dried beans, by soaking fava beans for twelve hours or longer. This will loosen the outer skin. Then after draining the beans, use your fingers to remove the tough coating. Your fava beans are then ready to cook.

Here is a list of some of the grains and legumes available to the first-century cook:

- Barley
- Chickpeas (garbanzo beans)
- Fava beans
- Garden peas
- Lentils
- Millet
- Pulse (another word for beans, especially fava beans)
- Spelt
- Wheat

Vegetables

Vegetables were eaten raw, dipped in salted water or olive oil, cooked by boiling, and used as flavorings in stews and soups. They were also added to meat and poultry dishes. However, vegetables were seasonal foods, eaten fresh only when in season. So preserving them was an important aspect of first-century food preparation.

Garlic, shallots, and onions will last a long time when stored in a cool, dark place. They can also be pickled or added to the jar when other vegetables are pickled. Pickled vegetables were served as appetizers or as part of a meal. Leafy vegetables, like mallow and bitter herbs, had to be harvested before the plants went to seed and eaten fresh before they spoiled.

Onions, leeks, and garlic were very popular in Israel, Egypt, and throughout the countries of the Roman Empire. The Romans required that *divine distinction* be given specifically to garlic. The Egyptians even considered garlic to be "among their deities."[1] Ancient records describe how the laborers who worked on the pyramids and other Egyptian monuments were given onions, leeks, and garlic as part of their pay. No wonder the Israelites missed these staples while wandering in the desert for forty years (Numbers 11:5–6).

Several of the vegetables mentioned in the Bible are difficult to identify precisely. For example, gourds are mentioned in Jonah 4:5–7. Were they similar to our squash? Squash is a favorite summer vegetable for many people in the world, and we can imagine including a number of recipes like stuffed zucchini squash simmered in a rich chicken broth for one of these feasts.

But as much as we would like to include squash, our research suggests that it was not available. The gourds mentioned in Jonah were not squash and, if botanists are right, were not even used as food.[2]

As for the bitter herbs of Passover, historical documents such as the Mishnah tell us that lettuce was the vegetable most commonly used.[3] By the first century, lettuces were being cultivated and grown in kitchen gardens but did not have developed heads like iceberg or the soft, buttery flavor of Boston lettuce. As the reference suggests, these lettuces were bitter. Lettuce still grows wild in the countryside around the Mediterranean Sea, and Bedouins continue to eat these wild, leafy, bitter greens. We suggest you use a mixture of young baby lettuces, often packaged as "spring mix." This product will include lettuces such as frisée, endive, dandelion, and red oak that are slightly bitter. Place a bowl of bitter herbs on your table so your guests can dip them in a dish of olive oil, salt water, or red wine vinegar flavored with salt, pepper, herbs, or spices.

Here is a list of some of the vegetables available to the first century cook:

- Bitter herbs (wild and cultivated lettuces), including chicory, endive, chervil, purslane, dandelion, nettles, chard, and watercress.
- Cucumbers
- Garlic
- Grape and fig leaves
- Leeks
- Mallow (a leafy vegetable related to spinach)
- Mushrooms
- Mustard greens
- Onions
- Radishes
- Shallots
- Turnips

There were other vegetables that were available in other areas of the Mediterranean and were probably available to the cook in Palestine, though we cannot be certain. Some of these, like carrots and celery, seem most likely to have been available and we will use them in a few of the recipes. Carrots were used not only for their fibrous and starchy roots, but also for the green tops. We know that certain other vegetables, like cabbage and asparagus, were popular with the first-century Greeks and Romans, but we are not certain whether they were eaten in the Middle East. Use asparagus for a special banquet and serve it with homemade mayonnaise. Yes, mayonnaise made with eggs and olive oil was available in the first century! Broccoli and cauliflower are both a variety of cabbage; actually they were developed from the flower of the cabbage. Cauliflower was eaten by the ancient Romans and probably was available in the Middle East in the first century. The history of broccoli is less certain.

Jeff Smith, the famous *Frugal Gourmet* of cookbook and television fame, claimed that the omnipresent thistles in the Middle East were related to artichokes and that an ancient cousin of the artichoke was available and was eaten in the first century. There is evidence that he was right, but that the artichokes were not as nicely developed and well formed as their modern equivalent. Artichokes are delicious. You can serve a steamed artichoke as an appetizer and use the leaves to scoop one of the dips described in this book. You may also chop or shred artichoke hearts and add them to one of the stews or salad recipes.

Here is a list of some additional vegetables that may have been available to the first-century Middle Eastern cook:

- Artichokes
- Asparagus
- Beets
- Cabbage
- Carrots
- Cauliflower
- Celery
- Fennel
- Parsnips

Fruits

Fruits and nuts also played a significant role in the first century diet. Nuts provided an important source of protein in the first century just as they do now and were served with meals as an appetizer, as an element of the dinner, or as part of the dessert. Nuts were also added to both sweet and savory foods. Try adding slivered almonds or roasted pine nuts as a garnish to one of the stew recipes in this book. Nuts ground with a mortar and pestle were used to thicken dips and sauces. Using roasted nuts instead of raw ones adds depth and character to the flavor. Nuts can be roasted in the oven or in a skillet over a burner. Roast nuts in a roasting pan at 300 to 350 degrees, stirring them occasionally. They generally take twenty to thirty minutes to roast, but cooking time depends on the amount roasted, the size of the pan, and the size of the nuts. Whole almonds take longer to roast than slivered almonds. Use the pan and burner method if roasting just a few or if roasting small seeds such as sesame seeds. Cook the nuts over medium heat stirring them so that they roast evenly. You can also sauté the nuts in butter or oil to give them a different flavor.

Unlike nuts, which can be stored indefinitely, fresh fruits were available only during harvest time. As with vegetables, storing this highly perishable food was a critical issue. How different it is today when we can find most fruits in our supermarkets every day of the year. This is true even of exotic fruits that are not grown in our country. Yet even with refrigeration, fresh fruits only stay fresh for a short period of time.

In the first century most fruits were preserved by drying. Once dried, fruits such as apricots, grapes (raisins), dates, and figs were eaten as a side dish with meals. They were also reconstituted by soaking them in hot water or by using them in stews. Special desserts were prepared by poaching dried fruit in water or wine and honey.

Fruits were also harvested for their juice. Some of the juices were consumed fresh as a special drink. Others were fermented and were consumed as a wine. Still others were boiled into a thick syrup and were used for cooking. The Bible sometimes refers to these as "honey," using the same Hebrew word as the sweetener produced by bees. Many of these syrups are available today in Mediterranean markets and some grocery stores and are frequently used in ethnic cooking. We use pomegranate molasses in some of our recipes.

Figs and dates were especially popular fruits in the first century and continue to be widely grown and eaten in the biblical lands and throughout the Mediterranean and Middle East. Like other fruits, they were eaten fresh or dried, were used to produce wine and syrup (honey), and were pressed into cakes that could be carried to work for lunch or on long trips. Like other fruits, they were added to stews and soups to give a fruity sweetness to the dish. For a special treat, dates were stuffed with cheese or ground nuts. It is difficult to imagine a first-century table without the presence of these two fruits.

Pomegranates were not only considered a delicious fruit, but were also admired for their beauty. Pomegranate designs were often used in ancient art, engraved on coins, carved into the tops of architectural pillars, and even used as a decoration on the hem of the high priest's robes. (see Exodus 28:33–34) One word of warning about using fresh pomegranates: the red juice stains are extremely hard to clean. We advise that you hold the pomegranate under water when cutting and cleaning.

The carob is an interesting fruit. Carob trees were found throughout the Mediterranean and Middle East and thrived in the semiarid climate. The seeds were used as a flavoring to sweeten wine. The flesh from the pods has a sweet flavor that is similar to cocoa and is also nutritious, providing various vitamins and fiber. The pods were used in a variety of ways. Sometimes they were added to foods to impart a sweet, chocolate-like flavor or boiled in water to make a sweet syrup. Carob pods were most often used as fodder for animals and as food for the poorest people, who used them to make porridge. Many scholars believe that the locusts eaten by John the Baptist in the wilderness (Mark 1:6 and Matthew 3:4) were actually carob pods. These pods were commonly known as "locust beans." Even though locusts were officially part of the kosher diet, carob pods were much more commonly eaten than the insect.

Olives are considered a fruit. In fact, it is the only fruit to our knowledge that was not eaten when ripe. Because the juicy, black ripe olives were used to make olive oil, only the green olives that were knocked from the tree during harvest were eaten, but not without being treated first. Raw olives, even ripe ones, are extremely firm and contain a chemical that makes them very bitter. So olives were treated in one of several ways. The most common was to soak the olives in brine, basically salt and water but with other flavorings, such as garlic and herbs and spices, added to enhance the taste of the olives. The process also leached the bitter chemical while making them softer. People ate the undeveloped green olives whole early in the spring, just as they ate green almonds.

Melons were widely available and were a popular first-century fruit. They were smaller than modern melons and had many more seeds. There were a variety of melons from which the first-century cook could choose, the fruit being quite similar to our watermelon, cantaloupe, honeydew, and musk-melons. We recommend you use melons as part of your first-century feast, especially when they are available locally.

The citron was the first citrus fruit in the Holy Land and northern Mediterranean. It is similar to the lemon in flavor, with a much stronger and bitterer taste. Citrons are difficult to find in the United States, so we use lemons in our recipes. Eventually lemons and oranges were grown in the hills of Galilee, but the date of their arrival is uncertain and their use was not widespread until later centuries.

Apples raise interesting questions. When did apples first arrive in Meso-potamia and the Middle East? And was the apple the forbidden fruit in the Garden of Eden described in the third chapter of Genesis? The Bible does not say; so, of course, scholars disagree. Most food historians believe that the references to apples in the Bible actually were referring to apricots. Apricots grew abundantly in the Holy Land and still do. Many of these same scholars believe that the apricot was the forbidden fruit in the Garden. They believe that the tasty, fragrant, golden fruit from a large, shady apricot tree better fits the biblical criteria as a tree "good for food and a delight to the eyes." (Genesis 3:6) A solid minority maintains that maybe the quince was actually the fruit of *good and evil*. However, at least one food historian writes that apples were present in Babylon and could be the infamous fruit, though the apple of antiquity was much more like our small, tangy crab apple than the shiny, sweet Fuji. Maguelonne Toussaint-Samat, in her book A *History of Food*, explains that these small fruits actually started growing in the Fertile Crescent before apricots.[4] However, it is the apple's Latin name that probably caused it to be connected to the Garden of Eden. The Romans called it a *malum*, a word that is very similar to the Latin *mal*, which means "evil." In many cultures, the apple was considered a symbol of the feminine (could this be a connection to Eve?); and in some circles, because when cut horizontally it makes a five-pointed star, or pentagram, it was connected with the knowledge of good and evil. But it still took Western Christians hundreds of years to associate the apple with the forbidden fruit in Genesis. There is no historical record of the apple being regarded as the fruit of Adam and Eve until the fifth century CE.

Here are some of the nuts and fruits available at the time of Jesus:

Nuts
- Almonds
- Walnuts
- Pine nuts
- Pistachios

Fruits
- Crabapples
- Quince
- Carob
- Citrons
- Apricots
- Figs
- Grapes
- Olives
- Mulberry
- Dates
- Pomegranates
- Melons (similar to modern watermelon, muskmelon, cantaloupes, and honeydew)
- Blackberries
- Figs

Meat, Poultry, Game, and Fish

Meat may not have been eaten often, but it was greatly enjoyed by the people living in the first century. The same was true of poultry and fish. The most commonly eaten red meats were goat and lamb. These meats were supplemented from time to time with game such as deer. Romans and Greeks were especially fond of boiled meats, while Jews preferred their meat roasted. Meat was often used in stews and soups so a small amount could feed a large family. After cooking for a time, the meat was removed from the bone and returned to the pot. The bone was crushed with a hammer and also returned. This allowed the marrow inside the bone to add flavor and richness to the broth. The first-century family typically used every part of the animal. Most parts were eaten or used to make stock. The stomach was used as a storage bag. The skins were used for clothing or storage. The intestines were a convenient package for sausage.

Poultry was also a first-century food source. The larger birds such as chickens and geese primarily provided eggs and feathers, but their flesh made for a nice feast on special occasions. When cooked, poultry was usually boiled, with the resulting broth used for soups and other foods. Birds were also roasted and grilled. The common people ate smaller birds, such as doves and pigeons, and game birds more often than chicken, ducks, or geese. Very small birds were sometimes pickled and eaten whole. The poor were allowed to sacrifice pigeons and turtledoves at the temple instead of sheep and goats (Leviticus 12:8). And just like cows and sheep, just about the entire bird was used once it was killed. Feathers became bedding. Everything else was added to the pot or fried. Sometimes birds were force-fed grains to increase their fat content and make them taste better. The very rich, especially in Rome, also ate exotic birds such as peacocks.

As often as not, chickens and other birds were kept for their eggs. An important source of protein, eggs were eaten often and were prepared in much the same way they are today: hard- and soft-boiled, fried, and scrambled. They were also used as an ingredient in other foods. For example, hard-boiled eggs were shredded and used in sauces and salads.

Pork was extremely popular and eaten throughout the world, except by Jews. First-century Jews were often derided for their refusal to eat pork. People in other parts of the Roman Empire who had little other knowledge of the Jews and their faith knew that they would not eat pork. This fact leads us to believe that even the Jews who were quite lax in following dietary and religious laws still kept the prohibitions against eating pork. Egyptians also considered pork unclean, thinking it caused leprosy, and passed laws forbidding their citizens to eat it. Unlike the Israelites, Egyptians generally ignored such laws! On the other hand, the Greeks and Romans enjoyed eating pork, and it was frequently the preferred meat for banquets. The Romans were especially fond of ham exported from Gaul (modern France). As with other meats, pork was both boiled and roasted. It was also ground and used to make sausages. The Romans and Greeks prized good sausages.

Fish was a very important part of the first-century diet. Most of the fish eaten in Israel were caught in the Sea of Galilee. Only those who were very rich or who lived near the sea had access to fresh fish, so most fish was dried and salted. When cooking, the fish was first soaked to remove most of the salt and to add moisture back to the flesh. Then it was usually added to soups and stews. The Israelites also liked their fish grilled. Typically, pieces of fish fillet or whole small fish were wrapped in fig or grape leaves and then cooked on the coals of the fire. Small fish like sardines were also pickled in vinegar or brine and eaten whole.

Those who lived by the Mediterranean Sea had access to a much-expanded variety of saltwater fish. The Romans, Greeks, and others who lived around the Mediterranean Sea not only ate many types of saltwater fish, but also had access to eels, shrimp, mussels, crabs, oysters, and other shellfish. However, like pork, shellfish and fish without scales, such as cat-fish, were forbidden to Jews by the law and were not eaten.

Here are lists of the meats most frequently eaten in Israel at the time of Jesus:

Meat

- Goat
- Lamb and Mutton
- Beef
- Ox
- Deer
- Pork

Fowl

- Chicken
- Geese
- Quail
- Partridge
- Pigeon
- Sparrow
- Turtledoves
- Eggs from all these birds

Fish from Galilee

- Tilapia
- Two species from the carp family: barbels and sardines
- A wide variety of saltwater fish and shellfish

Milk Products

Milk was an important food product. It was used as a drink and was often offered to visitors. But because it spoiled quickly in the warm Mediterranean climate, most milk was used to make other food products such as cheese, yogurt, and butter. By the first century, cheese making had become quite sophisticated. A wide variety of cheeses with many flavor variations were made to sell in the larger cities, but the vast majority of people, who lived in rural settings, ate cheeses that were typically much simpler.

Yogurt was another standard element of the Middle Eastern diet. It was similar to a soft cheese but had a creamier texture with a distinct *tang* in its flavor. It might be eaten plain, with fruit, added to other foods and sauces, or turned into a soft creamy cheese.

Butter was a secondary choice of cooks in the ancient Mediterranean world for flavoring and frying foods. Sometimes the word *butter* in ancient literature referred to a soft cheese or cream. Typically, though, it meant the same thing it means today, solid butterfat made by vigorously churning cream. Butter was then clarified by a process that removed the fatty solids and water, enabling it to be stored for an even longer period of time.

This is a list of the milk products consumed at the time of Jesus:

- Milk
- Cheese
- Yogurt
- Butter

Herbs, Spices, and Condiments

Herbs and spices have long been used to enhance the flavor of foods. Herbs are plants with flavorful leaves that are used when preparing food. When the leaves are chopped, they release an oil that makes the flavor even more intense. Herbs were used fresh and were dried. A general rule is to use three times as much of a fresh herb as when dried (one tablespoon fresh to one teaspoon dried). Spices are the other parts of plants that impart flavor and aroma. These include roots, seeds, bark, fruit, flowers, and buds. They are dried and usually crushed and pulverized before being used for food preparation.

Many of the herbs and spices listed below originated in the Mediterranean region and some still grow wild. Others gradually migrated from India and other regions and were then cultivated. Still others were native to some Mediterranean countries and not others. Herbs like oregano, basil, and rosemary grew and were used in Greek and Italian cooking, but we have no evidence that they were used in the Middle East during the first century.

Some herbs and spices were very commonplace and were universally used. Mint, parsley, mustard, dill, coriander, and cumin are examples. All of these were commonly available and used in the entire Mediterranean re-gion. Sumac is not commonly used in the United States but is a very popular flavoring for Middle Eastern food. It has a tart, almost lemony flavor, and it is especially tasty when used with poultry and fish. Try using it as a garnish on your homemade hummus. One word of warning please: do not use the red berries from domestic sumac; they are poisonous. Buy dried and ground sumac at your local Mediterranean grocery or health food store.

Other flavorings, such as saffron, were extremely difficult to harvest and were very expensive. Saffron comes from the stigmas of a flower that is a member of the crocus family. Each saffron crocus has three stigmas in its center and somewhere between 70,000 and 80,000 stigmas must be harvested for each pound of saffron. Harvesting is labor intensive with each of the stigmas collected by hand, thus the reason it is so expensive. Not only used as a flavoring for food, saffron was also used as a dye, a medicine, and as an aphrodisiac. Wealthy Romans sprinkled it on their wedding beds. And it was reportedly thrown before the feet of the Roman emperors and strewn around banqueting rooms of the rich and powerful.[5]

Here are some of the herbs and spices available at the time of Jesus:

Herbs

- Anise
- Dill
- Black coriander (nutmeg flower, fitches)
- Coriander (also called cilantro)
- Mint
- Rue
- Bay
- Parsley
- Savory
- Sage
- Thyme
- Fennel

Spices

- Cumin
- Coriander seed
- Mustard
- Pepper
- Saffron
- Cane
- Capers
- Cassia
- Cinnamon
- Sumac
- Poppy seeds
- Sesame seeds
- Carob

There were other ingredients commonly used in food preparation. Wines and vinegars were added during cooking to give additional flavor to foods and sauces. Recipes from the first century cookbook attributed to Apicius commonly call for a wide variety of wines, including honey wine, raisin wine, and wine infused with the flavor from rose petals.[6] Vinegar gave stews and sauces a characteristic tart flavor. Often vinegar and honey were added together in order to produce a "sweet and sour" taste. This combination is often used in Apicius's recipes and must have been a popular flavor combination, not only with the Romans, but also throughout the ancient Mediterranean countries.

Honey was the primary sweetener in the ancient world. As such, it was used in a wide variety of ways. Most obvious, it was used for desserts, sweet breads, and pastries. Yogurt, fresh fruit, and honey would have been a refreshing summer dish. A small amount of honey added to bread dough helped it to rise and gave a slight sweetness to the finished loaf. Several tablespoons of honey and a handful of raisins transformed the bread into dessert. Cakes had honey poured over them after they came out of the oven. But honey was also used for savory dishes. Just as a modern cook might add a pinch of sugar to a stew or vinaigrette to add balance to the food, the ancient cook used honey.

Garum, also called liquamen, seems a most unusual flavoring ingredient. It was a sauce made from dried fish that were left in brine to ferment in the sun for several months. At first mention, the sauce sounds unsavory to modern ears. But many food experts believe that the texture and flavor was very similar to the oriental fish sauce becoming more readily available in markets. Fish sauce from Thailand is called *nam pla*; from Vietnam, *nuoc mam*. The modern cook recreating ancient cuisine can use either of these products. Fish sauce was quite salty (and still is) and must have satisfied that universal craving for salty foods. Garum was especially popular and often used by the Romans. Those wealthy Jews who were the most influenced by Roman fashions and tastes would have tried and served Roman foods and flavorings like garum. These were the same Jews that sometimes mingled with Greeks and Romans at banquets, where they had to be careful not to eat unclean foods such as pork or shellfish.

Salt was extremely common both as a flavoring agent and as a preservative. It is actually not a food in the way foods have been described in this chapter, but is a mineral. Salt was just as important a seasoning for cooking in the first century as it is now. Unlike herbs and spices, it does not add fragrance to the food, but it does significantly enhance the other flavors. Salt is also essential for human life.

This is a list of some of the condiments available at the time of Jesus:

Common Condiments

- Wine
- Vinegar
- Honey
- Salt
- Garum (fish sauce)
- Meat broths

Reflections on Nutrition

As we mentioned earlier, the first-century diet could actually be quite healthy, though not necessarily, and certainly not by choice. The Bible often uses the image of *fat* as a good thing. We have seen that eating meat with fat was a luxury or a blessing, and the diet consisted mainly of whole grains and legumes. This foundation was supplemented by fresh fruits and vegetables in season and dried fruits and pickled vegetables during the rest of the year. Nuts, dried fish, and small fowl such as pigeons and doves were added to the diet to round off the meal. Olive oil was the principal fat used for cooking instead of butter. Vinegar, wine, herbs, and spices were used to add flavoring to stews and soups. This was nutritionally a very good diet, especially when supplemented by a substantial amount of exercise. The average person walked almost everywhere. Wealthy people could afford to ride on donkeys, and only the most powerful leaders and military officers had the luxury of riding horses. If this lifestyle had been coupled with modern medicine, people of the first century would have been very healthy.

Perhaps there is a lesson for us. Certainly our hearts and lungs would benefit if the vast majority of us spent more of the day walking. Ironically, current research in nutrition teaches us that we should eat a diet that is much more like the food Jesus ate: more whole grains, olive oil as the primary fat, and a lot of fresh or dried fruits and vegetables. Instead of foods packed with salt and chemicals, we should season our meals with vinegars, herbs, and spices. Meat and other foods high in cholesterol then can be enjoyed as an extravagance and a treat. Notice that processed sugar was absent from the diet entirely, as were all artificial sweeteners and flavorings.

Can you imagine children for whom raisins and dates are a special dessert? It might not be such a bad thing.

This completes the survey of ingredients for the first-century pantry. Now our task is to combine these foods and ingredients in such a way that we create feasts for our family and friends.

A wealthy landowner pays each olive laborer a silver drachma at the end of each work day.

CHAPTER THREE

Our Daily Bread

For the Lord your God is bringing you into a good land . . . a land of wheat and barley, of vines and fig trees and pomegranates, a land of olive trees and honey, a land where you may eat bread without scarcity, where you will lack nothing. . . . You shall eat your fill and bless the Lord your God for the good land that he has given you. (Deut. 8:7–10)

Not every meal is a feast. In fact, most meals are not. There are times, for special occasions, when we spend days in the kitchen and prepare multicourse banquets for friends and family. Everything is the best quality we can afford. Every recipe is for a dish that typically evokes rave reviews. In essence, we kill the fatted calf. But most of the time we eat ordinary food at ordinary meals. Maybe supper consists of a pepperoni pizza and tossed salad. Maybe we buy a roasted chicken at the local deli and add rice and steamed vegetables to make a nice weekday dinner. During the summer it might be bratwurst and corn cooked on the grill in the backyard. Six months later we sit down to a steaming hot bowl of chili and a wedge of corn bread. The food can be handmade and it might taste quite good. But it is not the same as a feast.

It will provide a helpful context if we first understand everyday cooking and food before studying and recreating first-century feasts and banquets. Just as today, an ordinary dinner two thousand years ago that was lovingly and carefully prepared was a satisfying experience. Jesus must have shared hundreds of these meals with his disciples and closest followers. We should do the same with our family and friends.

Bread is the food of emphasis for this chapter. After all, bread was the cornerstone of the cuisine in the world of Jesus and his friends. It is difficult, if not impossible to understand first-century life and culture without understanding the place of bread at the table.

Galilee of the Nations

Galilee is the setting for the everyday meal. We will join a common family, maybe a farmer, maybe a fisherman, certainly someone who could have been Joseph and Mary's neighbor. Just like Jesus, some of our meals will be with common folk; others will be with those who are quite well off, if not wealthy. Galilee is the region where Jesus spent most of his life and ministry.

A little background information about Galilee might be helpful. It was the northernmost section of first-century Palestine and home to four of the ancient tribes of Israel. It is a small region, only about thirty-five miles north and south and twenty-five miles east and west. Because it was on the northern fringes of ancient Israel, it was never completely Jewish and was occupied by an ethnically mixed population; this explains the nickname by Isaiah: "Galilee of the Gentiles." It was conquered by the Assyrians in 763 BCE and was not governed by the Jews again until eighty years before the birth of Christ. A short seventeen years later, in 63 BCE,[1] Galilee and the rest of Palestine were conquered by the Romans, though Jewish leaders continued to have authority over their people with a fair degree of autonomy from Rome.

Geographically, Galilee is divided into two regions. Southern Galilee is primarily plains and valleys and includes the great Plain of Esdraelon. The northern section is truly hill country, within the southern range of the Lebanon Mountains. Eastern Galilee borders the Sea of Galilee and the Jordan River. At the time of Jesus, around 350,000 people lived in the region of Galilee. It may be surprising to discover that the Jews were a minority, with only 100,000 in the region. The primary language in Galilee was Koine Greek, the Greek language as it was spoken in the Eastern Mediterranean countries, with most of the Jews speaking both Greek and Aramaic. The Jews in Galilee lived quite a long way from Jerusalem. Mary and Joseph's home in Nazareth was approximately seventy miles from Jerusalem, requiring a three- to four-day journey by foot. Nazareth is almost in the middle of Galilee, so Jews in Northern Galilee had to travel even a greater distance to reach their holy city. Because of the distance from the temple, the Jews in Galilee were known for being lax in the practice of their religion, including their attendance of major festivals. Surrounded by Gentiles, speaking Greek, lax in religion, rarely taking time to visit the temple in Jerusalem, no wonder Galilean Jews had such a bad reputation among their southern brothers and sisters. When Philip told him that the Messiah was from Nazareth, Nathaniel responded, "Can anything good come out of Nazareth?" (John 1:46) Nathaniel's question to his friend Philip certainly made sense to a first-century Jew.

The region truly reflected the meaning of the reference from Deuteronomy that begins this chapter. It was a "good land," especially when it received the average annual rainfall or above. Terraced farms and orchards covered much of the land. The plains were blanketed with grass for grazing animals and grains for bread. Olive orchards, grape vineyards, and groves thrived in the moist northern hill country. The fishing industry flourished around the Sea of Galilee. Streams and rivers from all over the region ran into the Sea and Jordan River and provided water for crops.

Somewhere between 80 and 90 percent of the people in Galilee were directly involved agricultural work.[2] Livestock, olives, and grapes were their chief products. Olive oil, wine, fish, and grain were all exported and brought income into the region. In addition, several major international trade routes passed through Galilee on the way from the areas of modern Iraq, Iran, and India to the Mediterranean Sea. From there, spices and other exotic exports were shipped to Rome, Greece, and Egypt. Taxes and tolls were collected from the caravans and helped provide money for extensive building programs—including baths, gymnasiums, theaters, coliseums, and entire new cities. Biblical scholars wonder if the disciple Matthew was this kind of tax collector, taking tolls and taxes from caravan merchants.

The little town of Nazareth was located only four miles from Sepphoris, one of the cities that benefited from this wealth. Approximately 45,000 people lived in Sepphoris, and new grand homes and public buildings constantly were being built during the first century. Scholars wonder if this is where Joseph did most of his carpentry work. It is certainly possible that Joseph and a young Jesus walked into Sepphoris each morning and spent the day working on different construction projects. Our suspicion is that most of the skilled craftsmen in that vicinity dedicated at least part of their careers to the building boom in Sepphoris.

Standard First-Century Diet

When we tell people we are writing a book about first-century food and feasts, the first response we receive is a look of pity. Apparently most people believe that Jesus lived some ten thousand years earlier, during the time of hunter/gatherers. After all, how many recipes for gruel and pottage can there be? In all truth, if we carefully consider the historical evidence, we discover that first-century Mediterranean culinary life was highly evolved. The first-century cook had access to the large variety of vegetables, grains, herbs, and spices that we described in chapter 2. They were capable of making delicious breads and sophisticated sauces. What they did not have were modern methods for storing and preserving food. Remember that two thousand years ago there were no refrigerators or freezers, no canned goods, no prepackaged foods, and certainly no frozen TV dinners.

Despite some similarities, there are many differences between the first-century diet and a modern one, and in many ways, the first-century diet was quite healthy. The largest part of their diet consisted of foods made with grains and legumes. In fact, well over 50 percent of their calorie intake came from grains and legumes. Wheat, barley, and other grains were significant crops for the Middle East, and grains found their way into breads, stews, porridges, and other dishes. Legumes, especially chickpeas, lentils, and fava beans, were dried and used as a staple throughout the year. During years of bad harvest or famine, when the supply of grain fell short, dried beans were ground into a powder and were added to the flour for making bread.

Grains and legumes sustained the common people when most vegetables and fruits were out of season. Leafy vegetables had to be eaten fresh while they were in season. Others could be pickled. We forget about the seasonal nature of vegetables. Because of refrigeration, freezers, greenhouses, and the swiftness and openness of national and international trade, we purchase whatever vegetables we want, whenever we want. This is both a blessing and a curse. It is a blessing when we crave a tomato salad in January. By January in Texas or Colorado, tomatoes are very much out of season. Yet our markets have tomatoes that are grown in greenhouses in the United States or shipped from South America. They do not have the quality and intensity of flavor of the locally grown tomatoes we buy during the summer, but they are tomatoes. If we shun these hothouse fruits then we can always turn to canned tomatoes, another option not available two thousand years ago. Canned fruits and vegetables are also a blessing. But they can also be a curse: most of us have become very accepting of inferior-tasting vegetables and fruits. We tolerate tomatoes without the sweet acidity of the vine-ripened product, just as we endure starchy corn or tasteless melon. There is a movement in this country that is demanding high-quality, locally grown produce. We approve, of course, unless we are craving tomatoes in January.

The other half of the curse is that we have lost the sense of the *specialness* of the harvest. What was it like two thousand years ago, or even two hundred years ago, when local farmers harvested their crops and brought them into the local market for sale? The community celebrated and everyone feasted on fresh and delicious produce. They recognized the connection between the seasons, the right weather, hard work, God's blessing, and a good harvest. We lose the need to celebrate and be thankful if the same product is on the grocers' shelves every day of the year.

Even though many vegetables and fruits had to be eaten while they were fresh, many others were dried or pickled with vinegar and spices. Ancient cooks knew that exposure to moisture and air caused food to spoil. They also discovered that moisture could be extracted from foods by laying them in the sun and using salt to extract the water. Drying vegetables, legumes, fruits, meats, and fish in this way enabled them to keep the food for months or longer if stored in a cool, dry place. Figs and apricots are examples of fruits that were often dried and eaten later. Likewise, raisins are dried grapes and were found in a bowl on the table or as part of a recipe for a savory stew or a sweet cake. Moisture was also added back to dried meats, fish, and fruits by soaking them in hot water or some other liquid before cooking. Then they were used in the same way as fresh foods.

Pickling such foods as vegetables and small fish protected them from water and air by completely submerging them in brine or vinegar. The pickled foods were made even more flavorful by adding seasonings such as garlic, dill, cumin, coriander, and other herbs and spices. Platters and bowls of pickled vegetables and dried fruits were often served as part of a special meal.

As one might expect, there were significant differences between the diets of the very rich and the vast majority of average people. One of the major differences was the access to meat. In the first century average people rarely ate meat with their meals. Another difference was the availability of some of the more exotic spices and flavorings. A number of herbs and spices came from plants that grew wild or were easily cultivated. Others were not so easy to come by, especially in rural areas, and were imported from Babylon (the area of modern-day Iraq) and some spices even came from as far away as India.

The First-Century Kitchen

We cannot emphasize enough the challenge of cooking and storing food for the first-century cook. Just imagine no electricity, no gas, no side-by-side refrigerator/freezers, and no self-cleaning ovens. None of the appliances that we take so much for granted existed in the first century. Preparing food for cooking and storage was a major occupation of almost every ancient family.

Most people in the first century lived in towns and communities and not in isolated homes. Even the farmers and shepherds lived in settlements and walked into the fields to farm or take care of their flocks. Families typically used their courtyards, located toward the front of their house, or a large open room that was often shared with the family livestock as their kitchen space. The fire was built on a brazier, or large curved metal plate. During bad weather, the brazier was moved and the meal was prepared inside the home instead of in the courtyard. Can you imagine walking into a small town just before dinner and smelling everyone's dinner being prepared in their courtyards? All the neighbors would know exactly what you were serving for dinner.

Mediterranean and Middle Eastern cooks used a variety of tools to prepare their meals, including mixing bowls, pots, kettles, and casseroles for stewing, braising, boiling water, and deep-frying. Some of the cooking vessels had a narrow opening on top to keep the water from evaporating and escaping during cooking. These pots were ideal for making soups and porridges and were used to cook beans and lentils. First century casseroles were similar to a pottery Dutch oven. Baking pans and even pans designed to bake an egg pie similar to quiche were common in Italy and Greece and were beginning to appear in Middle Eastern kitchens during the lifetime of Jesus.[3]

Most cooking vessels were pottery, though some of them, especially those used by wealthier families, were made of metals such as copper or bronze. We know that metal pans are much better conductors of heat than clay pots, but pots and pans made of materials like copper were very expensive, just as they are today, and were well beyond the means of the average family. Pots and pans were made by professional potters and metal workers and were made to standard sizes, as they are today.

The home cook at the time of Jesus also had griddles for frying breads and meats. Griddles were constructed of some type of metal such as iron or copper. Cooks used kitchen aids and utensils such as mixing bowls, strainers, mortars and pestles, funnels, cooking and serving spoons, and knives. The first-century cook even had a utensil similar to a modern fork that they used for cutting and serving meat.

Dinner with the Family

Creative and even gourmet foods can be prepared in the open air by using only wood or charcoal as fuel. But imagine preparing every meal in this manner. Breakfast and lunch were always simple meals, consisting perhaps of leftovers from the previous evening: cheese, maybe a handful of olives and raisins or pickled vegetables or maybe simply bread and milk. But always bread. The primary meal of the day was in the early evening. The evening meal might be the only one for a poor family. The *denarius* was considered a day's wages for a laborer. It just so happened that dinner for a large household costs around one denarius. If the men of the household were day laborers, then it was extremely important that they find work for the day or everyone in the family went hungry.

Dinner was a family meal and the family was a community in and of itself. Not only did it consist of a number of generations of those related by ties of blood or marriage, the family also included slaves, servants, and foreigners who lived in the village and became connected to that particular household. Families also had a role as a religious community. They were the fundamental organization that preserved traditions and passed them to new generations through instruction and worship. Yet biblical period families suffered from pressures similar to those we face today. Forces such as political and economic changes, as well as cultural and social order transformations can play havoc with family life and structure. Such was the case in the first century. Jewish families lived in occupied lands. They were subject to extensive taxation. Their culture and religious traditions and structures constantly were being challenged by the presence of Greek and Roman values and society. Some teachers and religious groups within Judaism were demanding radical reforms. Others called for open rebellion. After the death of Jesus, the country was plagued by civil war, resulting in the devastation of Jerusalem and the temple. The destruction of the temple ultimately led to significant shifts in the ways Judaism was practiced and God was worshiped. Strong family networks helped those living in the Middle East survive a time of upheaval. Still, these external forces placed great stress on family systems.

How did these families eat? Our common family in Galilee gathered around one or more small wooden tables and most likely sat on benches, stools, and chairs. Some families might have reclined, though for most Jews, reclining was reserved for special meals. The poorest families probably squatted on the ground around a common bowl on a low table. All the furniture had to be portable and was moved after the meal so the space could be used for work during the day. Bowls of food to share, plates of bread, and cups and goblets for the wine were placed on the tables. Bread was an appetizer, dipped into olive oil and then into herbs and spices. And remember, the bread also served both as eating utensil and as a napkin. Family members ate with their hands or scooped stews and vegetables with pieces of bread. Bread was used to "sop up" broth, sauces, and gravies as the meal ended.

Typically, the women of the family served the meals. Remember the story of Peter's mother-in-law? After being cured of fever, she served dinner to Jesus and his disciples (Mark 1:29–31). The story might seem odd to us. We would expect someone recovering from an illness to rest and be the center of attention. But the message of the story was clear: the cure was so complete that she was able to immediately resume her functions within the family unit. And in that case, her tasks included an act of thanksgiving by serving an honored guest, Jesus (Matthew 8: 14–15, Mark 1:30–31, Luke 4:38–39). So Peter's mother-in-law, like the other women in the household, served the food and then joined the meal.

As one might expect, wealthier families were the exception to many rules. The women in a wealthy family could afford to have dinner brought to the table by a slave or servant. There was a saying recorded in the Mishnah:

> If [a wife] brought in one bondswoman [as dowry] she need not grind or bake or wash; if two, she need not cook or give her child suck; if three, she need not make ready his bed or work in wool; if four she may sit [all the day] in a chair.[4]

Did the Galilean families strictly observe kosher regulations? We will address the whole subject of kosher regulations in another chapter. But the issue should also be considered to some extent within the context of Galilee. Historical evidence tells us that Jews were quite strict in avoiding at least some of the foods explicitly forbidden by their scriptures, especially pork. But they were also forbidden to eat most fowl; catfish and other fish that do not have scales; and shellfish, such as shrimp, lobster, and oysters. How strict were they at avoiding these foods? And what about some of the other regulations? The law stipulated that all of the blood must be drained from the meat before it was cooked. It also was interpreted to require that milk-based foods and meats were not to be served at the same meal. Did the Galilean Jews follow these practices? We know that Galileans were lax in other practices. They did not always follow the rules for washing before meals and were notorious for failure to pay the temple tithe. We suspect that they may also have been just as lax following the dietary laws, at least some of them.

Bread; the Staff of Life

In her book A History of Food, Maguelonne Toussaint-Samat refers to three food products as the "fundamental trinity" because of their impact on Western civilization.[5] We join Toussaint-Samat in calling bread, olives, and wine the *holy* trinity of food. Olive oil and wine are discussed in later chapters. Toussaint-Samat goes on to say that food "is a doubly divine gift: the gift of skill given to mankind, and brought to bear on the fruits provided by nature."[6] The ancient Israelites certainly would have agreed. Bread was God's gift of both the earth for growing grain and skill for baking. Moreover, bread was considered essential for life: "the essentials for life are water and bread and clothing and a house to cover one's nakedness" (Sirach 29:21).

For rich and poor alike, bread was the heart of the first-century Mediterranean diet. It was made every day. It was eaten at every meal. It was simply the most important food product of the entire biblical period and continued to be the most important food for centuries to follow. It was so important that it was included in the religious rituals of almost all the Mediterranean religions, including Judaism and Christianity. When Jesus told the crowd and his disciples, "I am the bread of life," he was using an extremely powerful image, much more powerful than the modern image of the loaf of soft, inexpensive bread in a plastic wrapper that we find in the grocery store today. Bread was what people ate to live. In essence Jesus was saying, "The message I give you is nothing less than the message you need to live." During times of famine, long after all the meat and vegetables were depleted, the people still were making and eating bread. When the bread was gone, everything was gone.

For the people of the ancient world, bread making was a miracle. Thousands of years before Jesus, the wives of farmers and shepherds made flat bread with dough from flour and water. In the arid world of much of the Middle East, the amount of yeast existing naturally in the air is quite significant. One can imagine that one of these women made a mistake and waited too long before baking her bread. The dough began to grow and bubble with life from the yeast in the air. Fearing the wrath of her family when there was no bread with dinner, she baked the dough anyway. What a surprise when it tasted so much better than the dry, cracker-like unleavened bread she usually made, and a gift was given to civilization, literally from thin air. Eventually the same wife and perhaps some of her friends reasoned that they could separate a portion of the risen dough from the rest and mix it with the next day's flour and water, causing the leavening action to begin much faster. That was the common practice by the time of Jesus.

The typical household had someone designated to make the bread. That person was a wife or daughter unless the family was wealthy enough to have slaves or servants bake the bread. She saved a small amount of dough the day before and carefully stored it and used it as the leaven for the next day's bread. She would light the fire in the bread oven and then begin the task of grinding wheat for flour, making the dough, and mixing in the leaven from the previous day. Once the oven was hot and the fire had burned down, she would sweep out the coals and ashes and replace them with the dough. The oven was warmed to around 800 degrees. The other women in the household spent the day tending the garden, and preparing foods for the evening meal.

Because of its culinary importance, bread was made every day, except on the Sabbath. Jewish families made twice the amount of bread on Friday so they had enough for Sabbath meals. Most of the homes in the towns and settlements had bread ovens. Neighborhoods in the cities had community bread ovens. Bread was also fried on an iron griddle, just as it still is today in some areas of the world. In earlier times, before the bread ovens, the dough was placed on a flat rock and covered with hot coals. The coals were removed halfway through the baking cycle and the bread was turned. Then the coals were replaced.

Bread was used as an eating utensil to scoop beans and grains and absorb sauces and gravies. It was also used as a napkin. Diners wiped the grease and sauce from their hands with a clean piece of bread and then dropped the soiled bread on the floor to be eaten by the family dogs. Can you picture this in your dining room? We can imagine that these dogs were actually quite well fed, eating bones and scraps along with the soiled bread. When the Canaanite woman said to Jesus that even the dogs eat the crumbs from the table, she was talking about some pretty substantial crumbs (Matthew 15:27). Certainly this picture is different from the image of the crumbs under our dinner table. Unless you have a two-year-old child who is just learning to eat, your pets would starve if they lived off of the crumbs from your tables. The Canaanite woman was referring to something more substantial in terms of her request from Jesus. "There is enough bread on the table that you throw entire pieces on the floor after wiping your hands," she was saying. "Surely you have enough left over from the bounty of your ministry to your own people to help my sick daughter?"

Eating bread was a common experience that united all the people of the Roman Empire. But the type of bread eaten clearly separated people into their various classes. The poorest and most common folk ate bread made of barley. Successful merchants and wealthy farmers made their bread from wheat. Some could afford bread made by their own slaves and servants. City dwellers baked their bread in community ovens or bought it at the market.

Only the wealthiest and most powerful families ate white bread made from the most refined wheat flour. Isn't it curious that, in the final analysis, the wealthiest people ate the bread that was the least healthy?

Ancient Middle Eastern bread was much like it is today. Most of the bread was large and fairly flat. Perhaps the Jews were introduced to leavened bread in Egypt. Certainly they were exposed to it by the Canaanites when they came into the Promised Land. Twelve hundred years later, by the time of Jesus, bread making had become quite sophisticated. The Egyptians, Greeks, and Romans had access to a wide variety of types of bread, and to some extent, so did the Jews. Those who lived in large cities had the option of buying their bread from professional bakers. And for the wealthy there was not only bread of good quality, but also a wide variety. There was Cappadocian milk bread baked in molds and "boletus," a loaf that was shaped like a mushroom with poppy seeds on top. There were plaited loaves, square loaves, rustic breads, flat breads, whole-grain breads, rye breads, and dark bran breads.

Unleavened Bread

The Jews most likely ate unleavened bread back when they were nomads before making their way to Egypt. Unleavened bread is made with just flour and water and perhaps a little salt, and is cooked before it has time to attract yeast and rise. The taste and texture were much more like crackers than our idea of bread. Nomads in the Middle East have continued that practice of making unleavened bread down through history. Even after the advent of leavening, unleavened bread continued to play a role in Jewish life and worship. Only unleavened bread was offered in sacrifice in the temple in Jerusalem.[7]

The use of grains was quite important to the Jewish sacrificial system of worship. Grains and unleavened bread were often offered along with an animal sacrifice. This offering was called a *cereal offering* and typically was burned on the altar in a sacrifice of thanksgiving for the grain harvest. But why not offer regular leavened bread to God? Standard bread certainly was readily available and tasted better, not that God actually tasted the foods that were sacrificed in the temple. None of the surrounding nations and peoples had religious qualms about offering regular, leavened bread at their temples. Scholars really do not have an answer. Perhaps it was because unleavened bread, with its connection to the Passover event in deliverance of the Jews from slavery in Egypt, played such an important role in Jewish history and worship. Other scholars believe that yeast, with its ancient relation to Canaanite culture, especially wine and beer making, was considered unworthy as an offering to God. These connections might have meant something to the Hebrews some 1,200 years before Jesus, but would have been lost by the first century. By then, they used unleavened bread primarily because of tradition and God's commandment.

Unleavened bread was and is the bread of Passover. It was also eaten for the following week during the Feast of Unleavened Bread. In doing so, that simple exercise of eating bread invoked a corporate memory that took them back thousands of years to a time when they were nomads and unleavened bread was the norm. And it helped them remember that pivotal night in Egypt when death passed over their ancestors and they passed from slavery to freedom.[8]

At the Last Supper, Jesus reinterpreted the Passover Event in light of his own situation. He used bread to reinterpret a meal that remembered the past so that it would have an impact on people's lives in the present. He did this by giving thanks for the bread and saying, "This is my body, which is given for you. Do this in remembrance of me" (Luke 22:19, I Corinthians 12:24; see also Matthew 26:26, Mark 14:22).

Bread as a Symbol
Bread was a symbol of life. When Jesus asked God to "give us our daily bread," he was asking for the things needed for survival. Moreover, a family without bread was a family in dire circumstances, with no food at all. Bread was also a symbol of something that was "universally present" as with the phrase from Isaiah, "the bread of adversity and the water of affliction" (Isaiah 30:20). It was also used as a metaphor for the coming of God's kingdom: "Blessed is he who shall eat bread in the kingdom of God." Quite frankly, it is a metaphor that still resonates with us today. We relish the idea of sitting at a banquet table and sharing good bread and delicious food with all the other people of God.

Bread was also a symbol of hospitality. Many meals and especially feasts and banquets began by blessing, breaking, and sharing a loaf of bread. People in the ancient world understood intuitively that broken bread was a symbol of food that was to be shared with family and friends. And sharing food with guests and even strangers was an extremely important aspect of Middle Eastern culture. Hospitality was a cardinal virtue. As the Letter to the Hebrews taught, "Do not neglect to show hospitality of strangers, for by doing that some have entertained angels without knowing it" (Hebrews 13:2). For early Christians, the phrase "breaking of bread" came to be synonymous with worship. Breaking bread as a sign of human hospitality became for the young church the symbol of God's hospitality as well.

There were several food prayers at a special Jewish meal, a prayer at the beginning of the meal offered in connection with the bread, and a prayer at the end of the meal offered with the wine. These prayers emphasize the importance of both of these food types. The prayers thanked God for the gift of the earth that makes grain and grapes possible. But God was also thanked for the talents of the farmer, winemaker, miller, and baker who were able to take advantage of God's creation and use their skills to make bread and wine.

How to Eat a First-Century Dinner with your Family

Set the table with all of the food at once. Choose one of the dining postures mentioned above, including reclining or sitting on the floor. Because the first-century household was both large and diverse, try to share this meal with friends and neighbors. It is authentic if they eat from several common bowls, though your guests may prefer to have their own plate and a soup bowl. Eating utensils can be optional for you. Place them on the table, or wait to offer spoons only *after* your guests notice the absence of flatware. A rule: do not run out of bread. Napkins were not an option; nor were plates. We are truly the product of a more refined time. We want our private space and our own food. And we are concerned with cleanliness and germs. Your table will be covered with bowls of food. This may be an everyday meal, but it is a delicious and abundant everyday meal. Remind your group that day laborers might have eaten the soup, bread, and little else.

The host should start the meal with this simple prayer while holding a loaf of the bread:

Blessed are You, Lord, our God, King of the Universe who brings forth bread from the earth. (Amen)

You may then add an additional prayer of thanksgiving for the meal and the occasion of fellowship. After the prayer, tear the loaf of bread in half and pass the pieces around the table. Family and guests should tear their first piece of bread from this one loaf. The symbolism of *sharing* and *community* should be obvious to everyone. Broken bread represents a meal that will be shared. Then the meal begins. We recommend that you do not serve dessert at this meal; though, if possible, seasonal fruit can be served.

It is appropriate to serve wine, water, or milk with the meal. Coffee and tea were still many centuries away from arriving to the Mediterranean countries. Iced beverages were still unknown in much of the world; only the

Emperor and a few extremely rich and powerful Romans had occasional access to ice in the first century. Many Gentiles drank beer, but our research shows that the Jews did not.

Menu for a Daily Meal with Family

- Mediterranean Grain Bread*
- Feta cheese (from the market)
- Yogurt* (two recipes or from the market)
- Yogurt Cheese*
- Soft Cheese* (this recipe or from the market)
- Hummus*
- Bowls of Olives and Raisins* (olives in chapter 4; raisins in chapter 7 or from the market)
- Pickled Onions*
- Cucumber and Cheese Salad*
- Lentil and Chickpea Soup*
- First-Century Chicken Stock*
- Fresh or dried fruit (from the market)

The Recipes

Instructions for Baking the Bread Recipes in This Book

Bread can be a joy to bake. The smell of baking bread fills your house with the most amazing and inviting perfume. Watching a mass of dough and water rise and turn into delicious brown loaf is fulfilling. And the loaf you made yourself always seems particularly tasty. For the beginner, however, the idea of making bread can be daunting. We are offering several suggestions that should make the experience more rewarding.

We use a heavy-duty kitchen mixer (KitchenAid) with a dough hook to make our bread. Of course you may make the dough without this or any other machine. It simply assists with the initial process of mixing and kneading the dough. If you use an electric bread machine, we suggest that you remove the dough after the first rise cycle and finish the bread by hand. Be forewarned that we both wore out several bread machines before switching to the mixers.

The bread recipe in this chapter is our standard and can be used with all the menus in this book. Even though first-century cooks used starters that consisted of dough from the previous day, we suggest you use yeast, especially if you are a beginner. These recipes recommend fast-rising dry yeast. We use either Red Star or Fleischmann's fast-acting yeast and have used both for years with good results. If you want to bake a loaf that uses a starter, then try the recipe for Barley and Wheat Bread in chapter 7.

Yeast is a living organism that feeds on starches and sugars. As the yeast feeds, there is fermentation, and carbon dioxide is released. This gas is trapped in the dough creating small bubbles. The gas bubbles are what cause the bread to rise. However, you should be aware that salt kills yeast. Make sure, as you start your dough, that you keep the salt and yeast separate. If not, you will be very dissatisfied with the way your bread rises.

Use exact measurements. Use *dry* measuring cups to measure the dry elements, like the flour, and *liquid* measuring cups for the liquids. When measuring flour, we use a smaller measuring cup to fill the larger one so that the flour is not compacted by scooping with the larger cup. Then we use a chopstick or the back of a knife to scrape across the top of the cup to remove the excess.

We tell you to use exact measurements, and now we warn you of exceptions. Factors beyond your control, like the weather and humidity, can impact your dough. If it is raining outside, you may need to use a little extra flour. If you are experiencing a drought, you may need more water. With a little experience, you will know after a few minutes of mixing or kneading whether to add more flour or a little more water. The dough should be spongy to the touch. If the dough is dry and hard, add more water. If the dough is too sticky, add more flour. Leave the dough alone if it is only slightly sticky and spongy. Add only small amounts of flour and water at a time when making adjustments.

The temperature will also impact the speed that your dough rises. The ideal room temperature for the dough to rise is 80 degrees. If your kitchen is cooler, the dough will rise slower and may need an extra twenty or so minutes. The process can be accelerated if the dough is placed in an oven for the first rise. Turn your oven on "preheat" for one minute. Then turn it off and it is ready for your dough.

For these recipes, we recommend that you cook the bread directly on a pizza stone, on oven tiles or on a baking sheet. Again, we recommend that if you use the baking sheet that you have heavy-duty industrial aluminum pans. The thin cookie sheets you might have purchased years ago at a grocery store typically do not heat evenly and will not stand up under the high temperatures required for making this type of bread. Cheap pans will also cause your bread to bake unevenly and burn on the bottom.

Always cool your bread on a rack for several hours before cutting and eating. If you do not have a cooling rack, you can use a rack taken from the oven or the grate over the burner of a gas stove. Bread left to cool on a flat surface will be soggy on the bottom. We know from personal experience that you will be sorely tempted to eat your bread as soon as it is taken from the oven. However, the bread will still be cooking and forming on the inside. Fight temptation and wait. If temptation is too great, then wait at least fifteen to twenty minutes. Your bread will continue to give off moisture for another six to eight hours. We suggest you leave the bread on a rack or store it in paper sacks during this time. This process is called *curing* the bread. After eight hours, your bread can be wrapped in plastic without the crust becoming soggy. It will remain delicious for days and will keep for a week. If you wrap your bag in plastic before it has time to cure, then the excess moisture trapped inside will cause the bread to mold in a couple of days.

Mediterranean Grain Bread

This bread was developed by Joel for this book and is absolutely delicious. Doug used it for the catering business and it always receives rave reviews. For a crustier bread, use only water (2½ cups) and not milk, do not use butter, and use 3 tablespoons of olive oil instead of 2. Use a grain mix that is made up primarily of whole wheat and barley that is ground to the size of couscous. We often use Bob's Red Mill 10 Grain mix because it is readily available at most markets. Do note that it contains several grains, such as corn, that are not authentic to first-century Palestine.

1 tablespoon yeast	2 tablespoon butter (soft or melted)
1½ cup warm water (apprx. 110°)	2 tablespoon olive oil
6 cups unbleached flour	1½ tablespoon honey
1 cup whole grain mix	1 cup milk
1 tablespoon salt	

Place the yeast and warm water in the bowl of your mixer. Wait until yeast begins to activate, approximately 15 minutes. It will change color and begin to bubble. Add the flour and the grain mixture. Then add the rest of the ingredients. Add the oil first and use the same tablespoon to measure your honey. The oil will keep the honey from sticking to the measuring spoon.

Mix with the dough hook for five minutes. Start on the slowest speed to keep the flour from splashing out of the bowl and then increase the speed to medium slow. Let the dough rest for 15 minutes and then mix for another 5 minutes. The dough should be slightly sticky and springy to the touch. Add flour 1 tablespoon at a time if the dough is too sticky or water if it is too dry.

Turn the dough out onto a floured surface and knead for about 30 seconds. Place in an oiled bowl and cover with a cotton kitchen towel or oiled plastic wrap. If your KitchenAid bowl is large enough, you can leave the dough in the bowl to rise. Punch down and knead by turning the machine on low for 1 minute. Let rise until it has doubled in size, about 1 hour at 80° (1½ hours at 65°).

After rising, turn out the dough onto the floured surface again, punch down with your fingers to allow the gases to escape and knead for about 1 minute. Form the dough into 4 loaves about 6–8 inches in diameter and 1–1½ inches thick in the center. Lightly spray baking sheets with cooking oil and place the loaves on the sheets. Cover with the floured towel and let rise for another hour. After 40 minutes, preheat the oven to 400°. Cook your bread on a rack in the center of the oven for 20–25 minutes.

Remove bread and let it cool on a rack for at least 2 hours. Makes 4 small loaves.

Joel likes to let his bread rise the second time, after he has formed the loaves, directly on a cold pizza stone. He then cooks the bread for 25 minutes at 400°. This method works very well. Another alternative, the dough formed into loaves can rise on a floured pizza paddle (or another piece of wood used for that purpose). After rising, slide the dough onto a preheated stone.

Yogurt I

We have included two recipes. One is very similar to the way yogurt was made almost two thousand years ago. The other involves the use of as starter and is a little more fool proof.

1 quart milk

Pour the milk into a saucepan and bring to 180° in order to scald. Remove from the heat, pour into a glass bowl, and allow it to cool to a warm temperature (110°). Stir in 1 tablespoon of unpasteurized plain yogurt. Cover with a kitchen towel and place in a warm location, such as the oven of a gas stove or in an electric oven that has been preheated only for one1 minute. Do not disturb the yogurt and allow it to stand for 10–12 hours. Then refrigerate your yogurt and eat it cool.

Yogurt II

This recipe is based on one from Ricki Carroll's book, Home Cheese Making; Recipes for 75 Homemade Cheeses. *We are big fans of Ricki Carroll, her book, and cheese supply store. We have tried many of the recipes, making mozzarella, ricotta, farmer's cheese, farmhouse cheddar, chevre, and this recipe for yogurt. All have been great successes. You must check her web site www.cheesemaking.com to learn more about making your own cheese. It is fun and easy.*

   1 quart milk
   ¼ cup dry powdered milk, optional to make thicker yogurt
   1 packet yogurt starter

Combine the milk and powdered milk in a stainless steel saucepan and heat to 180°. Let the milk cool to 116° then add the starter and mix.

Keep the pan covered and the temperature at 116 for at least 6 hours or until it is the consistency of thick cream. The pan and milk will stay close to temperature in a warm oven. After 6 hours, place in a clean container and refrigerate, covered. Yogurt will last up to 2 weeks.

You can keep a tablespoon of this yogurt and use it to make the recipe for Yogurt I.

Yogurt Cheese

You will certainly taste the first century when you spread a bit of this creamy cheese on a piece of homemade bread. Yogurt cheese will have the consistency of cream cheese with significantly less butterfat and a sharper flavor. Try rolling the finished product in herbs or spices before serving. Dill, coriander, parsley, cumin and sliced roasted almonds are all excellent. Minced garlic is always good, as is lemon zest to add a nice bright taste.

    2 cups yogurt, or any amount, homemade or plain yogurt from the
       market

You will need cheesecloth, string, a colander, and a bowl to make yogurt cheese. Cut a large piece of cheesecloth and place it in your colander. Spoon the yogurt in the center of the cheesecloth. Pull the corners of the cheesecloth up over the yogurt and tie them together. Hang the cheesecloth and yogurt over a bowl and let it drain for about 12 to 24 hours. Refrigerate after it has finished draining.

Soft Cheese (Fromage Blanc)

This is an easy cheese to make. Again, the recipe is based on the one from Ricki Carroll's book, Home Cheese Making. *You will need a colander, butter muslin and a packet of direct-set fromage blanc starter from www.cheesemaking.com or some other source. The recipe for goat cheese (chevre) is very similar, using pasteurized goat's milk (not ultra-pasteurized) and a chevre starter.*

    1 gallon pasteurized whole milk
    1 packet direct-set fromage blanc starter
    ½ teaspoon salt

Fill a sink with hot water. Pour the milk into a stainless steel pot and place in the water. Leave it there until the temperature of the milk is 86°. Remove the pot from the water and add the starter, mixing thoroughly. Cover and let it sit for 12 hours.

    Line a colander with the butter muslin and ladle the curd into the colander. Tie the corners of the muslin in a knot and hang the bag to drain at room temperature for 6 to 12 hours. A shorter hanging time produces a spreadable cheese; with a longer time, the cheese will have the consistency of cream cheese. Mix in the salt and store it in a covered container in the refrigerator. It will last up to 2 weeks. Makes 2 pounds.

Doug uses a plant hook over his sink and a bungee cord with hooks for hanging the cheese. We typically let ours drain from 10 to 11 hours. Try adding herbs, garlic and/or lemon zest to this cheese to make a delicious dip.

Hummus

This is a delicious dip to serve with bread, crackers, or raw vegetables. It is based on a recipe given to us by a friend who lived in Lebanon for a number of years. Her Lebanese mother-in-law gave it to her. You can cook your own chickpeas for hummus using the recipe for Lentil and Chickpea Soup. For an adventure, make hummus with a large mortar and pestle.

2 garlic cloves
1 (15- or 16-ounce) can chickpeas, rinsed (or 1½ cup cooked chick peas)
2 small lemons, juiced

½ cup tahini (paste made with sesame seeds)
1 teaspoon salt, or to taste
¼–½ cup water
Olive oil and/or chopped olives and parsley to garnish

Place the garlic in a food processor and process until finely minced. Add the chickpeas and process. Then add the lemon juice, tahini, and salt and process. Gradually add water until you achieve the desired consistency.

Serve on a plate or in a fairly flat bowl. Traditionally olive oil is drizzled over the top when served. Chopped olives, chopped parsley, or olive tapenade also make tasty and attractive garnishes.

Pickled Onions

2 cups water
¼ cup salt
2½ cups vinegar
1 yellow or red onion, sliced into quarter ¼-inch rings and then cut in half

Heat the water and salt in a saucepan until the salt dissolves. Take off the heat and add the vinegar. Allow to cool to room temperature. Place onions in a bowl or glass jar and cover with the pickling solution. Cover the container and refrigerate for 7–10 days.

Cucumber and Cheese Salad

This salad will not need much salt because both the cheese and olives are typically stored in very salty brine.

2 cucumbers, peeled
12 Greek-style olives, pitted and
   chopped
3 green onions, chopped, both green
   and white part
4 oz. feta cheese, crumbled

1–2 tablespoons red wine vinegar
1 tablespoon fresh dill, finely
   chopped or 1 teaspoon dried dill
½ teaspoon salt, or to taste
freshly ground pepper to taste

Cut the cucumbers in half, lengthwise. Scrape the seeds out using a spoon and then chop. If olives are not pitted, press each one with the side of a large knife to loosen the pit and then remove. Mix the cucumbers, olives, onion, and feta cheese. Splash on the vinegar and add the dill and seasonings. Serves 6.

Lentil and Chickpea Soup

We anticipate that you will enjoy this soup. It is easy to make, especially if you use canned chickpeas. It is good as part of a first-century meal and it is just as good as twenty-first century comfort food. Lentils are legumes and are easy to prepare because they do not require prior soaking and cook quickly. Dried lentils are found in most markets and grocery stores. You can use any stock, including vegetable stock.

¼ cup olive oil

1 onion, chopped

2 garlic cloves, finely minced

2 cups cooked chickpeas, or 1½
   (15 ounce) cans, rinsed

1 cup dried green lentils, rinsed

4 cups chicken stock

4 cups water

½ teaspoon ground cumin

½ teaspoon ground coriander

½ teaspoon ground mustard seed

2 teaspoon salt, or to taste

¼ teaspoon ground pepper

1 bay leaf

To cook dried chickpeas: cover 1 cup of chickpeas with water and soak overnight. Drain the chickpeas and place in a 4-quart pot. Cover with water and bring to a boil. Reduce to a simmer. Add a bay leaf and parsley stems for additional flavor. Simmer for 1 hour and drain.

In a large soup pot, heat the olive oil over medium-high heat. Add the onion and sauté. When translucent, add the garlic and sauté for 30 seconds, or until translucent. Then add the chickpeas, lentils, stock, and water. Bring to a boil and then return to a simmer. Add the rest of the ingredients and continue to simmer for several hours. Remove the bay leaf. Adjust seasonings and serve.

To make the soup thicker or to give it the texture of soup that has been reheated several times: take 2 cups of the soup, making sure to include some chickpeas and lentils, and place in a blender. Cover and puree, then return to the rest of the soup. Alternatively, use a hand blender and blend for several seconds.

First-Century Chicken Stock

This is a simple chicken stock recipe and its use will improve the flavor of your soup and legume recipes. Do not use salt so it does not interfere with the seasoning levels of your recipe.

1 onion, roughly chopped

1 carrot, roughly chopped

1 celery stalk, roughly chopped

chicken, cut into 8 pieces

2 sprigs fresh thyme

2 sprigs fresh parsley

1 bay leaf

Place all ingredients in a 12-quart stock pot. Cover with water by 2 inches and bring to a boil. Immediately turn down to a simmer and cook for 1 hour. Use a spoon to scrape out any fat or foam that rises to the surface.

After 1 hour, take the chicken pieces from the pot and carefully remove the chicken meat from the bones. It will be hot. Save the chicken for another use. Crack the bones with a meat clever and return the bones to the stock. Continue to cook for several hours, scraping any fat or foam that rises to the surface.

Partially fill a sink with water and ice. Strain the stock into a large bowl or pot. Place in the ice water until temperature is reduced. Then place in a covered container and refrigerate.

A family warehouse, mostly underground, could store five years' worth of food, serving as the neighborhood bank with strict repayment rules.

CHAPTER FOUR

The Farmer, Food, and Social Responsibility

Listen to another parable. There was a land owner who planted a vineyard, put a fence around it, dug a wine press in it, and built a watchtower. Then he leased it to tenants and went to another country. (Matthew 21:33–34)

There is a disconnect between most modern people and the production of their food. Unlike the vast majority of people who lived before the twentieth century, most of us have lost touch with the art of growing and harvesting the food for our table. For example, when was the last time you harvested grain from your fields and ground it into flour to make your own bread? How often have you butchered your own cow in your backyard to provide T-bone steaks to cook on the grill or the roast for Sunday dinner? If you have a vegetable garden, is the produce used to supplement the vegetables you buy at the supermarket, or do you grow enough to last the entire year? Do you keep bees to pollinate your fruit trees and supply you with honey? Have we proved our point?

The opposite was true at the time of Jesus. Most of the population in the first century was somehow involved with the growth and production of food. In fact, this was true of all people until very recently in the history of humanity. It is true that the creation of cities and empires allowed some of our ancestors to engage in other vocations. Armies were formed to protect cities and farms. Priests prayed to the gods and taught morality. Artists made beautiful objects and craftsmen and women produced items that eventually became necessities. Still, farming and food production were the most common of all professions.

Jewish laws and traditions at the time of Jesus still assumed that nearly all people were farmers and shepherds. Most of life revolved around the rhythms of planting and harvesting, including celebrations and religious festivals. Moreover, the family's security depended on the ability to store food for the future. A well-stocked storehouse ensured a household's survival during times of drought and famine. The Bible depicts a social system that required neighbors and communities to provide for those who did not have the resources to feed their households.

This procedure for storing food and helping neighbors served Israel well until the political and economic chaos of the first century. Taxation under Herod the Great and his sons depleted the food stores of many farmers. Many others lost their land and became tenet farmers or day laborers. The outcome was revolution, with the resulting destruction of Jerusalem and the temple by Roman troops.

Along with bread and wine, olives and olive oil were an essential food. The oil was used for cooking, cosmetics, medicine, and fuel. A bowl of brined olives was featured on many tables. Gallons of oil were in every kitchen. And large crocks of oil shared a prominent place in the storehouse. Oil was an important element in both Jewish and Christian worship. All in all, it is impossible to imagine first-century Palestinian and Mediterranean life without olives.

The noonday meal was a simple one. A farmer's land was often miles from his home. During harvests, the farmer and his family often spent days in the field, living in temporary shelters. The simple food of the farmer and his family while they worked their crops intrigues us.

The Ancient Farm

It is most likely that our experience of the North American farmer is the basis of our image of any family farm, including one in first-century Palestine. We see a farm family living in a house located on the edge of their property. Other buildings usually surround the house: a barn to hold crops and equipment, stables for livestock, and maybe a chicken coop or a tool shed. Depending on the size of the farm, the American farmhouse might be miles from a neighbor and even farther from the nearest town. But in the first century, the farmer and his family lived in the town. The farmer's land might be miles away. In this way, the farmer had the safety and other advantages of living in a community. The town typically had a public water supply.

First-century homes were built around courtyards. These were used to keep livestock, grow vegetables, and house dovecotes and chicken coops. During summer months, the oven, stove, and millstone were moved outside, so the courtyard was also used for cooking and grinding flour. Families would also eat in the open air. In many cases, courtyards were shared by several homes, and households often worked and ate their meals together.

Many of the farmers in the Holy Land, and in fact in the entire Mediterranean region, were "subsistence farmers." The purpose of the subsistence farm was simply to provide food and security for the family that owned it. Most of the farms in the hill country of Galilee were small, subsistence holdings. The average family owned approximately seven to eleven acres of land with some holding as small as one-half acre.[1] On this small piece of land, the family grew its own flax for clothing, wheat and barley for bread, grapes for wine and raisins, and olives for oil and brining. They had enough livestock to provide milk for cheese and yogurt, wool and skins for clothing, and occasional meat for a special meal. The family might have several fruit trees in the courtyard and maybe a few more near the olive orchard. In a good year, the farmer sold some of the surplus to buy storage jars and other supplies and then stored the rest for drought years. The women in the household made cloth from the linen and wool and tended the vegetable garden. They sold their extra cloth and vegetables in the marketplace to make money for the family.

Not all first-century farmers worked small family farms. Archaeologists have found the remains of larger commercial operations. There were certainly wealthy families with large, prosperous farms. These farmers grew crops for export to large cities or to other countries. Southern Galilee and the Plain of Esdraelon were major producers of grain and exported wheat and barley to cities as far away as Rome. The wines produced in Galilee were well respected and were exported to Greece and Rome. Remnants of olive presses are still found all over the Holy Land and suggest that olive oil was also an export crop. There are first-century records that tell of farmers who grew crops specifically for transport to larger communities. Chickpeas were grown in large fields in Judah, where they were then transported and sold in Jerusalem. No doubt Jesus walked along these fields and passed a number of olive groves on his last trip to Jerusalem.

Archaeologists have also found examples of *communal* storehouses where farmers in the community stored their crops. One such example was found at Gibeon. The community had ten centralized winepresses and sixty-three cellars where the wine was stored. The storehouses in Gibeon contain the remains of jars that were engraved with numerous names, demonstrating that a large number of vintners shared the storage facilities. The sheer volume of wine stored was vastly greater than was needed by the population of the community, leading archaeologists to conclude that most of the Gibeon wine was produced for export. One well-respected scholar, J. B. Pritchard, called the site "the 'ancient Bordeaux' of Palestine."[2] These cellars were hewn from rock and were an average of over seven feet deep. They were too damp for storing other commodities like wheat or dried fruit but were perfect for storing a liquid like wine that was sealed in airtight containers. The temperature in the cellars was and still is a full twenty degrees cooler than the temperature outside in the sun, creating a perfect environment for storing wine. A few of these cellars are still used by a modern winery near the site.

There were also very large farms, owned by very wealthy families. King Herod, who lived from 73 to 4 BCE, possessed a number of large farms that specialized in a particular crop: for example, dates near the desert in the south and grain in the Valley of Esdraelon. Many of these large farms surrounded a "manor house," a large home that must have functioned as a small town, housing as many as fifty to seventy-five people, with its own wine and olive presses, banquet rooms, and private quarters for the owners. The residents of the manor house included managers, servants, accountants and their families. The landowner and his family lived there as well, at least for part of the year. Many of the wealthy land owners also owned a second home in Jerusalem or Sepphoris.

The passage from Matthew that opens this chapter describes an instance where a vineyard was given to tenant farmers. Jesus describes a new but operational vineyard that was leased to farmers who would run the operation and give a share of the income or produce back to the owner. There were a number of types of tenant relationships in first-century Palestine. In some cases the tenant rented the land for a fixed percentage of the harvest, usually between one-third and one-half of the produce. Others paid a fixed amount, in money or produce, regardless of the success of the harvest. Some tenants were given seed which had to be repaid. In some cases, the tenant was expected to develop the farm or plantation and then received part of the land once it became profitable. The tenants usually paid the owner half of the produce until the time that they were compensated for the development of the farm. Copies of some of the contracts between owner and tenant still exist that tell the amount of the rent and the term of the lease. Leases were typically for five to six years. In addition, tenants paid the tithe and taxes on their shares.[3]

The first century was a time of significant consolidation of farmland. Many farmers with small holdings lost their land for a variety of reasons and wealthy landowners were able to acquire it. Nearly a century earlier, all Jewish settlers along the fertile coastland were moved inland to the hill country, thus creating a large population of landless farmers and adding many to the classes of tenant farmers and day laborers. It is believed that, by the time of Jesus, as much as 70 percent of the farmland was owned by a gentry class.[4] As we will see, it also added to a sense of political and economic unease that eventually resulted in revolution.

Harvest, Gleaning, and Social Responsibility

From the most ancient books in the Old Testament we discover that the Israelites had a system of social welfare designed to help the poorer members of their community and even for those non-Jews and strangers who were not part of their community.[5] This system was especially designed to help those who were the most powerless, especially widows and orphans. Farmers were required to allow the poor to *glean*, that is, to go through the fields, orchards, and vineyards and gather what the harvesters missed and left behind:

> When you reap your harvest in your field and forget a sheaf in the field, you shall not go back to get it; it shall be left for the alien, the orphan, and the widow, so that the Lord your God may bless you in all your undertakings. When you beat your olive trees, do not strip what is left; it shall be for the alien, the orphan, and the widow. When you gather the grapes of your vineyard, do not glean what is left; it shall be for the alien, the orphan, and the widow. (Deuteronomy 24:19–21)

Also in Leviticus, ancient Jews were warned not to reap to the edges of the field, to strip the vineyard bare or gather fallen grapes. Here again, the portion of the field or vineyard closest to the road or path was intentionally left untouched for the poor (Leviticus 19:9–10). In fact, the poor were allowed to pluck enough grain to eat at any time, as long as they did not use a sickle to harvest and thus steal someone's crops (Deuteronomy 23:25).

This was a primitive method of social welfare, based on an agricultural society. Certainly the practice of gleaning was unable to help the poor meet all their needs. There was no guarantee of work or shelter. Yet it helped those who were most destitute have access to the ancient world's three most important agricultural products, grain, olive oil, and wine, and to keep them from starving to death. The poor had grain to make bread and porridge, oil for cooking and for their lamps, and a little wine to drink with their meager meals. The Book of Ruth in the Old Testament gives us an excellent example of a widow who provides for her mother-in-law and herself by gleaning in the fields of a wealthy landowner (Ruth 2). As it happened, Ruth eventually married the prosperous farmer. But had she not, the system was in place to supply the two of them with key commodities for survival. There is no reason to believe that this social system had been replaced by the time of Jesus, especially in small, rural communities. Jesus, his family, and disciples certainly took advantage of these and other regulations. It is characteristic that, when Jesus and his disciples took wheat from a field, they were criticized for working, plucking the wheat on the Sabbath, and not for stealing (Mark 2:23–28; Luke 6:1–5).

But what about the widows and others who lived in the cities? Admittedly, life was not easy for widows and orphans, even with the benefits of harvest gleaning. But life was especially difficult in the cities. The cost of living was significantly higher, with the price of food and other necessities costing three times as much or even more.[6] Sadly enough, many people in dire situations, especially women, children, and those who were crippled, were forced to beg in order to survive, or turn to theft or prostitution to provide for their support. The number of beggars and those engaged in crime continued to grow throughout the first century with gangs of thieves and beggars eventually terrorizing all of precincts of Jerusalem. Some gang members became revolutionaries and patriots during the revolution of 66 CE; others simply saw the growing political instability as opportunities for theft and violence.

It was also true that Judaism fostered an environment of generosity. This was especially true in Jerusalem. The wealthy were considered blessed by God when they gave alms to the poor. Beggars tended to gather around the holy sites where they solicited charity from the great number of people who visited Jerusalem during religious holidays. While this generosity must have helped many that were in need, it also reflected a safety net system that was designed primarily for agricultural communities rather than cities.

The Family Storehouse and Social Responsibility

One of the reasons Jesus' parables were so poignant was because his stories painted vivid pictures in the minds of his audience using common experiences and images. This was certainly true of the parable of the rich man and his barns:

> Then Jesus told them a parable: "The land of a rich man produced abundantly. And he thought to himself, 'What should I do, for I have no place to store my crops?' Then he said, 'I will do this: I will pull down my barns and build larger

ones, and there I will store all my grain and my goods. And I will say to my soul, Soul, you have ample goods laid up for many years; relax, eat, drink, be merry.'" (Luke 12:16–19)

The "barns" in this translation were actually storehouses. After each harvest, the grain, fruit, wine or other crop or food product was moved to a storehouse where it was kept until needed. Every farmer had one. For a farmer with limited means, it might be a large room connected to his house or a shed in the family courtyard. On bigger farms, it was one or two separate buildings near the fields. A farmer and his family could store several years of crops in these storehouses.

Usually the first-century storehouse was a structure that was twelve meters square and was at least partially built below ground level in order to keep the wine and food cool during the hot Middle Eastern summers. It was likely that the crowd hearing Jesus tell the parable of the rich farmer were also farmers who had storehouses exactly like the ones in the story. It was also likely that his audience was praying for exactly the same problem as the farmer, a harvest so large they had to build new storehouses.

Imagine entering a first-century storehouse. The floor was at least several feet, and as many as five or six feet, below ground level, so the farmer descended stairs or a small ladder to get to the floor. Behind thick stone walls it was dark, cool, and dry with the overwhelming smells of grains and dried fruit. The wine was stored on the floor. These large cone-shaped, airtight containers, called amphorae, held seven gallons of wine (equivalent to thirty-five modern bottles) and had a handle on each side so two men could carry the jar. Imagine six rows in the back of the storehouse with the cone portion of the container resting in a hole dug in the ground. Each year, one row was emptied and then refilled at harvest when the grapes were pressed. The vineyard rested on the seventh year, the Sabbath year, so the farmer relied on the surplus from other years. By then one entire row was completely empty, ready to be replaced. Above the jars there may have been racks built to hold earthenware containers of dried beans and lentils. Olive oil was stored in three-gallon crocks. The taste of the oil remained excellent for the first year and was better used as fuel the next. Wheat, barley, and other grains were dried and then stored in crocks for five to six years. Maybe dried figs, raisins, apricots, and dates rested on racks above the wheat. These were eaten during the year and replaced with the next harvest.

The first-century storehouse was the family's 401(k), IRA, pension fund, and emergency bank account rolled into one. It was their security for the future. Rainfall in first-century Galilee fluctuated as much as 30 percent, just as it does today. Almost all the rain fell during the five months between October and the end of February. The summer months experience almost no rain at all. Without winter rains the size of the all-important grain crops suffered considerably. If the drought was severe, then the farmer and his family relied almost entirely on extra grains and other foods stowed in the storehouse. The more food in the storehouse, the more secure the future.

The surplus stored in the storehouse also provided the average farmer with the extra resources to purchase and barter for the things his family and he could not make or do themselves. Barley, figs, wine, and olive oil were sold at market so the family could buy more storage jars or tools. The dowry for a wedding might cost a number of amphorae filled with wine or even an ox from the field. Salaries for laborers had to be paid by the end of the day. Did the average farmers keep enough money on hand to pay the laborers of the harvest, or was the surplus from another crop sold for the purpose?

Assume that you had to live six months without any income. How would you make your house payment, buy food, and pay the bills? Use your savings account? Cash in the 401(k)? Borrow money from relatives or friends? First-century Jewish farmers did not have the advantages of modern banks and stock portfolios. They used their storehouse and they had each other. The family with an empty storehouse was in crisis. Ancient Jewish laws provided a framework for helping families experiencing a time of distress. In fact, members of the community were required to open the family storehouse whenever a needy neighbor asked for help, in essence asking them to share their retirement:

> If there is among you anyone in need, a member of your community in any of your towns within the land that the Lord your God is giving you, do not be hard-hearted or tight-fisted towards your needy neighbour. You should rather open your hand, willingly lending to meet the need, whatever it may be. Be careful that you do not entertain a mean thought, thinking, "the seventh year, the year of remission is near," and therefore view your needy neighbour with hostility and give nothing; your neighbour might cry to the Lord against you, and you would incur guilt. Give liberally and be ungrudging when you do so, for on this account the Lord your God will bless you in all your work and in all that you undertake. Since there will never cease to be some in need on the earth, I therefore command you, "Open your hand to the poor and needy neighbour in your land." (Deuteronomy 15:7–11)

This passage describes a significant sacrifice. It is not asking a neighbor to gather a few cans of beans from the pantry to take to the local charity.

It states that the loan to a neighbor was to meet the need, *whatever it may be*. If someone lost a wheat crop, if fire destroyed a storehouse, if soldiers or thieves raided their harvest, then their neighbors opened their storehouses and provided enough food to last until the next harvest. Deuteronomy included the instruction to give both *liberally* and *ungrudgingly*. It must have been very difficult for a farmer to open his storehouse and give his "pension fund" to his neighbors. It was especially difficult right before a Sabbath year. Every seven years all debts were to be forgiven (Deuteronomy 15:1–6). Jews were required to be generous with their charity and loans, even if the seventh year, the *year of remission*, was pending and chances of being repaid were negligible.

The Bible records other regulations for helping needy neighbors. Every third year, a tenth of the produce that was harvested was stored within the town for the sole purpose of providing food resources for the needy and poor. This included assistance for the Levites, members of the priestly tribe who had no land, and the "resident aliens, orphans and the widows" (Deuteronomy 14:28–29). The law also provided for the poor in other ways, including a prohibition against charging interest on money or resources loaned to a needy neighbor.

These passages from Deuteronomy paint the picture of a remarkable social system for security. The family and community storehouses were, for hundreds of years, the foundation of the social safety net. The contents in the storehouse clearly belonged to the farmer and his family, in the same way families and individuals in our capitalist economic system own property. But the family was obligated to share with their neighbors from their stores. As long as this system was in place, at least in theory, no ordinary Jew went hungry, at least as long as members of the community had storehouses with grain and wine saved from harvests of the good years.

Of course there were situations that were not ordinary. How does a society that believed diseases and bad luck are a sign of sinfulness and punishment respond when a farmer suddenly is diagnosed with a skin disease like leprosy? Were the storeroom doors open, or was the person ostracized from the rest of society? What about times of famine or war when almost all storehouses were impacted? And what about times when wealthy farmers refused to share with the less fortunate? Centuries before the birth of Jesus, the prophet Amos railed against Israel for oppressing the poor and crushing the needy: "they sell the righteous for silver, and the needy for a pair of sandals, they who trample the head of the poor into the dust of the earth, and push the afflicted out of the way" (Amos 2:6–7, also 4:1). This is not the description of a caring and generous people, opening their storehouses to their needy neighbors.

This understanding of the storehouse may even help us see some of the well-known teachings of Jesus from a slightly different perspective. For example, from the Lord's Prayer we read the text: "and forgive us our debts, as we also have forgiven our debtors" (Matthew 6:12). This phrase occurs immediately after the sentence, "Give us this day our daily bread." The context of this section of the prayer is food. So what were these debts that are the subject of this petition in the prayer? The Greek word in this passage clearly referred to "what is owed," as in paying back something that is borrowed.[7] But the word "debts" in this passage is commonly understood to refer to sins or acts of wrongdoing against another person. In fact, Luke's version of the prayer actually uses both "sins" and "debts": "and forgive us our sins, for we ourselves forgive everyone indebted to us" (Luke 11:4). But is it possible that Jesus was referring to the debts of those borrowing from a neighbor's storehouse? After all, the context for the sentence is "our daily bread." The meaning Jesus gave this petition was likely much broader than the giving and forgiving of agricultural debts. But it is certainly possible that storehouse debts were the underlying image. We believe that Jesus was using a concept that was clearly understood by the farmers in his audience in order to teach something more universal, the forgiving of sins. A dialogue between Jesus and Peter in Matthew might be another example:

> Then Peter came and said to [Jesus], "Lord, if another member of the church sins against me, how often should I forgive? As many as seven times?" Jesus said to him, "Not seven times, but, I tell you, seventy-seven times." (Matthew 18:21–22; see also Luke 17:4)

It might be difficult imagining what sin a neighbor might commit with such frequency that it would warrant this teaching. One exception, especially during difficult economic times, would be the borrowing of large amounts of food from neighbors' storehouses without repaying. How many times must this behavior be tolerated? Seven times? In order to feed a neighbor and perhaps keep that family from losing their farm, Jesus might have taught that they must forgive this sin seventy-seven times, or every time it happened. Like the discussion of "sins" and "debts" above, this is a concept that was very familiar to the people in Jesus' audience and also had a universal message regarding the forgiveness of all sins.

There is another very curious regulation in the book of Deuteronomy that may well illustrate the importance of the storehouse:

If someone has a stubborn and rebellious son who will not obey his father and mother, who does not heed them when they discipline him, then his father and his mother shall take hold of him and bring him out to the elders of his town at the gate of that place. They shall say to the elders of this town, "This son of ours is stubborn and rebellious. He will not obey us. He is a glutton and a drunkard." Then all the men of the town shall stone him to death. So you shall purge the evil from your midst, and all Israel will hear, and be afraid. (Deuteronomy 21:18–21)

Many Old Testament scholars simply dismiss this passage by stating that there is no historical record of this law ever being enforced. However, it does address an important question. What if someone had a son whose behavior placed both the family storehouse and then the community storehouse in jeopardy? The decision to execute a member of the community was difficult, but this regulation realizes that a young man who was "a glutton and a drunkard" could threaten the security of a family and a small community that must ultimately open their storehouses to support their unfortunate neighbors. Were young men executed for threatening the food supply of a community? As already stated, there is no historical evidence to answer the question "yes" or "no." But we believe the possibility exists and the presence of this regulation demonstrates the draconian measures an ancient community might have to take to ensure the safety of its food supplies.

Herod and the Threat to the Family Farm
Jesus said, "For the kingdom of heaven is like a landowner who went out early in the morning to hire laborers for his vineyard" (Matthew 20:1). As part of the story, the landowner also hires idle workers at 9:00 A.M., noon, 3:00, and 5:00 P.M. The parable in Matthew gives the impression that there were a large number of laborers available for work despite it being harvest time. It is reasonable to ask, "Why were they not already working?" The question can also be asked in relation to other accounts in the gospels. Why were so many people free to follow Jesus and spend their days listening to him teach? The work of a farmer was rarely completed, especially during the spring and summer, when conditions were also best for travel. So how was it possible that Jesus' outdoor teaching sessions, like the Sermon on the Mount (Matthew 5:1–7:29), the Sermon on the Plain (Luke 6:17–49), and the feeding of the 5,000 (Matthew 14:13–21, Mark 6:30–44, Luke 9:10–17, John 6:1–14), were able to attract such large crowds? Even if the numbers were

exaggerated by the gospel writers, a very substantial following was present to hear Jesus teach at these and other occasions, people who should have been working on the farm!

By the time of Jesus, many of the social systems in Israel had broken. Large numbers of men were unemployed and were attempting to support their families as day laborers or servants. Families that had owned farms for many generations were selling or losing their lands and livelihood. Some became tenant farmers or day laborers. Others migrated to larger towns like Jerusalem and Sepphoris in hopes of finding work or charity. Some of the most desperate became servants to the wealthy landowners who bought their farms or even sold themselves into slavery.

Religious leaders and teachers of the time bemoaned the disintegration of traditional families and Mosaic values. Crimes like theft of personal property were increasingly a problem. There may be a number of factors contributing to this societal breakdown, but one significant cause was socioeconomic. King Herod introduced an onerous level of taxation, one that was continued by his sons during the lifetime of Jesus. A tax of 10 percent was levied on most agricultural products and 20 percent on foods that were processed. In other words, the tax collector took 10 percent of all the grains, fruits, and vegetables harvested and charged 20 percent tax on food products like wine, dried fish, and olive oil. This amount was collected not only in surplus years, but in the bad years as well. In addition, Rome levied a smaller tax of 2–3 percent. For the subsistence farmer and his family, who ate most of what was raised, Herod's tax pulled food straight off the table, turned it into cash, and placed it in his treasure room. By the time of Jesus, Herod and his sons had likely managed to empty thousands of storehouses in the Holy Land by burdening a successful agrarian economic system with disproportionate taxation. In doing so, Herod became the equivalent of a modern billionaire, perhaps the first such person in the long history of Israel. We know from Herod's will that he left approximately half of his treasury, "ten million of coined money (of drachmae), besides vessels of gold and silver" and "garments exceedingly costly to Julia, Caesar's wife; and to certain others, five million."[8]

Moreover, farmers were still expected to pay the temple tithe to support the priestly hierarchy and its ministry of sacrifice. I think one can legitimately question how many Jews, especially Galileans, were actually giving their tithe. There is ample evidence of Pharisees and rabbis exhorting the faithful to continue to tithe despite the financial and social insecurity. For the Pharisees, tithing was one of many signs that a Jew remained truly faithful to God and had not acquiesced to Greco-Roman culture. The need for this kind of teaching was a sign that at least some of the faithful were not giving the full, required amount to the temple.

Consider for a moment the amount of taxation levied on the first-century farmer. It is likely that many readers are thinking, "Only 10 percent, what's the big deal?" Many of us are taxed at rates much higher than 10 percent. But we also have deductions for mortgage debt, dependent children, medical expenses, charitable donations, and for the costs of "doing business." At the end of the nineteenth century, when lifestyles and the economy were much more similar to the first century than today, there was no federal income tax. The few taxes that farmers did pay were more equivalent to 1–2 percent of the value of the crops they grew, not 10 percent and certainly not 20 percent.

Some might say that, as in our country, many good things were done with the tax revenues. And this was certainly true. Herod built buildings, towns, fortresses, palaces, harbors, and roads. These projects employed a large number of people, likely including Jesus and his father, Joseph. Tax revenues also paid for an army that protected the main roads and, along with Roman centurions, helped keep the countryside safe. But still, the equivalent of $1 billion was taken out of the economy of a small, primarily rural country, out of the storehouses of the people of Israel, where it did nothing but gather dust in treasure rooms. This left the farmers, as well as the merchants, craftsmen, fishermen, and others extremely vulnerable to a time of crisis.

Empty storehouses meant that families lost their ability to respond to a bad harvest or to help an even less fortunate neighbor. In essence, the situation was similar to a modern collapse of a national banking system. It meant that dispossessed farmers lost their land and farms that had belonged to their families for hundreds of years. In order to survive, land was sold to wealthier landowners. The common farmer then became a sharecropper, day laborer, servant or slave—or a beggar, a thief, or in some cases, a zealot or rebel. This trend continued to grow after the death of Jesus. The country was then left increasingly unstable and vulnerable to the revolt that resulted in the destruction of Jerusalem and the temple.

Olives and Olive Oil

Several years ago, UPS delivered twenty pounds of Manzanilla olives to Doug's front door. These were green olives, rock hard, straight from trees in California to a cardboard box and then to Texas. After their arrival, the olives were sliced, smashed, soaked, brined and anything else that might possibly make these solid green orbs into the delicacies we buy at our favorite Mediterranean markets.

Olives and olive oil join bread and wine in Toussaint-Samat's fundamental food trinity.[9] It is difficult to imagine first-century life without olives and olive oil. They were essential to very many aspects of ancient culture and existence. In fact, one modern author suggests that the history of the olive tree is closely linked to the history of agriculture itself.[10] Archaeologists know that olive trees have been cultivated for at least the last five thousand years. In addition, all the geographical regions discussed or even mentioned in this book—the Holy Land, Greece, Italy, Egypt, and in fact the entire Mediterranean region—the areas where Jesus' disciples and the early Christians lived and traveled, these were places where olive trees flourished. Olive oil became such an important commodity that the forests of ancient Greece were razed and replaced with olive trees. Unfortunately, the shallow roots of olive trees were unable to hold the soil and prevent erosion. By the first century the hills and mountains of Greece looked much like they do now: stark and rocky with very little topsoil.

Olive trees were a distinctive part of the Mediterranean landscape and were common in both the hills of Judea and Galilee. The trees grow to be fifty feet tall and can have a canopy of thirty feet. Olive trees are evergreens with grayish leaves. The trees are tenacious and hearty, sprouting and growing even when cut down level with the ground. The average life of an olive tree is five hundred years, though some live much longer. When we buy and eat those deliciously tangy cracked green Lebanese olives from our favorite Mediterranean market, we might be eating the fruit from trees that are the children or grandchildren of ones that produced olive oil for Jesus and his family.

Olives are actually fruit. Botanists call the olive a "dupe," or fruit with a single seed or pit, like peaches. Olive trees bloom in the spring and the fruit remains green until turning ripe in the fall. Ripening olives first turn a darker color of green and then finally turn a dark blackish purple. Yes, black olives and green olives come from the same trees and differ only in degree of ripeness. Olive blossoms require mild weather but the fruit needs a long, hot growing season like that found in the Holy Land. A late freeze will kill the blossoms, but it was the farmers of Northern Italy who worried about cold weather. The growers in Israel more often feared the hot winds and weather that would sometimes penetrate the Holy Land between Passover and Pentecost from the southern deserts. The heat could sear the blossoms and ruin the crop. After the petals dropped, the fruit was safe through the summer.

Olives were the last agricultural crop to be harvested before winter. The ingathering began in October with a process that remained basically the same until large growers began using machines to help with the harvest. The workers spread a tarp of some sort under the tree. One of the workers climbed into the tree to shake branches and pick olives he could reach. Another used a long pole to hit branches so that fruit fell onto the tarp. The third worker gathered and separated the olives and placed them in baskets.

Can you picture teams of three working their way through the orchard in late October? Their goal was to harvest just the ripe, dark olives. These were the ones that were best for olive oil and the farmer wanted to produce as much oil as possible. Olives did not ripen all at once. At the time of harvest, most of the olives were ripe and had turned, but some of the olives were still hard and green. Shaking and hitting the branches caused some of the green olives to fall, though most remained on the tree for the second harvest. Because the green ones were not quite ripe and did not produce nearly as much oil, they were set aside to be cured and eaten.[11] But the laborers did not have that much control over which fruit fell from the tree as the branches were being whacked with a pole. Olives rained from the tree, mostly ripe ones, but green ones, too. A week or so later, the farmer and his crews worked their way through the orchard one more time, harvesting as many ripe olives as possible. The olives remaining after the second harvest were left on the tree for the poorer members of the community to glean and press into oil. This practice enabled the families of unemployed fathers and husbands, widows, those who were crippled and sick, and others from the poorest segment of the community to have fuel for their lamps and oil for cooking.

As with the other crops at this time, the size of the olive orchards varied greatly. Small subsistence farms had several trees, enough to produce oil for the family to use during the year. Other producers had enough trees that they could sell their extra oil at the local market, while wealthy landowners had groves that produced oil for export.

Ripe olives are usually about 20 percent oil, though the oil could be difficult to extract. First, the olives had to be crushed and mashed with a mill stone. The olives were then placed in a press and the liquid was extracted. By the time of Jesus, most olives were pressed with a screw-type press. The mashed olives were scooped into thin baskets and the baskets were stacked ten or twenty high. The screw press was tightened and the olives were pressed for an extended period of time. The liquid then flowed through a trough and was collected. Finally, the lighter, watery oil was separated from the higher-quality oil. The liquid was poured back and forth from several containers until separated. The leftover olives were then pressed several more times, extracting additional oil. So that nothing was wasted, the lees, the pressed skins and pits, were then used to fertilize the soil around olive trees.

All varieties of olives contain a chemical called glycoside oleuropein that makes them so bitter that they cannot be eaten. This chemical must be removed before olives are brined. By the time of Jesus, a number of methods had been developed. Olives were packed in salt for an extended period of time, allowing the glycoside oleuropein to be drawn out. Alternatively, olives were soaked in lye, which is a mixture of ashes from hardwood trees, animal fat, and water. Lye is extremely alkaline and poisonous, but it makes green olives soft and extracts the bitterness. The olives then must be thoroughly washed before eaten. The method of using lye was particularly favored by the Romans. Olives also were split and soaked in water for several weeks. Because it draws the bitter chemical out of the olives, the water has to be changed every several days. These methods are still being used today. After removing the glycoside oleuropin and softening the olives, they were then brined. The brine was a mixture of salt and water to which flavorings, including vinegar, herbs, and spices, were then added. Once brined, the olives lasted for a long time.

Olive oil was the preferred oil or fat used for cooking. Cooks used it as an ingredient just as we do today. It was also added to a pan for browning or frying meats and it was added as a flavoring after the food was cooked. Deep frying was not as common a method of cooking in the ancient world, but it was used, and olive oil was the most common fat for the task. Olive oil, with or without additional herbs and spices as flavorings, was also present on the ancient table as a dip for bread, vegetables, and for meats.

Olive oil was much more than a food for people in the ancient world. It was an important fuel for lamps and lighting. Torches using pitch or some other fuel were used for exterior light after dark, but olive oil was the choice for lamps. One can hope that an inferior grade was used for fuel while the quality oil was reserved for the kitchen and dining table. The most ancient lamps were simply bowls of oil with cloth wicks. By the first century, the vessels looked more like a small pottery version of Aladdin's lamp. There were also seven-branch oil lamps for Hanukkah and other festival days.

Olive oil had still other uses as an ointment and as a medicine. Both women and men anointed their faces to keep the skin from becoming too dry. Middle Eastern summers were hot and dry with strong southern winds. The climate was especially rough on skin that was frequently exposed. Olive oil helped keep the skin moist and protected. Scented oil ointments were usually provided to guests during banquets and other special occasions. In addition ointments and makeup were made from an olive oil base, though other oils, such as sesame oil and rendered animal fat were also used. Oil-based ointments were often scented with perfume. Wealthier women usually wore makeup, though most women wore makeup and ointments only on special occasions. Their wedding feast was one such occasion. Anointing oils and ointments were kept in special jars and flasks. Alabaster was supposedly the preferred material for keeping expensive ointments. But it was very expensive, and only the richest people could afford expensive ointments stored in alabaster. Matthew's gospel refers to an alabaster jar of ointment (Matthew 26:7), as does Pliny's *Natural History*.[12]

Anointing with oil also had a religious significance. The act of anointing with oil blessed a person or object, that is, it *designated* or *set apart* a person or object to be used by God for a special purpose. For example, the king was anointed with oil, setting him apart as God's chosen leader for the kingdom. In like manner, it was the custom to anoint the priests, prophets, furnishings, and tools for use in the temple and even shields used for battle. Olive oil was an important aspect of temple worship as well. The grain offering required that grain was first mixed with olive oil and then presented in the temple (Leviticus 3). For a thanksgiving offering, unleavened cakes were made using olive oil, oil was poured over unleavened wafers, and cakes were soaked in it (Leviticus 7:11–14). Early Christians were anointed as part of their baptisms, after the water ritual, and signed on their foreheads with the sign of the cross.[13] In essence these Christians were *set apart* for God and marked as Christ's own.

Jews and early Christians also used oil when praying for healing. Oils were mixed with roots and herbs that were known for their curative powers to make medicinal ointments. Doctors and healers used ointments to treat skin problems such as burns or rashes. The New Testament and other period literature provide examples of sick people being anointed with oil during prayers for healing. This second- or early third-century prayer for oil is from the ancient text by Hippolytus called *Apostolic Tradition*:

> O God, sanctifier of this oil, as you give health to those who are anointed and receive that with which you anointed kings, priests and prophets, so may it give strength to all those who taste it, and health to all that are anointed with it.[14]

Along with these, olives and the olive tree also symbolized joy, peace, and reconciliation. It meant strength and olive laurels were worn by the victorious in battle. But because of the very bitter flavor of uncured olives, they also described bad relationships and arguments. To be born under an olive tree brought good luck and in some cultures showed that the child was divine.

Menu for Light Lunch in the Field

- Leftover Mediterranean Grain Bread* (chapter 3) or bread from another recipe in this book
- Bulgur and Lamb Wrapped in Grape Leaves* or
- Goat Cheese Marinated in Olive Oil and Herbs*
- Date or Fig Cake*
- Brined Olives* (This recipe or from the market)

The Recipes

Bulgur and Lamb Wrapped in Grape Leaves

This is based on a recipe given to me by a friend decades ago. It was a family recipe from the Middle East, altered because not all the original ingredients were available in the first century. The combination of lamb and bulgur is still extremely popular in the Eastern Mediterranean.

1 tablespoon olive oil
1 medium onion, diced
1 clove garlic, minced
1 pound ground lamb
1 teaspoon salt
1 cup of cooked # 3 bulgur (course),
   or #1 bulgur (fine) rinsed, and
   the water squeezed out

½ teaspoon dried dill
½ teaspoon ground cumin
⅓ cup raisins
1 jar grape leaves, drained, washed,
   and dried

Add the olive oil to a 14-inch hot skillet or sauté pan. Sauté the onion until translucent, then add the garlic and cook 1 minute. Add the ground lamb and brown. Add the additional ingredients except the grape leaves and heat. Remove from the burner and allow to cool to room temperature.

Place approximately 2 tablespoons lamb and bulgur mixture into the center of a grape leaf. Fold the corners over the stuffing and then roll into a cylinder. Continue until all the stuffing is used.

Cover the bottom of a stock pot with several layers of unfilled leaves. Place the stuffed grape leaves in the pot, arranged in layers. Add ¼ inch of water to the pot. Cover and bring to a boil. Continue to simmer for 45 minutes. Carefully remove and allow to cool out of the water.

The idea behind this recipe is using leftover lamb and bulgur to make something easy to carry into the field for lunch while working. To cook coarsely chopped bulgur, see the recipe for Bulgur Pilaf in chapter 5.

Goat Cheese Marinated in Olive Oil and Herbs

This is a wonderful treat, making a great appetizer that can be spread on gourmet crackers or a crusty bread. For this recipe you will need a glass or ceramic container with a tight-fitting lid. Follow the recipe the first time you make it and then add your favorite herbs in the future.

8 ounces goat cheese (from the market, or use soft cheese from chapter 3)
1 teaspoon dried parsley

1 teaspoon dried thyme
2 garlic cloves, peeled and crushed
olive oil

Form the goat cheese into balls with the diameter of a quarter. Place the parsley, thyme, and garlic cloves in the bottom of a container. Place the goat cheese balls on top. Pour olive oil over the cheese until it is completely covered. The cheese should not be exposed to the air. Marinate for at least 3 days.

Date or Fig Cake

These are simply cakes of dried and chopped dates or figs. Once formed into a cake, they were easy to store and transport. Dried dates and figs make great snacks and are wonderful in stews.

Dried dates or figs, any amount

If using dates, remove the pits. If using figs, cut off the stems with sharp kitchen scissors. Place dates or figs in a food processor, 1 cup at a time and process until well chopped, stopping several time to stir and scrape from the side with a spatula. Remove from the processor and form into cakes, ½ inch thick and 6 inches in diameter. Wrap in plastic wrap to store.

You may have to clean the blade of the processor between batches if you intend to make more than one cup. Both fruits are very sticky.

Brined Olives

Our homemade olives are great fun to make, but a true project. Our supplier of fresh olives, when they are in season, is Penna Gourmet Olives at www.greatolives .com. *We use green Manzanilla olives. You can be quite creative with the spices and flavorings added to the brine. Try mustard and cumin seeds along with the flavorings we recommend.*

Fresh green olives of any amount, usually 5–10 pounds
Water

Brine (for 5 pounds)
¾ cup red wine vinegar
4 cups water
5 tablespoons table salt

Flavorings (for 5 pounds)

5–10 garlic cloves, crushed with the side of a knife

5 teaspoons dried thyme

5 teaspoons dried rosemary or 5 sprigs fresh rosemary

10 thin slices of lemon

Rinse the olives before beginning. Crack the skin of the olives, either by bashing them with a heavy skillet or a mallet or by slicing them on both sides with a paring knife. Place the olives in a very large bowl or in a plastic container. Cover with water and then place wax paper and a heavy object on top to keep all the olives submerged. Soak olives for 12 days, draining and replacing the water every day.

To prepare: sterilize five quart-size Mason jars and lids. Remove from the boiling water and allow to air dry.

To make the brine: place water and salt in a pan and boil the water until the salt dissolves. Take the water off the heat and add the red wine vinegar.

In each jar, place 1–2 garlic cloves, 1 teaspoon thyme, 1 teaspoon or 1 sprig rosemary and 2 lemon slices. Fill the jars with olives, cover with the brine, and then seal with the lids. Refrigerate for approximately 6 months before eating.

A typical family with three generations eats a Sabbath feast together from a common bowl.

CHAPTER FIVE

The Sabbath Feast

Moses said, "Tomorrow is a day of solemn rest, a holy sabbath to the Lord; bake what you want to bake and boil what you want to boil, and all that is left over put aside to be kept until morning." (Exodus 16:23)

It was not that long ago when the weekly "special" meal was part of our culture. The typical American family spent Sunday mornings at church. Then they returned home to *Sunday dinner*. In the South, this meal might have been fried chicken or ham. Mashed potatoes and gravy, green beans cooked with salt pork until they almost melted, a tossed salad or Jell-O with fruit, cornbread or biscuits or maybe even hot yeast rolls were the usual accompaniments. Butter was plentiful. Sweetened iced tea flowed like water. Peach cobbler, apple pie, or pound cake served with strawberries, whipped cream, and a cup of coffee completed the meal; but not enough caffeine to keep everyone from taking an afternoon nap.

The first-century Jews also enjoyed a weekly special meal. It was the Shabbat or Sabbath meal. It was shared with family, sometimes with special friends and neighbors invited to the table. For first-century Jews, the day started at sundown, so the Sabbath began at sundown on Friday and lasted until sundown on Saturday. The food for the Shabbat was prepared during the day on Friday, and immediately before sunset, it was placed on the table. Hands were washed; candles were lit; and special prayers of thanksgiving were offered for the gift of the Sabbath. Then the family enjoyed its special meal.

In this chapter, we are taking part in a first-century Sabbath meal. It was, and still is for contemporary Jews, part feast and part worship ceremony. The dinner was both a celebration of creation and a remembrance of the exodus from Egypt. It is appropriate that the two foods we study became the symbol of the land promised by God within the context of leaving slavery, milk and honey. These ingredients also helped make the Sabbath feast special.

The Sabbath in Belief and Practice

As a central principle in the practice of first-century Judaism, the observance of the Sabbath had a profound impact on the common, everyday life of the Jews. The weekly day of rest merged with the Jewish understanding of creation, the Exodus from Egypt, and the sovereignty of God. First-century Jews believed that God's creation was *good* and that its goodness should be enjoyed and celebrated. They were reminded of creation's goodness when they heard the first chapter of Genesis read at the temple or in the synagogue. After all, it was God who proclaimed that creation was good. Who could argue? Moreover, the Jews believed that God remained active in creation. The delivery from slavery in Egypt was the primary example. The inheritance of the Promised Land was another.

Almost from their beginning as a nation, the Jews were faced with this decision: are they going to follow God or are they going to be like the surrounding nations? The choice in the desert was whether to go on to freedom or go back to Egypt where they worked seven days a week but were guaranteed daily food. We know that they chose freedom. The laws that the Jews followed were a reflection of this decision and they were the framework of their relationships with God and with each other. This was especially true of the Ten Commandments and the Sabbath regulations. The earliest reference we have to these laws, including the Sabbath law to keep the seventh day holy and to refrain from work, is found in the book of Exodus (Exodus 20:1–11). The Ten Commandments in Exodus are found within the broader context of deliverance from Egypt and the journey to the promise land. And yet, even within this context, the commandment to keep the Sabbath day contained a reference to the other major Sabbath theme of creation:

> For in six days the Lord made heaven and earth, the sea, and all that is in them, but rested on the seventh day; therefore the Lord blessed the sabbath day and consecrated it. (Exodus 20:11)

But perhaps the clearest connection between the Sabbath observance and the Exodus is in the book of Deuteronomy:

> Observe the Sabbath day, and keep it holy, as the Lord your God commanded you. For six days you shall labour and do all your work. But the seventh day is a Sabbath to the Lord your God; you shall not do any work. . . . *Remember that you were a slave in the land of Egypt, and the Lord your God brought you out from there with a mighty hand and an outstretched arm*; therefore the Lord your God commanded you to keep the Sabbath day. (Deuteronomy 5:12–15)

The Exodus was a defining experience for the Jewish people. God had rescued their ancestors from slavery and given them fertile Palestine, a land of milk and honey, as their home. The Sabbath feast was experienced as a weekly symbol of God's presence and blessing. As they ate the fruit of the land, they remembered that both freedom and the fields where their crops grew were gifts from God. Keeping the Sabbath was just one way that they remembered their covenant relationship with God and celebrated their many blessings.

The Sabbath also shaped the Ancient Jewish understanding of time and creation. Without one day set aside as different, life was just an endless series of work days. Certainly there were the transitions to different seasons. The rains stopped and the barley and wheat were ready to be harvested. The temperature became hot and legumes and fruit could be picked. The hot season ended and it was time to produce wine and olive oil. Then plant the wheat and barley and wait for the rain. With the Sabbath, there was a time marker once every seven days, establishing a unit of time other than the day. Eventually the Jews established a calendar based completely on the Sabbath. Months were a Sabbath of weeks, seven weeks of seven days or forty-nine days, with one extra day. Each year had an extra seven-day festival. Every seventh year was a Sabbath year in which fields lay fallow and debts were forgiven. The Jubilee year was a Sabbath of Sabbath years plus one, just like the month. Because the Jews believed the Sabbath was established at creation, time and the calendar were holy and weekly rest was a part of God's purpose.

Sabbath practices were a defining characteristic of Jews in the ancient world. Almost all Jews abstained from most forms of work, especially the most obvious forms of work. They were not allowed to labor in the fields or carry heavy burdens. The women did not clean or cook. In addition, they celebrated the day with a special meal and by attending synagogue. Even servants and slaves were excused from daily chores. Remember that this was a time in which the vast majority of people from other cultures labored from sunrise to sunset, seven days a week.[1]

The observance of the weekly rest impacted the days and hours preceding the beginning of the Sabbath. Because cooking and other household chores were forbidden on the Sabbath, preparations began a day early. Special food was purchased; clothes were mended and washed. Friday was set aside to complete these tasks. The Sabbath feast and other meals were prepared, the animals were secured and fed, the fire tended, and candles lighted, all before Sabbath began at sundown on Friday. In most towns, the ram's horn, called the *shofar*, was blown before sundown to warn those working in the fields to walk back to the village. The horn sounded again at the moment the sun set to tell everyone exactly when the Sabbath began. After last-minute arrangements, the family began the feast.

The Sabbath rest was considered an extraordinary blessing. But it was more than a time of respite. An underlying purpose of the rest was to keep the day holy, to use the Sabbath as time to reflect on history and heritage and to consider their relationship with God and each other. It was a weekly day of celebration with time set aside for joyful worship of God. The Sabbath was also a time to pray and to study the scriptures. Many Jews in Palestine and beyond took the opportunity to attend synagogue. The synagogue was primarily a place to hear the scriptures read and to study the law and the prophets. By the time of Jesus, Sabbath time in the synagogue included other familiar elements of worship, including prayers and the chanting of psalms.

To some extent, the Greco-Roman culture scoffed at and criticized Jews for their observance of the Sabbath. But, because of Herod's support of Julius Caesar during the Roman civil wars, Jews outside of the Holy Lands were granted special favors, including the ability to keep the Sabbath. For example, the city of Ephesus decreed that "no one shall be prevented from keeping the Sabbath days nor fined for doing."[2] Jews were also exempt from military service because of the requirement not to work or fight on the Sabbath.

It seems to the authors that the loss of the Sabbath rest is one of the unfortunate circumstances of our time. The idea of a day away from work has remained, though the modern family often uses a day of rest for household chores and errands. One of the geniuses of the ancient Sabbath is that the family was together every week for a day of celebration and rest, and for a time of reflection. They were able to spend at least part of the day looking at their relationships with God and their neighbor. It might be an interesting experience for a modern family to find Sabbath time away from errands, television and malls and rediscover what it means to keep an entire day "holy."

Jesus and the Sabbath

There is no doubt that Jesus celebrated the Sabbath in a manner that was similar to his fellow Jews. We can be assured that he enjoyed Sabbath rests and feasts from the time he was a very young child. We know that he continued to engage in the practice of the Sabbath even during his ministry and travels. We learn in St. Luke's gospel that it was his custom to attend the synagogue on the Sabbath and that he was often allowed to teach (Mark 1:24; Luke 4:16, 31). Jesus also enjoyed Sabbath feasts, sometimes as a guest of the village rabbi.

We can suspect that, most of the time, Jesus observed the Sabbath rest, though we are told that some of his activities and those of his disciples were criticized by the rabbis. His disciples picked and ate grain from the fields. This was considered work and was prohibited (Mark 2:23; Luke 6:1). Jesus occasionally healed people on the Sabbath, even when present at a synagogue. This also was considered work and earned him significant criticism.

But we know that Jesus was a critic of many of the practices that had grown around the observance of the Sabbath. By the first century CE, a considerable number of regulations existed to help average Jews keep the Sabbath rest. There were rules for the distances one could walk or throw objects, or the size of crumbs one could remove from the dining table, or how food could be prepared and eaten. A person could add salt to water or oil and use it as a dip for bread, but was prohibited from using the same mixture as a brine to pickle vegetables, though some considered even mixing water and salt as a dip for bread to be work.[3]

It appears as though Jesus' primary objection was the practice of placing Sabbath regulations above the well-being of people. A rule or regulation might be helpful in living one's life, but the life or health of a fellow human being was more important. Apparently satisfying one's hunger was also more important, especially if that person was a disciple who was doing God's work! A Jew could be executed for working on the Sabbath, especially if the infraction was blatantly intentional. Typically though, the infraction was considered unintentional and the person could atone with a sin offering at the temple the next time he or she was in Jerusalem. If intentional work might result in death, then it was important to know exactly how work was defined.

Jesus was not alone in his criticism of Sabbath regulations. Ancient literature records a variety of rabbinical opinions regarding what was punishable work. For example, the rabbinical school of Shammai believed that it was inappropriate to spread nets to catch wild animals if there was the possibility that the animal would be caught on the Sabbath. The rabbinical school of Hillel disagreed.[4] One also wonders how strictly Sabbath regulations were followed by Jews that lived greater distances from Jerusalem. Without priests and rabbis looking over their shoulders, farmers and their families were freer to make their own decisions regarding what activities were *work* and which were not.

The Weekly Feast

Each Shabbat was the occasion for a feast, making the Sabbath a celebration as much as it was an obligation. We can assume that Jesus and his disciples celebrated a Sabbath feast together or with others every week of his ministry. What an amazing experience this must have been for his closest followers. Many gospel stories have Jesus teaching in a house on the Sabbath. Most likely, the Sabbath feast was the setting for these occasions.

In some ways the Sabbath meal was similar to the banquet and other feasts described in this book. Practical rituals such as washing hands and lighting lamps were characteristic elements. The meal started with the familiar blessing of bread and ended with a prayer of thanksgiving over the wine. There were important differences, however. The Sabbath feast was not a special meal shared by a small group of male colleagues or a harvest festival celebrated by the entire community. It was a feast just for family and friends, where everyone was involved, including women and children. The purpose was not philosophical discussion or musical entertainment. Rather the emphasis was the Sabbath itself, the one day of the week set apart by God, a reminder of the goodness of creation. Shabbat was first and foremost a family feast and the focus was God.

No matter how rich or poor the household, on this one night of the week, dinner was transformed into a special occasion. Since it was a celebration, the meal was expanded to include foods not eaten during the rest of the week. Meat was still considered too extravagant and was saved for the three most important feast days of the year, but smaller extravagances were added to the menu. Dried fish or squab would be added to the stew. A platter of fresh fruit might be placed on the table. Hard-boiled eggs might be dipped into olive oil and salt or even into a special sauce. Perhaps sweet cakes were enjoyed with the final glass of wine.

First-century rabbis interpreted the law in such a way to make it possible for friends and family to join in the feast. Pharisees devised special rules that allowed neighbors to carry food and dishes from one house to the next without violating the Sabbath prohibition against work. In this way, groups of friends could come together to celebrate the Sabbath. Religious leaders even debated whether someone could move the ladder in the dovecote to remove a pigeon or dove for the special dinner.[5] To this issue however, the answer was clear: all preparations occurred before sundown. Cooking, lighting fires and candles, fetching a bird for dinner were all considered work and were forbidden after sundown on Friday. So everything was prepared beforehand. The mother lighted the lamps even though it was still light. Dinner was already prepared and the stew was bubbling away in a pot over the fire.

The meal itself was a combination of religious ceremony and family feast. The father of the house took bread and prayed the usual short blessing and then distributed pieces of the bread among family and guests. Broken and shared bread was and still is a symbol of unity and fellowship.[6] In the case of the Shabbat, the host also offered an additional prayer, the Kiddush, thanking God for blessing the Sabbath and making it a holy day. This is an example of a Sabbath Kiddush that is still used today:

> Blessed are you, Lord, our God, King of the Universe who sanctifies us with his commandments, and has been pleased with us. You have lovingly and willingly given us your holy Shabbat as an inheritance, in memory of creation. The Shabbat is the first among our holy days, and a remembrance of our exodus from Egypt. Indeed, you have chosen us and made us holy among all peoples and have willingly and lovingly given us your holy Shabbat for an inheritance. Blessed are you, who sanctifies the Shabbat. Amen.

One can then imagine bread being dipped into sauce, hands scooping lentils, onions, and little pieces of pigeon or fish from a large bowl while animated conversation flowed with topics ranging from crops and politics to what young girl might marry the blacksmith's son.

A Land of Milk and Honey

Milk and honey were two extremely important staples for the diet in biblical times and one or both would likely have been included in some way as part of a special meal or feast. In addition, both also had a significant symbolic meaning for Jews and later for Christians. For the Israelites, milk and honey were a symbol of the Land of Israel:

> Then the Lord said, "I have observed the misery of my people who are in Egypt; I have heard their cry on account of their taskmasters. Indeed I know their sufferings, and I have come down to deliver them from the Egyptians, and to bring them up out of that land to a good and broad land, a land flowing with milk and honey." (Exodus 3: 7–8)

Milk was a symbol of "abundance" and "fertility." The prophets sometimes used milk to mean the abundance of a coming age when God would rule the earth (see Isaiah 55:12 and Joel 3:18). Most important, the phrase "Land of milk and honey" referred to the fertility and abundance of the Promised Land while the Hebrews were wandering in the wilderness. We can almost hear them saying "We're in the desert and we want something other than water to drink and manna to eat. We want the time and resources to make cheese and yogurt. We're sick and tired of eating this bread without honey. We crave something sweet." Imagine how extraordinary a fruitful land characterized by the richness of milk and its by-products and the sweetness of honey must have sounded to that nation of nomads walking around the wilderness for decades.

Milk to Drink

Milk was an important product for the common people in Galilee and throughout the Mediterranean world. Ancient peoples used goats, sheep, cattle, and even camels for their milk. However, by far the most common milk-giving animals were goats and sheep. As one might imagine, people living in the country drank more of this beverage than their urban relatives did. Yet all people, regardless of their social status, drank milk from time to time, and it was often offered to guests as a treat. Milk was also used for cooking, making porridges and such. But milk spoils very quickly, especially in a world with no refrigeration, so most of it was made into yogurt, cheese, and butter. Once converted into one of these food products, it lasted for a considerably longer period of time.

Cheese to Eat

Using milk to make cheese is an extremely ancient undertaking and an efficient way to prepare milk for storage. Long before they were making pottery for storing their foodstuffs, people made cheese and used it as a major part of their daily diet. Food historians believe that the first cheese was probably created quite by accident. Not wasting any part of the animals they butchered for dinner, nomads used the bladders and stomachs of the sheep and goats to store milk from the other animals in the herd. It turns out that the stomachs of very young animals contain rennet, a natural enzyme that causes milk to curdle, forming curds, which are the building blocks for making cheese. The curds were eaten as they were, with a taste and texture much like cottage cheese, or they were salted and separated from the residual liquid, called the whey, by straining. The curds then were formed into a disk and dried in the open air. The result was cheese.

The Israelites took the process of making cheese to a new level by using plants that contain rennet to begin the curdling process. Plants with rennet, like fig tree sap or thistle buds, were common in the Middle East. These cheeses had different colors, textures and flavors according to the type of plant or sap that was used. This process is still used today in some areas and has been reintroduced in places such as Corsica and the lower Alps to make artisan cheeses. By the time of Jesus, utensils like ceramic strainers and wicker baskets were used to strain the curds from the whey. The curds were then molded with baskets or wooden boxes. It was also during the first century that cheese makers began to compress the cheese by placing a plate over the curds and weighting the plate with stones. The people of the first-century Mediterranean had cream cheeses, cottage cheese, cheese curds, and a large variety of harder cheeses, many with textures and tastes similar to cheddar and feta cheese. They also produced flavored cheeses, adding ingredients such as garlic, herbs, and spices. Some cheeses were flavored by soaking them in a brine of salt, water, and other flavorings. The more sophisticated Roman cheese makers even developed the technique of setting their wheels of cheese near smoking and smoldering fires in order to give the product a smoky flavor. Apparently smoked flavored cheeses were as popular two thousand years ago as they are now. The farmer and his family in Galilee certainly did not have access to these sophisticated flavored cheeses. But they did make or purchase a variety of both soft and hard cheeses.

Yogurt

Yogurt was also a popular food made from milk. It was used in a variety of ways: eaten plain, as a dip or sauce, or even made into a simple creamy cheese. Different flavorings such as garlic and herbs were mixed with it to form a dip for bread or vegetables. Fruits and fruit syrup were also combined with yogurt to produce simple desserts. Yogurt can be wrapped in cheesecloth and allowed to drain, producing a very primitive type of cream cheese that is very tasty.

Yogurt is actually milk that is fermented by the presence of two types of bacteria working together to form lactic acid from the sugars in the milk. Like cheese, the lactic acid causes curds to form; only these curds are much smaller than with cheese, and the end product is much creamier. Like cheese and many other food by-products, creation of yogurt must have seemed like a miracle of God to the ancient people. There was a fine line between the bacteria that cause milk to spoil and their relatives that caused milk to become a tasty treat like yogurt.

Yogurt was simple to make. Fresh milk was heated until it was warm and then a portion from the existing store of yogurt was added to the pot. The resulting mixture was left to stand for the rest of the day while the bacteria in the old yogurt worked to ferment the new milk.

There were additional benefits for ancients who ate yogurt. It is naturally low in fat and calories. A pot of yogurt has as many calories and as much fat as a glass of milk. The lactic acid produced in yogurt is also good for the digestive system. It works by destroying unhealthy microbes in the digestive system.

Butter as an Alternative to Olive Oil

Milk was also churned into butter. Even though olive oil was the principle fat used for cooking, butter was also used, especially in rural areas. We are part of a culture that loves the taste of butterfat in our foods, even as we are wary of its health downside. A modern food product has a much better chance of being popular if it tastes as though it was made with butter, even if the flavor is artificial. We appreciate, and even crave butter flavor in our foods. So it may seem strange to us that many Greeks, Romans, and sophisticated Jews chose not to eat butter, or ate butter only rarely, preferring olive oil and claiming butter was only for shepherds and other low-class country folk. Our ancient relatives eventually discovered that their butter lasted longer if the water and solids were separated and removed. This is the process still used to make clarified butter (called "ghee" in the Middle East).

Honey

Honey was considered one of the basic necessities of life and was a symbol of the good things that God's land produced. The Hebrew for "bee" has the same root as their word for "word," *dbr*. It is also where the Jewish name "Deborah" originated. At first thought, it may seem unusual to tie together bees and words. But the Hebrews saw honey, the by-product of bees, as a miracle that signified truth and God's word. Honey was one of very few foods that required no processing or treatment after it was harvested. It deteriorates so slowly as not to be noticeable and there was no real substitute for it. The bee seemingly created the sweet gift of honey out of nothing but God's own creation, which began with God's word. It was truly a gift from God, bees making honey by sitting on God's own flowers. Taking the similarity between the two words one step further, the writers of the Bible sometimes used the phrase "sweet as honey" to refer to receiving God's word (Ezekiel 3:3, Psalm 19:10, Revelation 10:10).

Can you imagine cooking in a kitchen without sugar? Not only for cookies and cakes, sugar is added to many of the foods we eat, including most drinks, breads, cereals and many prepared foods. We might even use a pinch of sugar to help balance a vinaigrette or encourage onions to caramelize. Now instead of sugar, consider what it would be like using only honey. For most of history, honey was the primary sweetener used both for savory foods and desserts. That was certainly true in the first century. Processed sugar as we know it was still centuries away. Honey and fruit syrups were not only the sweeteners of choice, they were the only sweeteners.

People in the Middle East harvested honey from both wild and cultivated hives that farmers kept on their property. The ancient Egyptians were the first to domesticate bees. After finding a wild hive in a hollow tree, they would cut the sections on either side of the hive and take it away. They also developed the use of smoke to temporarily sedate the bees when moving the hive and to harvest the honeycombs. This technique is still used by modern beekeepers. Apparently, later in history, the Egyptians decided that smoke failed to provide the royal beekeepers with adequate protection. Ramses III had archers escort his beekeepers to the hives in order to protect them; though it is difficult imagining arrows being much of a deterrent to a swarm of angry bees.

Using methods of domestication and smoke to stun the bees, first-century farmers harvested their honey twice a year. The first harvest was in early summer. The taste of this honey was the most intense because of the abundance of the flowering plants of spring visited by the bees. The second harvest was in late summer. Collecting honey, especially wild honey, was not for the faint of heart. It required skill and courage to face the stinging bees. This was one task that was traditionally regarded as a *man's work*, while many of the other tasks of gathering or harvesting food for the table were reserved for women.

In the Bible, and in other literature from biblical times, the word *honey* could also refer to fruit juices that were boiled into syrup and used to flavor foods. Juices from grapes, pomegranates, dates, figs, and other fruits were used in this way. Pomegranate and other fruit syrups are still common cooking ingredients in many Eastern Mediterranean kitchens.

How to Celebrate a Shabbat with Family and Friends

The Sabbath feast should feel as though it is part worship and part intimate dinner with family and friends. A Friday evening dinner for six to twelve is ideal. Make sure to include at least one candle on the table for the ritual candle lighting. Begin the dinner by washing everyone's hands; you will need a pitcher of water, a bowl, and a hand towel for each of the guests. The host can use this prayer:

> Blessed are you, Lord, our God, King of the Universe, who sanctifies us with his commandments, and commands us concerning washing of hands. Amen.

After hands are washed, the hostess or another member of the host family lights the candles on the table and elsewhere around the house. Begin the candle-lighting ceremony with this prayer:

> Blessed are you, Lord, our God, King of the Universe, who sanctifies us with his commandments, and commands us to light the candles of the Shabbat (Amen).

The dinner continues with the blessing of the bread and the Sabbath blessing. The host takes a loaf of bread and holds it during the blessing. After the blessing, the host tears the loaf in half and takes a portion. Then the bread is passed to the guests so that everyone present tears a piece of bread from the first loaf. These prayers can be used:

> Blessed are you, Lord, our God,
> who sanctifies us with his commandments,
> and has been pleased with us. For you have lovingly and willingly given us your
>   holy Shabbat as an inheritance, in memory of creation.
> The Shabbat is the first among our holy days, and a remembrance of our exodus
>   from Egypt. Indeed, you have chosen us and made us holy among all peoples
>   and have willingly and lovingly given us your holy Shabbat for an inheritance
> Blessed are You, who sanctifies the Shabbat. Amen.
> Blessed are you, Lord, our God, King of the Universe, who brings forth bread
>   from the earth. Amen.

After the main course is finished and the table is cleared, the wine should be blessed. The host should hold a cup of wine his hands and use this prayer:

> Blessed are you, Lord, our God, King of the Universe, who creates the fruit of the vine. Amen.

Menu for a Shabbat Feast with Family and Friends

- Egg Bread*
- Olive Oil and Thyme Dip*

- Olives* (chapter 4 or from the market)
- Chickpea and Cucumber Salad*
- Bulgur Pilaf*
- Braised Chicken with Figs and Apricots*
- Poached Apricots with Yogurt*

The Recipes

Egg Bread

There were several types of bread in the first century that included eggs in the dough. Egg bread was truly a special occasion bread for special guests!

1 tablespoon quick-rising yeast	1 tablespoon salt
½ cup warm water (apprx. 110°) and 1 cup additional water	2 tablespoons butter (soft or melted)
	2 tablespoons olive oil
2 eggs	1½ tablespoons honey
6½ cups unbleached flour	1 cup milk

Place the yeast and warm water in the bowl of your mixer. Wait until yeast begins to activate, approximately 15 minutes. It will change color and begin to bubble. Crack eggs into a liquid cup measure. Briefly beat with a fork and add some water to the eggs until mixture measures 1 cup.

Add the flour to the yeast mixture. Then add the rest of the ingredients, including the egg mixture. Add the oil first and use the same tablespoon to measure your honey. The oil will keep the honey from sticking to the measuring spoon.

Mix with a dough hook for 5 minutes. Start on the slowest speed to keep the flour from splashing out of the bowl and then increase the speed to medium slow. Let the dough rest for 15 minutes and then mix for another 5 minutes. The dough should be slightly sticky and springy to the touch. Add flour 1 tablespoon at a time if the dough is too sticky, or add water if it is too dry.

Turn the dough out onto a floured surface and knead for about 30 seconds. Place in an oiled bowl and cover with a cotton kitchen towel or oiled plastic wrap. If your KitchenAid bowl is large enough, you can leave the dough in the bowl to rise. Let rise until it has doubled in size, between 1 and 1½ hours.

After rising, turn out the dough onto the floured surface, punch down with your fingers to allow the gases to escape and knead for approximately 1 minute. Form the dough into 2 loaves about 10–12 inches in diameter. Oil or lightly spray baking sheets with olive oil or cooking oil and place the loaves on the sheets. Cover with the floured towel and let rise for another hour. After forty minutes, preheat the oven to 400°. Cook your bread on a rack in the center of the oven for 30 to 35 minutes, until nicely brown.

Remove bread and let it cool on a rack for at least 2 hours.

Olive Oil and Thyme Dip

For dipping bread or vegetables. Try using other herbs, too.

1 cup olive oil
1 tablespoon dried thyme
½ teaspoon salt

Mix the ingredients and let sit. Stir before serving.

Chickpea and Cucumber Salad

This is an easy salad to make, yet very tasty. You can use a 15-ounce can of chickpeas, but it only contains 1½ cup. If you do use canned chickpeas, rinse and drain first. To pit an olive, press down on it with the side of a chef knife. This loosens the fruit from around the pit.

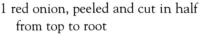

1 red onion, peeled and cut in half from top to root
2 cups cooked chickpeas
2 cucumbers, peeled and cut into chunks
¼ pound feta cheese, cut or broken into chunks

16 kalamata olives, or brined olives from chapter 4, pitted and cut in half
2 tablespoons parsley, stems removed and roughly chopped
lemon salad dressing

Slice the onion into thin half-moons. Mix all the ingredients and allow to sit so flavors can mingle.

Lemon Salad Dressing: Place 1 teaspoon of dried oregano and ½ teaspoon salt in a small bowl. Add ¼ cup of freshly squeezed lemon juice and ¼ cup of olive oil. Whisk or stir to combine and add to the salad.

Bulgur Pilaf

Perhaps the oldest recorded use of wheat was in preparing and using bulgur. Its uses are numerous, from salads to soup, breads to desserts. It has the same nutritive value as whole wheat. This dish is also very good served as a side dish with the stews from this book.

1 cup coarse cut bulgur (#2 or #3)
⅓ cup olive oil (divided use)
½ medium onion, chopped
1 garlic clove, minced
1 cup chicken stock or water

¼ teaspoon ground cumin
1 teaspoon salt
¼ teaspoon ground black pepper
chopped parsley and roasted almond slivers for garnish

Using a fine-mesh strainer, quickly rinse and dry the bulgur. Heat a 3-quart saucepan over medium heat and add oil. Add onions and sauté until beginning to turn brown. Add garlic and continue to cook until garlic turns translucent. Add the bulgur and sauté until it begins to toast and separate.

Add the stock (or water), cumin, salt, and pepper. Bring to a boil, reduce to a simmer and cover. Let it cook for approximately 20 minutes.

After the bulgur finishes, remove the lid and stir with a fork to separate. Then stir in several tablespoons of chopped, fresh parsley. Spoon the bulgur into a serving dish and garnish with roasted almond slivers. Serves 6.

Braised Chicken with Figs and Apricots

This is one of our favorites!

8 large bone-in chicken thighs
  (skins can be removed)
1½ teaspoons salt, or to taste
ground pepper to taste
flour for dredging
2 tablespoons olive oil
½ onion, chopped
2 garlic cloves, minced

1 cup chicken stock (or water)
1 cup white wine
1 cup dried figs
1 cup dried apricots
1 teaspoon cumin
1 teaspoon coriander
1 teaspoon mustard

Salt and pepper the chicken thighs and dredge them in the flour. Brown them, three or four at a time in a 14-inch skillet or 5-quart Dutch oven. Remove the chicken and sauté the onion in the same pan until it begins to caramelize. Add the garlic and cook for another minute. Return the chicken to the pan and add the rest of the ingredients.

Bring the liquid to a boil and then reduce to a simmer. Cover and cook for 40 to 45 minutes, until the meat easily pulls away from the bone, turning the thighs from time to time. Uncover and remove the chicken. Cook for an additional 5 minutes to thicken the sauce. Adjust the seasoning if necessary by adding additional salt or pepper.

Place the chicken on a serving dish and cover with the sauce. Or return the chicken to the Dutch oven and use it for the serving dish. Serves 8

Instead of finishing the cooking time on top of the oven, cover and place in a 350° oven. If you cannot find dried figs, simply use dried apricots.

Poached Apricots and Yogurt

Serve these apricots at room temperature over a bowl of unflavored (homemade, plain, or Greek) yogurt. Or if you want to leave the first century, try it as a topping for vanilla ice cream or pound cake. If you love lemon, add zest from one lemon to the poaching liquid before cooking the apricots.

½ lb. dried apricots, cut in half
2 cups water
1 teaspoon lemon juice

⅓ cup honey
1 cinnamon stick

Place the apricots in a mixing bowl and cover them with the water. Soak overnight.

Preheat the oven to 300°. Cut a piece of parchment paper the size of your medium saucepan and crinkle. Set aside.

Separate the apricots from the water using a strainer, retaining the apricot-flavored water. Pour the water into a medium ovenproof saucepan and add the lemon juice, honey, and a cinnamon stick. Bring to a boil on top of the stove and then add the apricots to the pan. Remove from the heat. Make sure the liquid covers the apricots; you may need to add additional water if it does not.

Cover the apricot sauce with the parchment paper. The parchment paper should rest on top of the sauce. Cook the apricot sauce in the oven for at least 2 hours, or until the apricots begin to break down. Serves 6 to 8.

At banquets and formal gatherings, the rich ate while reclining. Servants removed the inner table and replaced it with a table holding the next course.

CHAPTER SIX

The Banquet

When Jesus noticed how the guests chose the places of honor, he told them a parable. "When you are invited by someone to a wedding banquet, do not sit down at the place of honor, in case someone more distinguished than you has been invited by your host; and the host who invited both of you may come and say to you, 'Give this person your place,' and then in disgrace you would start to take the lowest place." (Luke 14:7–9)

Is there any culinary experience more universally enjoyed than a special dinner with friends? Yet the same experience can cause a fainthearted host to tremble with fear. There is the guest list to consider: how many people do we invite? Who will sit where? Is it wise to have Cathy and George under the same roof? Then there is the menu to prepare. Which friends have "sworn off" carbs? Can we get a nice salmon fillet and fresh asparagus this time of year? Chardonnay or Chenin Blanc with the fish? Espresso with the chocolate mousse or maybe serve seasonal fruit instead? The house is cleaned and the silverware polished. Do we really need three forks and four glasses? Finally, the big night arrives.

Is it worth it? These authors say absolutely. You know by the smiles and compliments as the food is served and by the way everyone lingers over that final cup of coffee. The conversation becomes more open and engaging with each glass of wine. All the guests have a wonderful time and the evening is considered a success by all.

These experiences are as old as recorded history. Ancient people from all cultures hosted dinner parties and formal banquets for friends and colleagues.

Wealthy Romans set aside rooms in their homes solely for that purpose. The world of Jesus and his friends and followers was no different. The banquet was an opportunity for companions to gather and spend an evening together. Entertainment and the opportunity to recline and enjoy the company of friends often followed tables full of fine food. Just as today, banquets were a setting for conducting business or engaging in political or religious debate. There were even banqueting clubs and associations. On many occasions, the purpose of the banquet was dictated by religious or social traditions. As we will see in a later chapter, even the poorest Jew reclined at the Passover feast, dined on roasted lamb, and enjoyed the prescribed four glasses of wine.

Figs, dates, and pomegranates were widely grown and eaten in the Holy Land and, whether served as appetizers, used as flavorings, or included with dessert, were most assuredly included as part of banquet menus. This chapter will include a closer look at these three fruits that are still very important for Mediterranean and Middle Eastern cuisine.

First-Century Banquet

Many of the customs and practices of the first-century banquet were common throughout the Mediterranean and Middle Eastern countries at the time of Jesus. These similarities included such details as singing hymns and reciting prayers, though the deity that was the focus of hymns and prayers would vary. Still the customs were the same, probably because many of the countries in question had been conquered first by the Greeks and then later by the Romans. Centuries of occupation gave countries the opportunity to mix and share their practices of banqueting.

The first-century banquet actually began with invitations. An invitation to a banquet was always considered a request to be part of a special occasion. In many cases the invitations were in writing. With wording very similar to cards printed by modern greeting card companies, these invitations were delivered by servants or members of the host's household. Ancient examples of these invitations continue to be discovered in archaeological digs in Egypt and the Middle East. In some cases we know exactly who was hosting the banquet, who was invited, and when and where the banquet was held. Yesterday's trash, today's archaeological treasure.

Just as today, some guests were verbally invited. The host would see friends at the marketplace or the baths and invite them to a special dinner just as we invite friends and neighbors to a backyard barbecue when we see them at the mall or grocery store. There were those who were so popular that they received many invitations and would try to attend several banquets on the same evening. We also have records of first-century "banquet crashers." These were men who heard friends were hosting or attending a banquet and arrived after the dishes and food had been cleared from the tables and just as the wine was being poured! The feast usually started at sundown and lasted three or more hours. The guests spent time before the banquet preparing themselves, wearing perfumes, oil, and special clothing.

Several factors influenced the number of guests invited to a banquet. Like today, many more people would have been invited to a wedding feast than to a dinner party. Also, a host was thought inconsiderate if the guests felt cramped because of too many people. But more than space, men in the first century appreciated the banquet because of the conversation and hospitality it promoted. With a small group, all the guests could engage in the same discussion. If too many were invited, the party broke into smaller groups and a sense of community was frustrated. Most hosts considered eight or nine guests to be the perfect number for a banquet. Writers like Plutarch criticized the wealthy who built "showy dining rooms that hold thirty couches or more. Such magnificence makes for unsociable and un-friendly banquets where the manager of a fair is needed more than a toast-master."[1] With a group of nine, all of the guests were seated in the same room and could be part of the same conversation.

The feast began in an anteroom. The guests had their feet washed and were sometimes anointed with perfumed oil. These customs were rooted in common sense. People wearing sandals and walking on dusty or muddy streets needed to have their feet washed before entering the host's home. The task of washing feet usually was given to a slave or servant. If the host did not have a slave or servant, then one of the women in the family was given that responsibility. Needless to say, washing feet was not considered an honorable job. That is one reason why Jesus' disciples were so troubled when he took that role at their last supper (John 13:2–11). The perfumed olive oil or ointment served both as a skin moisturizer and deodorant.

After a guest's feet were washed, his right hand was washed and he was offered a glass of wine. The assumption was that only one clean hand was needed to drink wine. The guests remained in the anteroom until all the invited guests arrived. Then they were shown to the banqueting room.

Men, Women, and the Banquet

By now you may have guessed that the guests were all male. Mediterranean cultures were solidly patriarchal, and women had very few rights and privileges. The difference in age between the husband and wife may also have been a rea-son why these dinners were *male only*. Men in their late twenties and thirties may not have wanted to include their young and uneducated teenage brides at dinners where conversation was focused on politics, religion, and philosophy.

There were exceptions to this practice. Some feasts and religious festivals were specifically designed to include women. For example, after a betrothal, the bridegroom gave the bride's family resources that enabled them to host a betrothal feast primarily for the bride and the women of the community. Both men and women were present at the wedding feast, but they sat at different tables. At both Greek and Roman banquets the male guests sometimes brought women with them, but these women were not their wives! It was common in the Greco-Roman culture for men to have concubines or to engage the company of prostitutes as companions for the banquet.

Egyptian customs were different. They more often included their wives and other women at their banquets. Eventually the men of other Mediterranean cultures saw the wisdom of having women, including wives, as guests. We know that by the first century, respectable women were attending Roman banquets with more frequency and that by the second century this practice was becoming more commonplace even among the Greeks, who were the last holdouts of the male-only parties.

In light of how women were understood in the first century, especially in the Middle East, Jesus' behavior was quite radical, especially for a respected rabbi. For example, consider the story of Mary and Martha. A common interpretation of this passage is that it occurred either while a banquet was being prepared or during a banquet where Jesus was the guest of honor. Martha was fulfilling the traditional role of women in such circumstances by performing her many tasks of cooking and serving (Luke 10:40). Mary, however, broke with tradition and was sitting at Jesus' feet and listening to his teaching. Apparently she actually *crashed* the banquet while it was in process and, forsaking her domestic responsibilities, chose instead to sit near his couch and listen to his message. Her presence was doubly shocking, first because women did not sit at the feet of a teacher and second, because Jewish women did not attend banquets, especially when not invited. The surprise is not that Martha becomes upset because she is left to fulfill the domestic duties without her sister. The surprise is that Jesus agrees with Mary, "Mary has chosen the better part, which will not be taken away from her" (Luke 10:42).

In the Dining Room

The typical banquet was divided into two parts. The first section focused on the meal. It was called, in Greek, the *deipnon*. By the first century, the deipnon included a first course of appetizers and a second course with the main dish. The second part of the banquet, called the *symposium*, emphasized entertainment and wine. A third course of the meal, a light dessert of nuts, fruit, and sweet cakes, was served during the symposium.

Once all the guests arrived, they moved to the banqueting room where couches for reclining had been placed against three of the walls. All the diners faced the middle of the room making it easy to share tables and talk with each other. The typical banqueting room held nine of these couches, though some held as few as five or as many as eleven. A few very large banqueting rooms were designed so that dining couches could be grouped in small clusters. Some homes were large enough to have banqueting rooms, but they were also available in public buildings and temples.

Couches were assigned to the guests according to their rank in society, and arranging the guests without causing insult or embarrassment was one mark of a good host. A guest of honor sat on the right side of the host. Other guests sat accordingly. As Jesus reminded fellow diners at such a banquet, better to sit too low and have the host ask you to join him than to take the seat of honor and be asked to move to the couch near the door (Luke 14:7–11).

Not only were seats assigned, but responsibilities were also designated. The host's responsibilities included securing the menu, preparing the guest list, providing the location for the dinner, and designating the order of seating for the guests. The host also appointed a guest as the *symposiarch*, who established the rules for drinking wine during the second half of the feast. This person decided the ratio of mixing wine and water and also determined how full the goblets and glasses were to be filled. The wine steward mentioned in the story of the wedding at Cana was probably a guest serving as the symposiarch. He was asked by the host of the feast, probably the groom's father, to mix the wine and water. One can hope that the person selected as symposiarch was chosen for his knowledge of wine and skill at adding water to a particular type of wine to produce the desired taste.

After the guests had reclined, servants or female family members washed the guests' hands, both of them this time. Then tables with food were carried into the room. If the tables were permanent fixtures, the servants brought the food on trays. Each table served two or three guests. The food was served on platters or in bowls and the guests at that table shared everything. There were no plates or bowls for the individual diners, just as there were no knives, forks, spoons, or napkins. All the more reason for the custom of washing hands before the meal!

The practices of the Jews were slightly different regarding posture during the banquet. Some Jews reclined to eat at banquets, just as their Greek and Roman neighbors did. This was certainly the case at the most formal of banquets. But research tells us that there were those Jews who sat to eat the first part of the meal and then reclined for the dessert and entertainment.[2] Regardless of exactly when relaxing on couches and cushions took place, reclining at meals was another sign of class differentiation. Only free citizens were allowed to eat while reclining, which meant that women, children, and slaves were not allowed to assume this posture while eating.

The host began the first part of the banquet by offering a prayer of thanks- giving for the bread: *Blessed are you, Lord, our God, King of the Universe who brings forth bread from the earth.* If the feast was for a special occasion or on a religious holiday, an additional prayer was offered that made reference to the occasion.

Then the feast began. The practice of the banquet was a formal meal in a luxurious setting with the best food and wine that the host and his family could offer. Hospitality in the ancient world, and especially in the Middle East, was practically a religion in itself. This was exhibited almost two thousand years before Jesus under the Oaks of Mamre, when Abraham and Sarah prepared a feast for three strangers (Genesis 18:1–8). The guests eventually revealed themselves as divine messengers, but it would have been the same feast even if they had been average human travelers. The author of the Epistle to the Hebrews also reminds us that it is also our responsibility to practice unbridled generosity with our hospitality (Hebrews 13:2). That part of the world is still famous for its practice of abundant hospitality. In her book on Eastern Mediterranean cooking, Paula Wolfert writes in the intro- duction about her many encounters with gracious and generous people for whom sharing food is an important symbol of hospitality. She tells this story:

> During my stay in Georgia, I and a friend were invited to the tiny autonomous republic of Dagestan, on the Caspian Sea. When we arrived at the ancient Caucasian village of Khunzakh, nine thousand feet above sea level, we were greeted by the mayor. . . . "Guests here are holy," he told us. . . . "You are guests of our entire village. By the end of your stay, all our women and children will have kissed you!"[3]

Just because the food was the best possible did not necessarily mean that meat was included in the meal. The feast certainly included a lot of bread and vegetables such as lettuce, onions, leeks, beans, herbs, and olives.[4] Cheese and other milk products also were part of the banquet. If the meal was im- portant, then fowl or fish was served. Meat was included only if the meal was especially extravagant. Both fresh- and saltwater fish were extremely popular throughout the Mediterranean world, though residents of Jewish Palestine tended to eat the freshwater fish from the Sea of Galilee. Doves and pigeons were the most common poultry served, though other wild and domesticated birds, including chicken, were also eaten. The most commonly served meats were lamb and goat, but beef and pork (for non-Jews) were also served. Sausages were commonly made in the first century and served at Greek and Roman banquets. Wild game also made its way onto the table.

After the meal, the tables and dishes were cleared from the room. Servants entered and swept the floor clean. New tables with fresh and dried fruit, pistachios, almonds, hard-boiled eggs, bowls of salt, and sweet cakes were brought into the room. With the lighter fare, the focus of the feast shifted. Instead of food, the guests now focused their attention on entertainment and wine. This marked the beginning of the *symposium*. Another table was carried into the room with a large bowl called the *krater* (also in Greek). Wine and water were mixed in the krater. Until this time, wine and water were mixed in each individual cup when given to a guest. But now, for the rest of the evening, the wine was served from the common bowl. At this point in the feast another prayer was offered, this time in thanksgiving for the wine. The Greeks and Romans offered their prayer to Dionysus, called Bacchus by the Romans, who was the god of wine, while the Jews prayed their prayer of thanksgiving to the one God: *Blessed are You, Lord, our God, King of the Universe, who creates the fruit of the vine.* After the prayer, those in attendance sang a hymn and then began to enjoy the entertainment while they ate their dessert and drank their wine.

There was the practice at Greek banquets that the first taste of wine during the symposium came from a common cup. After the blessing, a small amount of wine was poured from the cup into the fire or onto the floor as an offering of thanksgiving. The host then offered a simple thanksgiving, drank from the cup and passed it to the next guest. Each guest at the banquet did the same. After the guests drank from the common cup, each individual cup was filled from the common bowl.

Did the Jews at the time of Jesus have a similar custom? Because so many of the banquet customs were similar, it is very possible that they did, with the exception that the focus of thanksgiving was the God they worshipped. If so, was this how the cup was shared at the Last Supper, after Jesus reinterpreted the meaning of the cup of wine and commanded that his followers "do this in remembrance of me"? We can picture Jesus drinking from the cup and passing it to the disciple next to him, who then did the same. Though our investigation of the historical evidence is not conclusive, one can still wonder whether this drink of thanksgiving was from one cup or from many.

The themes of *equality* and *sharing* permeated ancient banquets. Customs like the assigned seating based on social position were certainly signs of cultural stratification, but once seated, everyone was treated as an equal. All ate the same food from common bowls. All drank the same wine from the krater. All enjoyed the same entertainment. All had an opportunity to speak their minds and share their opinions. All participated equally in the extravagant hospitality of the host. In fact, this was intentional. When not listening to flute music, one of the favorite topics of discussion was the equality of the participants of the banquet. Because the setting fostered equality and sharing, it also promoted such values as friendship and community. During the course of the evening, social separation and stratification were overcome and, in the midst of extravagant celebration, a new bond was created.

Certainly there were those who abused the banquet. The Old Testament condemns the overindulgence and excesses, even as it uses the feast as a model for the abundant life with God at the end time. The prophet Amos railed against the common practices of the banquet, citing examples of luxury while the plight of the poor was ignored:

> Alas for those who lie on beds of ivory, and lounge on their couches,
> And eat lambs from the flock,
> And calves from the stall;
> Who sing idle songs to the sound of the harp,
> And like David improvise on instruments of music;
> Who drink wine from bowls,
> And anoint themselves with the finest oils
> But are not grieved over the ruin of Joseph. (Amos 6:4–6)

In the first century, by its very nature, the banquet was still a feast that was reserved for the wealthier members of society. Very few farmers and vendors could afford the extravagance of this type of feast. It was certainly beyond the means of a tenant farmer or day laborer. As at the time of the prophet Amos, the extravagance of the banquet must have served to differentiate the rich and poor, especially as the first century progressed toward the Jewish revolution.

The Romans eventually took the banquet model to an extreme, where food and drink became excessive and the division of guests obscured the themes of sharing and equality. New and exotic foods were imported from all over the known world. Ostrich and peacock were banqueting favorites. A dinner for the Emperor Vitellius supposedly consisted of such foods as "pike liver, pheasant brains, peacock brains, flamingo tongues, and lamprey roe."[5] Guests were now segregated into different rooms based on their social position, which also determined the kind of food they were served and the quality of the wine they were offered. Were you given beef Wellington or round steak? Did you drink Chateau Lafite Rothschild or wine from a box? No longer were banquets concerned with creating a sense of equality. Instead, social stratification was emphasized. No longer was community promoted. Instead of extravagance being offered as a gift to friends, extravagance became an end unto itself. Guests threw food at the servants and humiliated their hosts if the food and wine failed to meet their expectations. Individual indulgence became the model. Feasters purged their stomachs in *vomitoriums* between courses so they could continue to eat and drink huge quantities of very rich food and strong wine. The feast was corrupted.

So marked the extravagance of the most powerful and wealthiest people in the ancient world. It also sealed their fall. But for many, the banquet remained the same. A host provided a feast of the best food, drink, and entertainment possible. He willingly shared this as a gift that promoted community and sharing. And on occasion, this was the feast of Jesus and his friends.

Banquet Entertainment

After the ceremony with the wine, the guests enjoyed some type of entertainment. In fact, the meal was not truly a banquet unless the host provided entertainment and wine. Music was a very popular amusement. There were also poetry readings by the guests; riddles posed that stimulated conversation; and different types of games, including drinking games. Very wealthy hosts provided even more elaborate entertainment, including dancers, acrobats, and entire musical ensembles. These types of feasts were also hosted by clubs, guilds, or other organizations that would use at least part of the entertainment portion of the evening for a business meeting. Many of the groups had *pleasure* and *social intercourse* as goals of their organizations that were fulfilled by enjoying the food, entertainment, and fellowship of the banquet.

Music was by far the most popular form of after-dinner amusement. Many ancient documents and works of art depict a *flute girl* entertaining guests with her music. Usually the flute player entered the room after the blessing of the wine and began to play. It was also written that at least some of these women were also prostitutes and that the flute players were often the targets of rude behavior from intoxicated guests. But surely this was not true of all the women musicians. In Greek and Roman culture flute girls not only provided music for banquets but also played their instruments for religious ceremonies.[6]

First-century Jews also enjoyed music as entertainment at their banquets with concerts from the flute and harp: "A ruby seal in a setting of gold is a concert of music at a banquet of wine. A seal of emerald in a rich setting of gold is the melody of music with good wine" (Sirach 32:5–6). This passage also includes a warning that the wise man does not interrupt the music with his conversation (Sirach 32:3).

Philosophical conversation was also a common type of entertainment. The host chose a guest in advance to pose questions for discussion. Common themes for discussion included topics such as the nature of friendship and community. The Jews preferred music for their entertainment, but also used conversation as a means of engaging the participants. Instead of philosophy, they discussed or debated the meaning of the Torah or Law of Moses. Politics and religion were always popular themes for discussion at banquets. And as we can imagine, the discussions became more animated and intense as the evening progressed and more wine was consumed. Sometimes a special guest was invited to the banquet. For the Jews, this guest might be a well-known rabbi or scribe. This part of the banquet was an opportunity for the guest to teach and ask and answer questions. After three or more hours of food, wine, and entertainment, the guests sang a hymn and left for their homes.

Knowing the model of the banquet, it is easy to understand the role of Jesus at the feast. Simply put, he was the entertainment. Jesus became a well-known if somewhat controversial rabbi. Even though his ministry was focused in Galilee, he had followers as far away as Jerusalem. Many religious leaders, especially the Pharisees, were sympathetic to at least part of his message. But a few of his actions and some of the tenets of his teachings were contentious and polarizing. So he was invited to banquets. The wealthy and the powerful wanted to hear what he had to say without fighting the crowds when he spoke at the edge of town or in the synagogue. Like everyone else, his feet were washed in the anteroom and he was offered a cup of wine mixed with water. Servants led him to a banqueting room where his hands were washed and where he ate from common bowls of vegetables, stews, and sauces. He tore bread from common loaves and dipped pieces in flavored olive oil and dips made from legumes. After dinner he watched as water was mixed with wine and as thanksgivings were offered.

Then came the questions. What are your views on fasting? Is it true you healed a man on the Sabbath? Should we pay taxes to the emperor? Jesus answered their questions with stories and talked about the Kingdom of God. Then he asked questions in return. Was the Sabbath made for us or were we made for the Sabbath? Who is the true neighbor? Which are the greatest of the commandments? We can imagine that sometimes his teachings and rebukes amused his host and fellow guests and sometimes they angered them. Sometimes they agreed with him; sometimes they disagreed. Some eventually became followers and some became enemies.

Is it any wonder that, despite shift in the practices and traditions, we continue to enjoy banquets today? The elements of bread, wine, prayer, discussion, good food, and good fellowship are catalysts for more than just an enjoyable evening. Relationships are established and friendships deepen. A common identity is forged. It is no surprise that the first century of Christian worship included a feast of good food along with a special blessing and sharing of bread and wine. It is also no surprise that there is a belief among some of those who study such things that the form of early Christian worship was likely very similar to the banquet.

Banquet Snacks: Three Holy Land Delicacies

The Mishnah, an important Jewish document written toward the end of the second century, stated that there were seven kinds of produce for which the land of Israel was noted: wheat, barley, grapes, figs, pomegranates, olives used for oil, and dates used for honey."[7] As this list expresses, figs, dates, and pomegranates join grapes and olives as being extremely important both as food and as biblical symbols. These fruits each had a prominent place in the first century diet and all three served an important role as part of the banquet cuisine.

Figs

Adam and Even may have lost their innocence and their home in the Garden of Eden by eating an apricot, or maybe it was an apple or a quince, but when they decided to clothe themselves, they chose fig leaves. The leaves are big and one can imagine that they could be used to make a not-too-revealing loincloth, or maybe even a primitive apron. However, our primitive ancestors must have quickly realized that the produce of the fig tree was better suited for cuisine than for couture. Archaeologists agree that figs and fig trees played an important role almost from the beginning of the history of civilization. They have found the remains of figs in a number of ancient sites that cause some to believe that the fig tree may have been one of the first fruits to be cultivated.

Because they are naturally high in sugar, figs were a popular snack and dessert. They are nutritious, being high in fiber, calcium, and many other healthy minerals. However, figs have a very short shelf life, perhaps the shortest of any fruit, so most of them were dried and eaten long after the harvest season. Dried figs were then pressed into cakes and used as a key ingredient in both sweet and savory recipes. Fig cakes were carried to work and eaten for lunch and were standard snacks for longer trips. Enterprising first-century cooks also used the sweet fruit to make syrups and other treats.

Figs are a most unusual fruit, if they are truly a fruit. Actually, the fig is a receptacle that contains and protects little flowers. Wild fig trees are either "male" or "female" and the fruit of the female figs must be pollinated or it falls off the tree before it is fully developed. A tiny wasp, conveniently known as a fig wasp, fulfills that role by crawling through a little hole in the outer skin and pollinating the flowers. The skin, the sweet fleshy fruit, and the small edible seeds then continue to develop. Because the figs are actually protected flowers, they appear each spring on the trees before the leaves emerge.

The figs were not the only part of the tree that was eaten. The leaves from fig trees and from grape vines were a standard part of Mediterranean cuisine. Because of their size, damp fig leaves were wrapped around fish fillets before being laid on coals for cooking. Ancient cooks soaked the leaves in brine and once soft, used them to wrap around all sorts of food. These little packets of wheat or barley, spices, and scraps of meat or fish were then steamed until cooked. We suspect that farmers carried stuffed fig leaves into the fields for lunch and cooks served them as a treat for supper. They were a wonderful way to use leftovers from a special dinner, and they continue to be popular in Greece and the Middle East today, except now rice is used as the primary ingredient in the stuffing.

Not only were fig trees prized for their fruit and leaves, the sap from the tree was also used for cheese making. Most people used animal rennet to curdle the milk and cause it to separate into curds and whey. The curds were then used to make cheese. The Jews preferred using plants, such as fig sap, that naturally contain rennet as the curdling agent, especially because regulations required that meat and milk food be kept separate. The fig sap gave the cheese a unique flavor and fig-ripened cheese was very popular in Rome as well.

Figs and fig trees are mentioned forty-three times in the Bible, forty-five times including the apocrypha, so we can assume that they were important not only as a food but also as a symbol. The fig tree was primarily a symbol of abundance. Figs certainly have an abundance of seeds, and fig trees produce an abundance of fruit. Perhaps because of the connection with abundance, the fig also used to represent faith. The life of faith was a life of abundance, perhaps material abundance, like the fig tree, but certainly spiritual abundance. The tree also represented safety and tranquility with the image of sitting under one's own fig tree becoming a picture of good life:

> During Solomon's lifetime Judah and Israel lived in safety, from Dan even to Beer-sheba, all of them under their vines and fig trees. (1Kings 4:25)

> Nathanael asked Jesus, "Where did you get to know me?" Jesus answered, "I saw you under the fig tree before Philip called you." Nathanael replied, "Rabbi, you are the Son of God! You are the King of Israel!" (John 1:48–49)

The prophets also used the fig as an image to represent the people of Israel:

> The Lord showed me two baskets of figs placed before the temple of the Lord. . . . One basket had very good figs, like first-ripe figs, but the other basket had very bad figs, so bad that they could not be eaten. . . . Then the word of the Lord came to me: Thus says the lord, the God of Israel: Like these good figs, so I will regard as good the exiles from Judah. (Jeremiah 24:1–4)

Because the tree symbolized abundance, Jeremiah also used the destruction of fig trees as a symbol of the destruction of the nation (Jeremiah 5:17, 8:13). Like other fruits, especially those with a large number of seeds, many ancient people also considered the fig a fertility symbol.

Dates

Dates are not actually mentioned in the Bible, though we know date palms were widely grown and their fruit eaten throughout the region. Writers like Josephus and rabbinical collections like the Mishnah do refer to dates. Archaeologists tell us that people living in the southern Jordan Valley were eating dates some 4,500 years before the birth of Jesus. By the first century, there were as many as thirty different varieties of dates growing in the Middle East. Date palms grew along the southern Jordan River and were cultivated around Jericho. In fact, Jericho was known as the city of date palm trees.[8] Herod the Great owned extensive date palm orchards that were confiscated by Mark Anthony as a gift to Cleopatra. We also know that the scriptures contain plenty of indirect references to dates and that it is likely that references to palm trees were likely referring to date palms: "the righteous shall flourish like a palm tree, and grow like a cedar in Lebanon" (Psalm 92:12).

Like figs, dates are extremely high in sugar and are a good source for vitamin C. They were eaten alone as an energizing snack or as the sweet part of a meal. Like dried figs, they could be chopped and pressed into small wheels or cubes that were stored or carried to work in the field or on trips. Once the one large seed was removed, dates were stuffed with soft cheese, almonds and other fillings as a special dessert at a banquet. Chopped dates or a paste made from dates might be added to pastries and sweet breads. Chopped dates also provided a touch of sweetness to savory stews and soups. Even the seeds were saved and, once softened by soaking in hot water, were fed to the livestock. During times of severe drought, date seeds were dried and ground so the powder could be added to flour to make bread.

The ancient Hebrew word for "honey" also referred to syrups made from fruit, and especially to date syrup. Dates were chopped and boiled in water. The resulting juice was then strained and boiled to the consistency of honey. Date honey was used in much the same way as regular honey and must have provided a special treat when poured over a cake or pastry at a banquet.

The juice from dates was also used to make wine. Because of the large amount of natural sugar in the fruit, date wine was probably quite high in alcohol. It is the sugar in the juice that is converted to alcohol by yeast, so higher sugar levels results in higher levels of alcohol. At least some researchers believe that date wine might have been the *shekar*, or "strong drink," that is mentioned some twenty-one times in the Bible. Scripture warned against drinking "strong drink" and John the Baptist refrained from both grape wine and "strong drink."[9]

Dates and date palms were symbolic of both life and faith. Because they grew tall near an oasis, the palms were a sign of the presence of life-giving water in an arid climate and gave hope for thirsty travelers. The palm fronds were also used for Jewish and later for Christian worship. The frond was part of the instrument of worship, the lulab, used to celebrate the feast of Tabernacles, and the followers of Jesus waved palm fronds as Jesus entered Jerusalem for the last time. Many Christians continue to use date fronds to celebrate Palm Sunday, the Sunday before Easter Day.

Because of its symbolism, the image of the date palm adorned the first temple and likely other important buildings as well: "He [Solomon] carved the walls of the house all around about with carved engravings of cherubim, palm trees, and open flowers" (1 Kings 6:29). The date palm was also a symbol of the land of Israel. After the defeat of the Jews and the end of the Great Revolt in the year 70 CE, the Romans minted a coin for the Holy Land with an imprinted date palm. A Roman soldier stood under the tree and both tower over a kneeling woman. The words *Judaea capta* described the scene.[10]

Pomegranates

Pomegranates were admired both for their taste and for the beauty of the fruit. They are mentioned many times in the Bible as an image for decoration. Pomegranates were painted on walls, carved into columns of important buildings, embroidered on the hems of priestly robes, and imprinted onto coins. Because they are bright red in color, at least one poet used them as an image of his beloved's cheeks: "Your cheeks are like halves of a pomegranate behind your veil" (Song of Solomon 6:7).

Like the date and the fig, pomegranates were used for a variety of culinary purposes, including making wine and a syrupy honey. Unlike figs and dates, pomegranates can have a degree of tartness to their flavor. At a banquet or special meal, the fruit was deeply cut and then broken in half. The word *pomegranate* is Latin for "seed apple" and is filled with a large number of seeds encased by red jelly-like seed casings or juice sacs. The seeds and juice sacs are found in channels that are surrounded by a white pith, which is not eaten. The seeds and juice sacs were lifted out of the pith and eaten raw or mixed with yogurt. The seeds were sometimes dried and used as a flavoring or garnish on salads or stews. Dried seeds were also ground into a powder and added to food as a spice.

Pomegranates can be juiced in much the same way as an orange or lemon, with a hand-held reamer or mechanical juicer.[11] In the ancient world, especially for larger-scale juice production, pomegranates were cut into smaller pieces and placed in a basket press or were crushed by stomping like grapes. The cook collected the juice and used it to make wine or syrup. Pomegranate syrup, usually called pomegranate molasses is more commonly available today than syrups made with figs and dates and can be found in stores specializing in Mediterranean food. The syrup was used to flavor soups and stews, make sauces, and marinade or glaze poultry and meat.

Because of the crown on top of the pomegranate, the fruit was sometimes used to symbolize the Torah, or the first five books of the Old Testament. The Torah was central to the belief and piety of all Jews and very important to early Jewish Christians as well. Silver smiths often made small silver pomegranates to adorn scrolls of the Torah. There was also a Jewish folk tradition that a pomegranate contained 613 seeds, one seed for each of the laws and statutes in the Torah. The large number of seeds were said to represent the good deeds of a righteous person, and the Christian church continued to use the pomegranate as symbol of righteousness. The image of the pomegranate even today is often woven into the fabric of Christian vestments.

Your Banquet for Friends on a Special Occasion

The banquet should be divided into two parts just as described above. Even though first-century banquets were only for wealthier males, or sometimes for those belonging to a trade guild, your banquet can include women, men, and any friends and family members you choose to invite. You can precede the meals with light appetizers and a glass of wine. If at all possible, recline on cushions and pillows for your feast, at least for the second part of the meal. Food and drink can be served on trays or a coffee table. Begin the banquet proper with the blessing of the bread, and then pass the bread around the table so all can take a piece. The second part of the meal should start with the blessing of a glass of wine. You may choose to serve the second part of the banquet in a different room to emphasize the shift to the symposium. Plan a discussion, perhaps based on one of the chapters of this book, or some other entertainment.

The Menu for a Special Banquet

Deipnon
- Bread (from one of the other chapters)
- Pickled Radishes*
- Asparagus with Lemon and Thyme*
- Green onions (from your market)
- Lamb Stew Apicius* or
- Baked Tilapia with Two Sauces*
- Chickpeas and Wheat Berries* or
- Bulgur Pilaf* (chapter 5)

Symposium
- Spiced Wine*
- Hard-Boiled Eggs and Fish Sauce*
- Pistachios (from the market)
- Fresh figs, pomegranate seeds, or dates (from the market)

The Recipes

Pickled Radishes

2 cups water
¼ cup salt
2½ cups vinegar
8 ounces radishes or more, washed and quartered

Heat the water and salt in a saucepan until the salt dissolves. Take off the heat and add the vinegar. Allow to cool to room temperature.

Place the radishes in a bowl or glass jar and cover with the pickling solution. Refrigerate for 7–10 days.

Asparagus with Lemon and Thyme

1½ pounds asparagus
1 tablespoon salt
2 tablespoons olive oil
1 lemon, juiced
zest from same lemon

1½ tablespoons fresh thyme or 2
  teaspoons dried thyme
1 teaspoon salt, or to taste
¼ teaspoon pepper, or to taste

Prepare the asparagus by breaking off the fibrous bottom section. The asparagus will typically break at the correct spot when bent. Save the bottom section for asparagus soup or for some other purpose.

Add 3 inches of water and the tablespoon of salt to a pot large enough to hold the asparagus spears. Bring to a boil. Add water and ice to another pot or large mixing bowl. Blanch the asparagus by placing half in the boiling water. Remove the asparagus after 20–30 seconds and place it in the ice water so that it stops cooking. Remove the asparagus from the ice water and dry. Repeat for the other half

Heat the olive oil in a 12-inch or 14-inch skillet or sauté pan. The pan should be hot. Add the asparagus to the pan and sauté until tender. Then add the lemon juice, zest, thyme, salt, and pepper. Serves 8.

Lamb Stew Apicius

This stew was inspired by some of the flavor combinations found in Apicius's first-century Roman cookbook. It is elegant and very good.

1 tablespoon salt (mixed use)
1 teaspoon pepper (mixed use)
3 tablespoons flour
1 leg of lamb cut into stew size pieces
2 tablespoons olive oil, plus an
  additional ¼ cup for separate use
2 carrots, julienned
1 onion, chopped

3 cloves garlic, minced
3 cups vegetable broth or beef broth
1 cup red wine
½ cup raisins
½ teaspoon ground cumin
½ teaspoon coriander
1 cinnamon stick

Slurry

1 tablespoon flour
2 tablespoons water
1 tablespoon honey
2 tablespoons red wine vinegar

Add the 1½ teaspoons salt and ½ teaspoon pepper to 3 tablespoons of flour. Place the lamb in a large bowl and toss with 2 tablespoons of olive oil. Pour flour mixture over the lamb and stir until lamb is coated. Heat a 5-quart Dutch oven and add ¼ cup of olive oil. Add the lamb and brown in hot oil. Remove lamb and cook carrots, onions, and garlic. Add the lamb back to the pot and then the stock and red wine, deglazing the bottom of the pot. Add the raisins and spices. Cover and cook for 1½ hours. Remove cinnamon stick.

Mix the slurry ingredients. Uncover the pot and add the slurry and cook until meat is tender and sauce thickens, an additional 20–30 minutes. Adjust the seasoning with the additional salt and pepper. Serves 8

Baked Tilapia with Two Sauces

You can serve this dish with one or both of the sauces. Fish fillets or whole fish would have been baked in the bread oven, once the bread was baked and the oven cooled a bit.

4 to 6 tilapia fillets
2 tablespoons olive oil
Juice from 1 lemon
2 teaspoons salt

1 teaspoon pepper
1–2 teaspoons Middle Eastern
    sumac

Yogurt sauce

1 cup grated cucumber, drained and
    dried with towels
1 garlic clove, minced and then
    mashed with the side of a knife

1 cup yogurt
½ teaspoon dill
½ teaspoon salt, or to taste

Parsley Sauce

1 clove garlic

1 cup parsley

juice and zest from 1 lemon

3 tablespoons bottled capers

½ teaspoon salt or to taste

Preheat the oven to 375°. Use a little of the oil and grease the bottom of a large baking pan. Rub the fillets with the rest of the oil and place in the pan. Squeeze the lemon over the fillets and then sprinkle with the salt, pepper, and sumac. Cover the pan with a lid or with aluminum foil. Bake for 20 to 25 minutes or until the fillets flake easily with a fork.

Yogurt Sauce: Peel then grate the cucumber. Put the cucumber in a strainer and press to remove liquid. Then remove and pat dry with a kitchen towel or paper towels. Add all the ingredients, including the cucumber to a bowl and mix. Can be covered and refrigerated. Stir before serving

Parsley Sauce: Place the garlic in the bowl of a food processor and then process until minced, scraping down the sides when necessary. Add the parsley, lemon juice, and zest. Process until the parsley is finely chopped. Remove and add the capers and salt.

First century diners would have broken off pieces of the fish and then dipped them in one of the two dips.

Chickpeas and Wheat Berries

The wheat berries add a different, pleasing texture to this tasty recipe. We use "hard" berries, but either hard or soft will work for this recipe.

2 cups dried chickpeas (garbanzo
    beans) or 2 (15-ounce) cans,
    rinsed

1 cup wheat berries

1 tablespoon olive oil

½ yellow onion, chopped

3 cloves garlic, minced

½ teaspoon ground cumin

½ teaspoon ground coriander

2 bay leaves

4 cups chicken stock

2 teaspoons salt, or to taste

½ teaspoon pepper, or to taste

Sort through the chickpeas thoroughly to remove any type of debris and then rinse. Place the chickpeas and wheat berries in a large bowl and add enough water to cover by 2 inches. Allow to soak for at least 4 hours or overnight.

Drain the chickpeas and wheat berries using a strainer. Heat a large pot or Dutch oven and add olive oil. Then add the yellow onion and sauté the onion over medium high heat until it begins to turn brown. Add the garlic and sauté until it turns translucent. Then add the chickpeas, wheat berries, and the rest of the ingredients, except for the salt and pepper. Bring to a boil and then turn down to a simmer. Place the lid on the pot so it only covers ⅔ of the opening, allowing some steam to escape. Add water if the peas begin to dry out.

Cook for 1 hour and 15 minutes and then add the salt and pepper. Continue to cook for another 15 minutes or until the chickpeas are tender and the wheat berries have split. If using canned chickpeas, add them 30 minutes before the wheat berries have finished cooking. The wheat berries should cook faster without the raw chick peas. Remove the bay leaves before serving. Serves 6 to 8

Spiced Wine

First-century cooks also added flavorings such as cumin seed, coriander seed, mustard seed, saffron, and mint to their wines. Start with the flavorings we recommended and then be creative. A nice inexpensive Shiraz is perfect for this recipe. Don't use an expensive wine!

1 bottle Shiraz or other dry red or
    white wine
½ cup honey

1 or 2 sticks cinnamon
4 whole cloves
lemon zest from 1 lemon

Empty the bottle of wine into a saucepan. Add the honey and cinnamon and other flavorings. Heat on medium low until the honey dissolves. Allow to sit for 10 minutes or more so the flavors continue to mingle. Serve at room temperature or warm during the winter.

Hard-Boiled Eggs and Fish Sauce

Everyone knows how to boil an egg. So why include a recipe? Just in case, we have found that this one adapted from Betty Crocker's Cookbook works very well. The fish sauce is typical from the period and is a tasty dip. It would work well as a marinade or dip for fish, beef, or pork. You may add your favorite spice, even a touch of honey, or just use straight fish sauce if you like the fish taste.

Eggs
Water

Fish Sauce Dip
3 tablespoons fish sauce
2 tablespoons soft red wine, such as a syrah or merlot

Place the eggs in a pot and cover with cold water. Do not crowd the eggs. Heat to a boil, remove from the burner and cover the pot. Allow to stand for 22–23 minutes. Remove the eggs and place in ice water so they do not continue to cook.

Mix the fish sauce and red wine and use as a dip for eggs, vegetables, or bread at the feast.

Wealthy men eat a chicken and salad together.

CHAPTER SEVEN

The Wedding Feast

My beloved speaks and says to me: "Arise, my love, my fair one; and come away; for now the winter is past, the rain is over and gone. The flowers appear on the earth; the time of singing has come, and the voice of the turtledove I heard in our land. The fig tree puts forth its figs, and the vines are in blossom; They give forth fragrance. Arise, my love, my fair one, and come away." (Song of Solomon 2:10–13)

The largest family feast two thousand years ago was the wedding feast. Just as it is now, the first-century wedding was no simple dinner party for a few friends and neighbors. Anyone who is married or has helped to plan a wedding knows the protocol. A long list of relatives, friends, and acquaintances must be invited to the festivities. If someone is forgotten, tensions may exist for years. Should we invite Uncle Saul, even if he is in Macedonia preaching to the Gentiles? Why was she invited and I was not? If the family is not careful, even the simplest ceremony with just a handful of relatives may become an event for hundreds.

As with a modern wedding, the bride and her bridegroom were concerned with their special clothes for the big occasion. But the similarity between first century and twenty-first century ended there. The ancient wedding was more concerned with fulfilling a contract than it was a religious ceremony. The bride and maids waited in front of the bride's house for the bridegroom to carry her off to her new home. Once the bride and groom arrived at their new home, the party began.

The first century wedding feast lasted for an entire week and was a grand affair for family, neighbors and friends. Our two foods for this chapter were important to the celebration. The ancient wedding cake was nothing like its modern counterpart and yet was the focus of several fun traditions. However, it was the wine that was absolutely essential. Wine was the third food for our culinary trinity and the daily beverage of choice for poor and rich alike. It is impossible to even begin to consider first-century food and feasting without studying the importance of wine.

First-Century Marriages

First-century Jews considered marriage a covenant relationship. It was an agreement not only between a bride and bridegroom but also between the two families. The covenant was a contract with a special set of terms. In Jesus' lifetime, the marriage covenant dealt with such issues as the "bride price" and the dowry.

Although the bride was loved and cherished by her family and later by her husband, still her status was very similar to that of property. This was reflected in the covenant. The groom paid for her and then took possession of her from her father. A woman's legal standing in the community was similar to that of a slave, except that she had the right to keep property and possessions, especially the dowry that she brought into the marriage. The covenant spelled out how much money or property would be paid to the bride's family and what size dowry she would bring into the relationship.

Old Testament covenants typically had three elements: the special terms of the contract, a description of the property that was being exchanged, and a description of the *part of life* that was exchanged. In the case of marriage, the covenant contained a number of special terms and descriptions of property exchanged. The terms included the money to be paid to the bride's family and the timing of the marriage. The covenant guaranteed the virginity of the bride-to-be and included the hope for many children.

The contract also described the obligations of the groom to provide food, clothing, and housing for the bride and family. The husband was required to pay ransom for his wife if she was kidnapped and he also had to guarantee that he would provide a funeral for her when she died, which included hiring flute players and female mourners. Similar to modern prenuptial agreements, the covenant detailed the money owed to the bride in case of divorce or the husband's death. On a more positive note, the covenant included promises by both the groom and the bride to love, cherish, and be faithful to each other. After all, the two were becoming "one flesh" and the bride was being incorporated into her new husband's life and family.

In the Middle East and in the Mediterranean world, it was normal for a man to be in his mid-twenties when he married, though some married younger. What is so shocking to our modern sensibilities was that women were usually in their early to middle teens. It is difficult picturing a twenty-five-year-old man marrying a fourteen-year-old girl or even understanding what they would have in common or what they would talk about in the evening. The husband was a man of the world with years of work experience, but his wife was still a child. The difference in the age was even greater if we consider that the average life span was significantly shorter.[1] To some extent, this societal norm made sense. If nothing else, it allowed time for the husband to learn and become established in a trade. Usually, young men became part of the family business, learning the necessary skills from their fathers. Young Roman men also spent time in military service before marriage. Whatever the reason, first-century society expected future grooms to settle down and learn a trade long before marriage.

The Role of Women in the First Century

Societal expectations were different for the women. It was more important that first-century brides were virgins and that they have many years for childbearing. A girl of fourteen was most likely still a virgin and had much of her life before her to create a big family. Childbirth was also much more dangerous for the mother than it is now. Unlike today, the life expectancy of women was shorter than that of men, and as a woman grew older, the likelihood of complications at childbirth increased. The difference today is that modern medicine is better able to deal with the complications that killed many first-century women.

A young bride was also more likely to be accepted into her new husband's family. Most sons stayed at home after their marriage and their young brides became part of the family. After the wedding, the groom's mother would have to become the young bride's mother. Like another daughter, she helped with the gardening, cooking, and cleaning. Imagine the potential for tension caused when another woman was added to the family. Comments like: "I can't believe you make bread like that," and "Didn't your mother teach you how to clean a room," must have been common. The pillow talk at night during the first year of adjustment must have been scathing. A friend of ours had the experience of moving to the Middle East with her Lebanese husband.

She tells the story of her mother-in-law and new sisters moving in with them and staying *until she learned how to cook*. That experience of joining the new family may not have been ideal, but we can vouch that they succeeded in teaching her to make wonderful Lebanese food.

The wife had many responsibilities. She had to grind meal into flour, bake bread, prepare meals, wash clothes, tend to the house, care for the children, and help her husband with his work. In a large household, some of these duties were divided among the women. One daughter was responsible for the bread. Another daughter helped prepare the meals. One son's wife worked in the vegetable garden. Another cleaned the house. If the family had no servants, then the wife was responsible for washing her husband's hands, face, and feet.

Daughters and the wives of wealthy men rarely left their homes. If they did, their heads were completely covered by veils:

> When the Jewess of Jerusalem left her house, her face was hidden by an arrangement of two head veils, a head-band on the forehead with bands to the chin, and a hairnet with ribbons and knots, so that her feature could not be recognized. It was said that once, for example, a chief priest in Jerusalem did not recognize his own mother when he had to carry out against her the prescribed process for a woman suspected of adultery.[2]

The wives and daughters of day laborers and farmers did not have the luxury of remaining hidden from public view. They helped their husbands with their vocations, including the harvesting of crops. The book of Ruth painted a picture of widows and other poor women gleaning grain from the fields. Young women, most likely servants or the wives and daughters of the farmers who could not afford servants and slaves, were also working in the fields helping with the harvest. A sensitive Boaz warned his male laborers not to bother Ruth, which would have been considered a public sexual solicitation and a stain on her reputation (Ruth 2:8–9).

This was the cultural situation in which Jesus talked with women and allowed them to support his ministry. Jesus conversed with a Canaanite woman in public, despite the effort of his disciples to send her away (Matthew 15:21–28). Jesus had a long conversation in a public place with a Samaritan woman that astonished his disciples (John 4:27). The unusual aspect of the conversation was not just the content, but the simple fact that it took place. It was even more astonishing that women followed Jesus as he traveled with his ministry. In Luke's Gospel we discover that some of these women also financially supported Jesus and his disciples (Luke 8:1–2).

To some extent, the attitude toward women established by Jesus found its way into the life of the early church. Women were described as prominent members of the young congregations (e.g., see Romans 16:1–16). In fact, the New Testament paints a picture of church leaders who struggled to balance the traditional roles of women over against the notion that the *dividing walls* separating male and female—as well as Jew and Greek, slave and free—were removed by Jesus. The fact that the apostle Paul addressed the role and dress of women in one of his letters leads us to conclude that at least some women were acting with even greater freedom than the surrounding culture allowed and the church found prudent (I Corinthians 11:2–16).

The Betrothal and Wedding

The marriage relationship between husband and wife actually started with the betrothal. The word *betroth* has a Hebrew root that meant "to pay a fine or price." Usually the bridegroom and his father visited the father of the bride and the two fathers negotiated the covenant agreement. A key element of the covenant was the amount paid by the bridegroom's family for the bride. After the negotiations, the future bride came into the room and the bridegroom asked for her hand in marriage. She accepted and he presented her with a gift, which sometimes included a ring. The bride, bridegroom, and their fathers then shared a glass of wine to seal and celebrate the betrothal. First and foremost, the betrothal was a legally binding relationship. The negotiated terms of the covenant relationship were recorded and the bride kept the document.

During the time between the betrothal and the marriage, the groom gave a variety of gifts to the bride and her family. Some of the gifts were given with the intent that they become part of the bride's dowry. Other gifts were part of the betrothal payment that was kept by the bride's family. These gifts demonstrated the groom's commitment to the relationship and confirmed that a new bond was being established between the two families.

The groom also gave the bride's family money to pay for a betrothal feast. This meal was a formal announcement and celebration of the engagement. Unlike most other types of feasts that were celebrated only by men, the women of the village were the ones who attended the betrothal meal. Typically it was an open celebration where female friends and neighbors came to congratulate the bride and her family and to begin work on the bride's trousseau. The groom was also present at the meal and part of the ritual was the recitation of the *groom's blessing*. This blessing was repeated at the wedding and was an important element of the wedding feast.

The actual wedding often occurred as long as a year or more after the betrothal. The bridegroom had to first prepare a place for the new couple to live and to choose one room to be the wedding chamber. Usually the bridegroom did this by building several rooms onto his family's house. During the betrothal year, the mother of the bride taught her daughter all she needed to know to become a good wife. In addition, she collected clothing, perfumes, cosmetics, and jewelry for the wedding day. These and other items became part of the dowry that the new bride took with her when she left home.

When the bridegroom finished building the new quarters, the rooms were furnished. The bridal chamber was decorated with garlands of flowers and sometimes a canopied bed. The groom's father inspected the new lodgings, and when all was completed to his satisfaction he gave his son permission to bring home his bride. Then, and only then, could the bridegroom and his friends begin their procession to the bride's house to take legal and physical possession of her.

The Wedding Procession

The first-century wedding procession was actually a parade through town, and it was usually quite elaborate. The groom and his friends dressed in special clothes and in many cases, they hired musicians to walk with them. The procession took place at night when everyone in the community was at home. In the days before television, glass windows, and air conditioners, we can imagine that the noise of a raucous and joyful procession created a lot of attention as it moved through the town. It is likely that friends and neighbors who were also waiting in anticipation for this evening joined the procession.

The bride and her bridesmaids knew in advance the approximate day and time that the bridegroom would come for her, but they did not know exactly. The commotion and noise, including the blowing of the shofar, or ram's horn, warned the bride in advance that her bridegroom and his friends were on their way. We suspect that word of mouth also gave her advance warning. She then prepared herself to be taken to her new home. She quickly dressed in special clothing and jewelry and covered her head completely with a veil. After being joined by the bridesmaids, she met the groom's procession. This meeting took place either in front of her parents' home or at another prearranged location. The bride was seated on a litter and then the parade to the bridegroom's house began. The procession, now substantially larger and even more boisterous, probably gained even more followers as it made its way to the feast.

Once back at the bridegroom's home, the couple completed a simple ceremony that might include spreading a robe or cloak over the bride. The cloak was symbolic of the bridegroom and represented him taking possession of his new wife. Even today there is a practice in areas of the Middle East where a cloak is thrown over the bride and the bridegroom proclaims, "None shall cover thee but such a one."[3] By the end of the first century, the groom and bride were using a festively decorated canopy called the *chuppah* for part of their ceremony. The chuppah was a symbol of the home to which the groom brought his new bride. The couple remained in the chuppah for most of the seven-day feast where they received money and other gifts. However, we have found no evidence of the use of a chuppah at the time of Jesus. Perhaps it came into use during the chaotic time after a revolution when many people were displaced and bridegrooms no longer had homes to bring their wives to.

A series of blessings known as the "groom's blessing" were repeated several times during the wedding feast. The only existing copy from the ancient world is found in the Babylonian Talmud and is a series of six blessings:

- Praised are you, Lord our God, king of the universe, who created all for his glory;
- And praised are you, Lord our God, king of the universe, who forms Adam;
- And praised are you, Lord our God, king of the universe, who formed Adam in his image, in his likeness he fashioned him and established for him, from him, an abiding abode. Praised are you, Lord, who forms Adam.
- Let the barren one rejoice and cry out when her children are gathered to her in joy. Praised are you, Lord, who causes Zion to rejoice with her children.
- Surely you will make the lovers rejoice, as you originally made your creation rejoice in Eden. Praised are you, Lord, who causes the groom and bride to rejoice.
- Praised are you, Lord our God, king of the universe, who created gladness and joy, groom and bride, rejoicing, song, mirth, delight, love, friendship, peace, and companionship. Lord our God, may there soon be heard in the cities of Judah and in the streets of Jerusalem the voice of gladness and the voice of joy; the voice of the groom and the voice of the bride; the joyous shouts of grooms from their bridal chambers, and of youths from their marriage celebrations. Praised are you Lord, who causes the groom to rejoice with the bride.[4]

Except for the groom's prayer, weddings were altogether secular arrangements. In later centuries, the village rabbi had a role in the wedding ceremony, but there is no historical evidence of the liturgical presence of a rabbi at first-century weddings. So the blessings might have been proclaimed by the father of the bridegroom or by some other elder male member of the groom's family. After this short ceremony the bride and bridegroom entered the wedding chamber where they stayed for as long as seven days. The groom's friends hovered around the door to the chamber where they engaged in the same type of pranks as contemporary groomsmen. At some point the newly married couple emerged from their rooms and joined the party, the bride with her veil now removed.

Meanwhile, the wedding feast continued while the bride and groom were in the wedding chamber and after they emerged. The guests sang love songs and danced. Wine flowed like water. Instead of the fatted calf, it was the cow that was roasted. Can you imagine a celebration lasting seven days? Can you imagine *paying* for a celebration that lasted seven days? Or preparing the food for a celebration lasting that long? Wealthy families had teams of servants and slaves to prepare the food and drink for the wedding, but we suspect that the feast for an ordinary couple was more of a community project. Historians tell us that family and guests brought wine for the feast. Without servants baking bread, roasting lambs and tending stews, the task of preparing the food was probably shared with relatives and neighbors. Because the feast lasted seven days, it probably had the look and feel of an open house, with friends and relatives dropping in on the feast, as they were able. Each evening, a large meal was consumed followed by more revelry. The guests went home eventually, but they rejoined the feast the next day as soon as they could. Documents from the period acknowledge that the food and wine were the best possible, and were accompanied by music, dancing, and great joy.

The wedding feast for a wealthy family was a grand affair. Jesus sometimes used the image of an extravagant wedding when he taught, "The kingdom of heaven may be compared to a king who gave a wedding banquet for his son" (Matthew 22:2). Servants bearing invitations were sent. The food was cooked. Musicians were hired. Wine was opened. Banqueting halls were decorated. Cattle and fatted lambs were roasted. A feast for seven days was ready. Servants and cooks were working overtime to make sure everything was perfect for the wedding banquet of the king's son. It was time for the feast, and once everything was prepared it had to be used. Without refrigerators, freezers, or preservatives, food began to spoil. Wine turned to vinegar. If the guests cannot come, go into the villages and byways and invite everyone you find. Because the party must go on (Matthew 22:9).

Except for its length and the number of guests, the form of the wedding feast was probably very similar to an ordinary banquet. During the day, wine and lighter foods such as bread, dips, dried fruits, and cheeses were available for the guests. Most of the guests arrived late afternoon after work. A meal was provided each evening. Though women were present, they ate at separate tables away from the men. First the food was served. Then wine was served, along with sweets and lighter foods. There was dancing and singing during the second part of the feast. The revelers returned to their homes late in the evening only to start celebrating again the next day.

Most weddings were in May and June even in the ancient world. Very few homes had banqueting rooms large enough for a wedding so most of the feasts were celebrated in courtyards or out-of-doors. That is why most of the weddings were held in late spring and early summer when temperatures were comfortable and there was very little rain. At that time of year, the weather was perfect for outdoor feasting.

The Wedding and Wedding Feast as Religious Symbols

Even though weddings in ancient Israel were not religious ceremonies, biblical writers and teachers frequently used wedding customs and marriage as religious symbols. Perhaps the most powerful of these biblical images compares the relationship of husband and wife with that of God and Israel, and later to God and the church. Sometimes the image is a positive one, illustrating compassion and faithfulness in a relationship. For example, Isaiah painted a picture of the faithfulness of God with these words:

> For your Maker is your husband,
> The Lord of hosts is his name;
> The Holy One of Israel is your Redeemer,
> The God of the whole earth he is called.
> For the Lord has called you
> Like a wife of a man's youth when she is cast off,
> Says your God. (Isaiah 54:5–6)

And there is this passage from the prophet Jeremiah that speaks of the devotion that should be found both in a marriage and in our relationship to God:

> Thus says the Lord:
> I remember the devotion of your youth,
> Your love as a bride,
> How you followed me in the wilderness,
> In a land not sown. (Jeremiah 2:2–3)

The biblical writers also used this same imagery to illustrate the rebel-
liousness and infidelity of Israel. The prophet Hosea compared Israel to an
unfaithful wife (Hosea 2:5). Yet his message was ultimately one of forgiveness
and reconciliation that offers a beautiful image of hope:

> On that day, says the Lord, you will call me, "My husband," and no longer
> will you call me, "My Baal." For I will remove the names of the Baals from
> her mouth and they shall be mentioned by name no more. I will make for you
> a covenant on that day with the wild animals, the birds of the air, and the
> creeping things of the ground; and I will abolish the bow, the sword, and war
> from the land; and I will make you lie down in safety. And I will take you for
> my wife forever; I will take you for my wife in righteousness and in justice, in
> steadfast love and in mercy. I will take you for my wife in faithfulness; and you
> shall know the Lord. (Hosea 2:16–20)

In the New Testament, marriage was seen as a metaphor of the relationship
between Christ and the church: "I feel a divine jealousy for you, for I promised
(betrothed) you in marriage to one husband, to present you as a chaste virgin
to Christ" (II Corinthians 11:2). And St. Paul further developed the symbol in
his teaching on the relationship between a husband and wife: "The husband
is the head of the wife, as Christ is the head of the church" (Ephesians 5:23).
These passages affirm that the relation of husband to wife is more than one of
authority. A husband must love his wife, and cherish and nourish her, just as
Christ loves, cherishes, and nourishes his church (Ephesians 5: 25).

The wedding procession became a symbol, naturally enough, of preparing
and waiting for the coming of the Kingdom of God. Jesus told the story of
the ten bridesmaids (Matthew 25 1–13). They knew approximately when the
groom was coming to take the bride. They were dressed for the occasion, wearing their best gowns and garlands of flowers in their hair. And they had their
lamps. The wise ones also had flasks of extra olive oil so that they could refill
their lamps when the oil ran low. The foolish ones did not. The bridegroom
came at midnight and only the wise maidens were prepared for the procession.
This story painted a familiar picture for the first-century audience and most
likely elicited a chuckle. The image spoke to them because they saw these
midnight processions from time to time with young maids carrying their little
pottery lamps filled with olive oil. The message was clear enough: be prepared.

The wedding feast itself was an ancient symbol. The feast was an oasis of
great celebration during a period of history marked by social upheaval and
violence. It was unbridled joy and abundance. For many in the church, this
joyful feast was a powerful symbol of existence with God at the end of time.
Jesus used this image in his parable of the king's wedding banquet for his son.

The king sent his servants into the streets and byways to find guests, thus offering the unexpected gift of the feast to all people (Matthew 22:1–10). In John's vision of God's ultimate victory over evil and the emergence of a new heaven and a new earth, the angel announces, "Write this: Blessed are those who are invited to the marriage supper of the lamb" (Revelation 19:9).

> Hallelujah
> For the Lord our God the Almighty reigns.
> Let us rejoice and exult and give him the glory,
> For the marriage of the Lamb has come,
> And his bride has made herself ready,
> To her it has been granted to be clothed
> With fine linen, bright and pure. (Revelation 19:6b–8)

The Wedding Cake

The menu for first-century wedding feasts certainly included wedding cakes, but these cakes were nothing like their modern counterparts. First-century cooks and bakers made their sweets and pastries without ingredients such as refined sugar and chocolate and without leavening agents like baking soda and baking powder. First-century cakes were much more like flat cheese cakes or modern fruitcakes, using dried fruits like dates and apricots and honey or fruit syrup as the sweetener, or like raisin bread, small pieces of dried fruit added to standard bread recipes.

Throughout the Mediterranean, there were a number of different traditions involving the wedding cake. Ancient Romans used cakes made of wheat or barley, and a cake was broken over the bride's head as a symbol of her fertility. Also, the wedding party would stack the cakes, one on top of the other, as high as they could be stacked. The bride and bridegroom then had to kiss each other over the tower of cakes without knocking them over. If they were successful, the couple looked forward to a lifetime of prosperity. Among Greeks and Romans, the bride and bridegroom took several wedding cakes to the local temple or shrine and sacrificed them to the appropriate god or goddess. This practice was eventually imitated by first-century Jewish couples, who began offering a wedding cake as a sacrifice to God during the wedding feast.

This practice is hard to imagine, since the sacrifice must have taken place away from the temple. Perhaps it consisted of a special prayer of thanksgiving or a prayer for fertility as the wedding cake was first offered to God and then was broken and eaten by the bride and bridegroom.

Wine to Make Hearts Glad

The consumption of wine was a major element of all feasts and banquets, including the wedding feast:

> Wisdom has built her house, she has hewn her seven pillars. She has slaughtered her animals, she has mixed her wine, she has also set her table. . . . "Come, eat of my bread and drink of the wine I have mixed." Proverbs 9:1–2, 5

The second half of any banquet began by mixing wine with water and giving thanks for the fruit of the vine. The blessing was typically followed by a hymn. Then the festivities continued with music, discussion, snacking on sweet foods, and drinking wine.

The same was true of the wedding feast. The importance of wine to the wedding feast is the subject of one of the most widely known stories about Jesus, the turning of water into wine at the wedding in Cana (John 2:1–11). One of the underlying issues in the story is the importance of the wine for the party and the embarrassment caused to the bridegroom and his family if the wine ran out. Another important aspect of the miracle is the amount of water Jesus turned into wine. If each of the six stone jars held 20 to 30 gallons, then there must have been between 120 and 180 gallons of wine. That is the same as 600 to 900 modern bottles. That much wine would have made for quite a party, especially if the group had already depleted the existing supply. On a symbolic level, the vast amount of wine speaks to the abundance of grace given by God through Jesus. On a more practical level, it speaks volumes about the nature of wedding feasts and the amount of wine that was consumed at them.

All Mediterranean cultures frowned on drunkenness, which was one of the reasons that the wine was mixed with water before it was consumed. But they did not frown on using wine to become more relaxed and less inhibited. This was especially true of the Greeks and Romans. They believed that alcohol contributed to political and philosophical debate because it caused the participants to become less guarded and more honest in stating their opinions. The Greek philosophers believed that this characteristic of wine could expose hidden truths. "Wine reveals what is hidden," declared the Greek philosopher Eratosthenes.[5] "Quickly, bring me a beaker of wine, so that I may wet my mind and say something clever," added the Greek comic Aristophanes.[6]

The Hebrews, however, were much more critical of drunkenness than the Greeks and Romans, except at wedding feasts. It was as though the entire community was suddenly given permission for excessive celebration, including consumption of wine. The celebratory aspect of a wedding and the feast was so important to the community that even the religious obligations of the merrymakers were suspended for seven days.

Wine is the third element of that all-important *holy trinity* of food. In the first century, a family typically consumed about 350 liters of wine a year. Families in France are the largest consumers of wine today and they only consume an average of about 60 liters a year. Of course, in the first century the households were larger, encompassing several generations of sons, with their wives and children. Still, 350 liters of wine a year is an astonishing amount. Wines were often mixed with herbs, spices, fruit juices, and other flavorings. Cinnamon, saffron, and pomegranate were especially popular.

Today in the United States, when we think of kosher wine, we think of a sweet wine made with concord grapes. However, concord grapes were not and are not grown in Israel nor were they grown anywhere else in the Mediterranean region. There were a number of varieties of grapes that were grown in the Middle East in the first century. In fact, archaeologists believe that the wild grapes in the Fertile Crescent were the ancestors for almost all of the varietals used to make modern wines and that wine production originated somewhere in this region. The ancient Phoenicians, who were a seafaring people that lived on the coast of Palestine, developed and grew large amounts of grapes and exported wine around the Mediterranean, introducing both the drink and a wine culture. Later the Philistines, Canaanites, and eventually the Jews also grew grapes and produced much wine from the same region.[7]

Shiraz and the sweet Muscat are believed to be two varietals that were widely used and loved in the ancient Middle East, with the Shiraz grape originally coming from the area around Shiraz, Iran. These and other Palestinian grapes provide an interesting study. These two varieties continued to grow in that region for centuries after the death of Jesus. Even after the Muslim conquest, there were small vineyards that provided wine for Jews and Christians still living in the region. Some vineyards were still there when the Crusaders invaded the Middle East. They used the existing vines to increase the size of the vineyards and to produce even more wine. They also took cuttings of the vines back to Italy and France, and after five or six years, the amount of time necessary for the vines to become established and produce fruit, began using Shiraz and other Palestinian grapes in Europe. Because of the Muslim ban on alcohol, the Middle Eastern vineyards were finally destroyed after the European Christians were defeated. Unlike the olive trees, which can live as long as a thousand years, a vine lives only up to around one hundred years. Ironically, about 1820, the French took cuttings from the ancestors of those vines and planted them in California, Australia, and Israel. Descendants of those ancient vines finally came home. Today Shiraz and other varietals are once again predominant grapes in Israel.[8]

Since beer was actually the first alcoholic drink and was widely available in Mesopotamia and in Egypt by the time of Moses, it seems strange that beer is not mentioned in the Bible or in any ancient Jewish literature. A great deal was written about beer in both Mesopotamian and Egyptian literature, and much later in Greek and Roman sources. But the Jews wrote nothing. It appears that the Jews so preferred wine that they did not make or drink beer. This preference was not because of crops or geography. The Hebrews grew a large amount of barley, the primary ingredient in beer, and could have brewed great quantities. The Jews chose, perhaps intentionally, not to adapt their tastes to that of their neighbors and conquerors. They stayed with the diet they knew, and that diet often differed from that of all their neighbors.

Family vineyards were typically grapevines grown around the trunks of the olive trees. The fruit of these vines was also used to make wine for private consumption. Grapes were pressed in family-owned or community wine presses. There were also larger commercial vineyards. These were much more like their modern counterparts, with many rows of grapevines. A family vineyard might produce enough grapes that excess wine was sold in the local market. Wine made from commercial vineyards was made for export, some of it shipped around the entire Mediterranean region.

Wine from family producers was stored in wine skins or in pottery crocks. Families with bigger vineyards and larger producers used larger crocks or amphorae. To keep air from touching the wine and turning it to vinegar, the tops of the crocks were often sealed with pitch, a thick, dark, sticky substance made from the resins of pine or fir trees. Sometimes the entire jar was covered with pitch to keep air from seeping through the tiny holes in the pottery. Another method of sealing a jug of wine was to float a thin layer of olive oil on top of the wine. This too kept air from reaching the wine. The wine was kept in a storeroom in the family's house or in a storage shelter. Thus sealed, the wine was good for years, and even decades if it was a good vintage year and stored in a cool location.

At harvest time, the ripe and overripe grapes were taken to the wine press, a shallow basin carved from a large granite rock. The grapes were left to partially dry in the pool and then the juice was crushed out of them by barefooted men and women. Using people to mash the grapes actually produced a better tasting wine than a mechanical press, as long as the feet were clean. Grape seeds produce a bitter flavor when crushed, and people feeling the seeds under foot, would push them to the side when crushing the grapes, thus yielding a less bitter-tasting wine.

There are two varieties of yeast on grape skins; one of those begins the process of turning the sugar in the grape juice into alcohol as soon as the juice comes into contact with the outer skin. Within one or two days, this yeast converts nearly half the sugar in the grapes to alcohol, producing an alcohol level between 4 and 5 percent. The initial yeast dies at this point, killed by the alcohol, and a secondary, slower fermentation begins. The yeast for this stage of fermentation was also present on the skins of the grapes. This stage of fermentation lasts anywhere from five to ten days, increasing the alcohol level to about 14 percent, depending on the amount of sugar in the juice.

Some wine makers allowed the crushed grapes to sit in the wine press for several days while the juice was exposed to the yeast. During this time, some of the water in the juice evaporated, making the sugars more condensed and the wine stronger tasting and more alcoholic. To make it even stronger, some of the juice was boiled to further condense the sugar and then the syrup was added to the fermenting wine. Wine produced for export was often quite strong, using the method of boiling the juice, and then was diluted with water once it reached its destination. After sitting and fermenting, a channel was opened and the juice was drained from the wine press to a smaller, deeper pool. The remaining grape skins and seeds were cooked to extract additional juice. This grape juice was used to fill the wine jars before they were sealed to protect them from air.[9]

The juice from the second pool was placed in barrels or jars to finish the fermentation process. After fermenting anywhere from four to ten days, the wine was transferred to a large jar called an *amphora*, which held seven to eight gallons. The *amphorae* (plural of amphora) were filled to the top with the juice from the cooked grape skins and then sealed. Amphorae were cylinders that had large handles at each side of the top and came to a point at the bottom. Sediment from the wine gathered in the tip at the bottom of the jar. Commercial winemakers stored amphorae in large cellars dug into the ground. The jars were lowered into a cone shaped hole or were stacked in racks built especially for them.

Because of the shape, amphorae were easily packed on wagons and merchant boats when the wine was transported. The wines from Palestine and Galilee were exported to countries all around the Mediterranean, especially to Rome and Greece, where they were famous for their quality. Wrecks of merchant ships have been found with literally thousands of amphorae.

Wine and Water
Mixing wine with water before drinking was a common custom. Ancient literature speaks of unmixed wine as being barbaric: "Mere mortals . . . could

only drink wine whose strength had been tempered with water; otherwise they would become extremely violent or even go mad."[10] Was the alcohol level in first-century wine that much stronger? Certainly, the flavor was stronger. The strength of flavor and to some extent the alcohol level in wine depended on the amount of water in the grape juice. For example, if it rained for weeks right before the harvest, the juice and the wine had a greater water content, less flavor, and slightly less alcohol. The opposite was also true; less rain means less water in the grapes and more flavor and alcohol. Location of the vines was also a factor. Vines planted with good drainage produced wines with less water and more flavor. Old vines also produce smaller grapes, which had less water in the grapes. As mentioned above, vines can live to a hundred years or more before they have to be replaced. Ancient winemakers often kept older vines and knew that the hillsides and rocky, sandy soil were ideal for growing their grapes. They also let water evaporate from their juice and mixed in syrupy grape juice, making the wine that much stronger.

Another benefit of mixing the wine was that the water became safer to drink. People in the ancient world were familiar with the dangers of drinking contaminated water. They preferred water from deep wells or rainwater from cisterns. They discovered that wine made the water even safer, even if they did not understand anything about the antibacterial quality of fermented drink.

The result was the almost universal practice of mixing wine and water. Mixing with the ratios of water to wine at 2:1, 5:2, 3:1, and 4:1 were common. Typically a mixture of equal parts water to wine was considered strong.[11] If an important person came to a feast, they might receive a 3:2 mixture, but for everyday drinking and for children and servants, the mix was more likely three parts water to one part wine. The Romans became infamous for segregating guests at their banquets. Honored guests were seated in the main banqueting hall and received the best wine with the least water. Other guests and the protégés of the honored ones received a lesser quality wine with more water. The Greeks were more democratic. Everyone's wine goblet was filled from a large common bowl, so all drank the same wine with the same mix of water.

The wealthiest people were able to purchase wine of the highest quality. Rich Romans imported wine from all over the known world. Many spent time learning about and tasting different wines, becoming connoisseurs. The poorest people drank wine that had more in common with vinegar. There is a story about the famous Roman politician Marcus Antonius. He found himself on the wrong side of a political power struggle and hid in the house of an associate of far lower social status. However, in an act of hospitality, his host accidentally caused Antonius's death. The associate sent his servant to a neighborhood wine shop to buy a bottle of wine for their guest. When he tasted the usual family wine, the servant decided the quality was not good enough for the noble Antonius. So he purchased a far better and much more expensive wine. When questioned by authorities, the wine merchant mentioned the servant's "suspicious" behavior. This led the authorities straight to Antonius's hiding place. All for a good glass of wine![12]

Your Wedding Feast

So Wisdom has slaughtered her animals, set her table, and mixed her wine. (Proverbs 9:1–2, 5) The wedding feast was an extravagant experience, so we recommend that you serve two meat dishes, the ones described below or favorite recipes from other chapters. You can replace the quail with Cornish hens if quail are not available at your local markets. You will have to adjust the cooking time for the bigger birds. This menu also provides plenty of variety for your vegetarian friends.

It is time for the feast! Bless the bread at the beginning of the meal with this blessing:

> Blessed are You, Lord, our God, King of the Universe
> who brings forth bread from the earth. Amen.

A special blessing of thanksgiving can be said for the bride and groom. This one is based on the Sanctification Prayer from a Jewish wedding liturgy:

> Blessed are you, Lord our God, King of the Universe, who created rejoicing and gladness, bridegroom and bride, mirth and exultation, pleasure and delight, love and friendship. Lord our God, let there be heard the sound of joy and gladness, the voice of the groom and the bride, the sound of jubilation of grooms from their canopies and of youths from their feasts of song. Blessed are you, Lord, who gladdens the groom with the bride. Amen

Bless the wine with this blessing:

> Blessed are You, Lord, our God, King of the Universe, who creates the fruit of the vine. Amen

Menu for a First-Century Wedding Feast

Mezza (Appetizers)
- Barley and Wheat Bread*
- Olive Oil and Thyme Dip* (from chapter 5)
- Almond Dip*

- Raw cucumbers, carrots and spring onions for dipping (from the market)
- Raisins* (recipe or from the market)
- Brined Olives* (chapter 4 or from the market)
- Pistachios and almonds (from the market)

Main Course
- Braised Cucumbers with Dill*
- Beef Short Ribs and Barley Stew*
- Regional Spices*
- Roasted Quail with Pomegranate Glaze*

Dessert
- Slices of honeydew and cantaloupe (from the market)
- Honey Lemon Dip*
- Wedding Cake*
- Sweet Bread*

The Recipes

Barley and Wheat Bread

The idea for this recipe came from the book, Baking with Julia. *The sponge for the dough is made the day before and gives the experience of saving dough and using it to leaven the next day's bread. It also uses barley flour, common in first-century bread making.*

Sponge
3 cups warm water (110°)
½ teaspoon yeast
2 cups unbleached all-purpose flour

Dough
1½ cups barley flour
4 cups unbleached all-purpose
   flour

1 tablespoon olive oil
1 tablespoon salt
1 tablespoon honey

First make the sponge. Place the yeast and warm water in the bowl of your mixer. Wait until yeast begins to activate, approximately 15 minutes. It will change color and begin to bubble. Add the flour and with a dough hook, mix on low 1 minute, until well mixed. Remove from the mixer and put dough in oiled bowl. Cover with plastic wrap and let sit for 1 day (24 hours). Some of the water may separate from the sponge. Do not discard.

Place the sponge, separated water, and all the dough ingredients into a mixing bowl. Using the dough hook, mix for 5 minutes. Allow to rest for 15 minutes and the mix for another 5 minutes. Remove the bowl and cover with a kitchen towel or plastic wrap. Allow the dough to rise until it doubles, approximately 3 hours.

After rising, turn out the dough onto the floured surface, punch down with your fingers to allow the gases to escape and knead for about 1 minute. Form the dough into 4 loaves about 6–8 inches in diameter and 1–1½ inches thick in the center. Lightly oil baking sheets with olive oil and place the loaves on the sheets. Cover with the floured towel and let rise for another hour. After 40 minutes, preheat the oven to 400°. Cook bread on a rack in the center of the oven for 20 minutes. Remove bread and let it cool on a rack for at least 2 hours.

Barley flour has less gluten and breads made with barley tend to be denser.

Almond Dip

1 slice white bread, crust removed	½ tablespoon salt
1 cup water, plus two tablespoons	¾ cup roasted almonds
1 garlic clove	Juice from one lemon

Soak the bread in 1 cup of water. Squeeze the water from the bread and dry. Discard the water. Blend together all the ingredients, including the bread, in a food processor or blender until smooth. Add additional water if needed for consistency. Serves 8.

This recipe also can be made with a large mortar and pestle.

Raisins

Yes, you can make raisins. Use your homemade raisins as a side dish with any of the meals in this book or as an ingredient in recipes, such as Lamb Stew Apicius in chapter 6. The raisins will dry better if blanched first, but that step is not necessary.

Any amount of grapes, removed from the stem

To blanch grapes: Fill a large bowl with ice water. Bring a large pot of water to a boil. Carefully place one pound of grapes in the boiling water and cook them for 30 seconds. Immediately remove them with a slotted spoon and place in the bowl of ice water. Cool completely and dry.

To make raisins: Preheat the oven to 170°. Place the grapes on baking sheet and slowly cook until the grapes are shriveled, approximately 5 to 7 hours. They should be completely dry when eaten or squeezed.

Cool the raisins and then place in a covered container for 7 to 10 days. Repeat the drying process if moisture collects on the inside of the container. Store in an airtight container for up to 1 year.

Braised Cucumbers with Dill

We predict that you will wonder why cooked cucumbers are not eaten more often. We did!

4 cucumbers, peeled
1 tablespoon olive oil
2 cups chicken stock

1 tablespoon fresh dill or 1 teaspoon
   dried dill
1 teaspoon salt
¼ teaspoon pepper

Slice cucumbers lengthwise and remove the seeds by scraping them with a spoon. Then chop the cucumbers into bite-size chunks.

Heat oil in a 12-inch sauté pan. When the oil is hot, sauté the cucumbers briefly. Add the chicken stock and spices. Bring to a boil and then reduce to a simmer. Cover and cook for approximately 10 to 15 minutes until crisp-tender. Adjust salt and pepper before serving. Serves 8.

This dish will look and taste more rustic if you do not remove the cucumber seeds. You can garnish with finely chopped green onions. For a different flavor, use a teaspoon of cumin and a bay leaf instead of the dill.

Beef Short Ribs and Barley Stew

This is a wonderful meal to eat with your fingers.

3 pounds short ribs	2 cloves garlic, minced
3 tablespoons olive oil	¾ cup pearl barley, rinsed and
1 tablespoon salt, or to taste	drained
1 teaspoon pepper, or to taste	3–4 cups beef stock
1 tablespoon regional spices (below)	1 tablespoon dill
1 onion, chopped	Additional salt and pepper to taste
1 carrot, julienned	

Preheat the oven to 350°. Place the short ribs in a large bowl and then coat with olive oil. Season them with salt, pepper, and regional spices. Heat a 5-quart Dutch oven on the stove top over medium heat, brown the ribs and then remove. Add the onion and carrot and cook until the onion begins to soften. Then add the garlic and cook for another 2 minutes. Return the ribs to the Dutch oven and add the pearl barley. Add the beef stock and dill. Cover and move to the oven. Cook for 1½ hours or until the meat is falling off the bone. Serves 4 to 6.

If you do not have a Dutch oven, you can brown the ribs and cook the vegetables in a 14-inch skillet and the place all the ingredients in a large baking dish or glass baking pan. Cover the pan with foil before baking and remove the foil for the last 15 minutes of baking.

Regional Spices

This is a helpful spice mix for first-century cooking. You may certainly omit any spice you do not have. You may also reduce the amount from 1 tablespoon of each spice to 1 teaspoon.

1 tablespoon ground cinnamon	1 tablespoon ground turmeric
1 tablespoon ground coriander	1 tablespoon dried dill
1 tablespoon dried rosemary	1 tablespoon. dried sage
1 tablespoon ground cloves	1 tablespoon dried cumin

Place all the spices in a jar. Put the top on the jar and shake vigorously. This recipe provides enough regional spices for several recipes.

Roasted Quail with Pomegranate Glaze

This is a big favorite, too.

8 quail, back and ribs removed	1 tablespoon fresh thyme or 1½
3 tablespoons olive oil, divided use	teaspoons dried thyme
salt and pepper to taste	8 thyme sprigs
	8 garlic cloves

Glaze

4 tablespoons pomegranate molasses	2 tablespoons olive oil
4 tablespoons red wine vinegar	2 tablespoons honey
4 tablespoons water	

Clean and dry the quail. Rub them inside and out with 2 tablespoons of olive oil. Rub salt, pepper, and thyme on the inside of the quail and the place 1 garlic clove and 1 sprig of thyme in each one. Generously salt and pepper the outside of the quail and add the remaining thyme.

Preheat oven to 350°. Lightly oil a roasting pan and set aside. Heat olive oil in a 14-inch skillet or sauté pan over medium-high heat. Brown the quail, several at a time, breast side down for approximately 10 minutes. Turn frequently so they do not stick to the skillet. Remove the quail, breast side up, to the roasting pan.

Combine the glaze ingredients in a small bowl and mix until combined. Be prepared to mix again before using if the oil separates from the other ingredients.

Spoon approximately ⅓ of the glaze onto the quail. Add a small amount of water to the roasting pan to keep the juices and glaze from burning, then place them in the oven. Roast for 30 minutes, adding additional glaze after 10 and 20 minutes. Let rest 5 minutes before serving. Serves 8 with another meat, or 4 if served alone.

Honey Lemon Dip

You may want a little of this with all your fruit. Recipe can easily be doubled or tripled.

⅓ cup honey
1 tablespoon lemon juice
pinch of cinnamon

Mix all three ingredients in a small serving bowl.

Wedding Cake

This recipe is our version of a wedding cake described by Cato. Living in the century before Jesus, he wrote about farming and wine making. His writings also included examples of how foods were prepared, including this sweet cake.

1 cup unbleached all-purpose flour
1 cup ricotta cheese
1 egg, beaten
1 tablespoon olive oil

½ cup and 1 tablespoon honey, divided use
Fresh bay leaves

Preheat the oven to 400°. Sift the flour. Place the cheese in the mixer and beat on low for 20 seconds. Add the flour, egg, olive oil, and 1 tablespoon honey and then mix until combined but still soft.

Grease a baking sheet. Divide the dough into 4 pieces and then shape into cakes, approximately ¾ inch thick. Place a bay leaf on the baking sheet and the cake on top of it. Tightly cover the baking sheet with aluminum foil and then bake for 30 to 35 minutes until beginning to brown, removing the foil for the final 5 minutes. Remove from the oven and form a cross on each cake with a knife. Pour the honey on the cakes and allow to sit for 10 to 15 minutes. Remove the bay leaves and serve.

Sweet Bread

Candied citron peel is usually available in the market between Thanksgiving and Christmas for use in making fruit cakes. You can use raisins or another dried fruit cut into raisin-size pieces instead.

1 tablespoon yeast
¼ cup warm water (110°)
4 cups unbleached all-purpose flour
1 cup milk
1 teaspoon salt

1 tablespoon cinnamon
¼ cup melted butter
¼ cup honey
1 egg
½ cup candied citron

Place the yeast and warm water in the bowl of your mixer. Wait until yeast begins to activate, approximately 15 minutes. It will change color and begin to bubble. Add the flour to the yeast mixture. Then add the rest of the ingredients, except for the citron.

Mix with the dough hook for 5 minutes. Start on the slowest speed to keep the flour from splashing out of the bowl and then increase the speed to medium slow. Let the dough rest for 15 minutes and then add the citron. Mix for another 5 minutes. The dough should be slightly sticky and springy to the touch. Add flour 1 tablespoon at a time if the dough is too sticky or water if it is too dry. Place the dough in an oiled bowl and cover with a cotton kitchen towel or greased plastic wrap. If your KitchenAid bowl is large enough, you can leave the dough in that bowl to rise. Let rise until it has doubled in size, about 1½ hours.

Turn the dough out on a floured surface and divide into 12 parts. Roll each into a ball. Place the balls on a greased baking sheet. Cover with a kitchen towel or greased plastic wrap and allow to rise another 45 minutes.

Preheat oven to 350°. Bake for approximately 25 minutes or until turning brown. Cool on a rack for 1 hour before serving. Serve with honey.

If your pan is not large enough for all twelve breads, put one of the pans in the refrigerator while the breads on the first pan rise. While first pan is cooking, remove the second pan and let come to room temperature and finish rising.

A multilevel townhouse in ancient Jerusalem with space to eat outdoors on the upper roof.

CHAPTER EIGHT

The Feast of the Passover

This day shall be a day of remembrance for you. You shall celebrate it as a festival to the Lord; throughout your generations you shall observe it as a perpetual ordinance. (Exodus 12:14)

The house is crowded. A family from Galilee gathers with relatives who live in Jerusalem. Several of the men spent the morning purchasing an unblemished lamb at a stall in the Kidron Valley. That afternoon they walked to the temple and stood in line, along with thousands of others, waiting for their turn to have a priest kill the lamb and take its blood to the altar. After the sacrifice, another priest took the lamb and returned it several minutes later with the skin removed.

But now it is dark. The lamb is roasted. The lamps were lighted before sunset and the families are reclining around tables in a large open room. Guests are casually helping themselves to bowls of lentils, stacks of unleavened bread, and the slices of meat that are heaped on the small tables. Everyone is drinking wine from simple pottery mugs when one of the children is prompted to ask, "Why is this night different from all others?"

Why indeed! It is the celebration of the Passover. Without a doubt, this feast was and still is the most important holiday of the Jewish year. It is the night that, in many ways, defines Judaism by setting the Jewish people apart and helping them to remember and relive their identity. There is no overestimating the importance of Passover for first-century Jews. It was certainly the most important feast of each year. Hundreds of thousands of Jews from all around the Mediterranean and from Babylon streamed into Jerusalem each year for this day. In looking for a modern equivalent, we concluded that it contained elements of the Fourth of July, Thanksgiving dinner, and a road trip with family and friends. One historian compared the ancient Passover celebration to modern Christmas celebrations: "a blend of piety, good cheer, hearty eating, making music, chatting with friends, drinking and dancing."[1]

Passover was more than just a feast. It celebrated what was certainly the seminal and defining event in the history of Israel: death passing over the Jewish firstborns and striking the Egyptians and the Jewish people passing over from slavery to freedom. The complex of events and people molded and shaped the Jewish people and made them who they were and still are. It was these events and people that they remembered and relived each year at the Passover or seder feast. In this chapter we will join the celebration of this very ancient feast. We will experience how it was celebrated at the time of Jesus and we will see how Passover impacted the young Christian Church.

This chapter is followed by a supplement with detailed instructions that explain how a family, church, youth group, or some other gathering can celebrate its own Passover feast. There are already many detailed scripts, or *haggadahs* (teachings), available at bookstores or online. But these contain traditions that have been added to the celebration over the centuries and do not necessarily reflect the practices of the first century. The haggadah following this chapter attempts to reconstruct a Passover evening much like the one shared at the time of Jesus.

Passover: the Feast of Feasts

At a time in which life for most people consisted primarily of hard labor, the people who lived around Jesus found ample reasons and opportunities for celebrations and feasting. In chapter 5, we described the weekly observance of the Sabbath feast by first-century Jews. For one day each week, everyone was excused from labor and enjoyed the Sabbath. There were other celebrations as well, such as the monthly observation of the new moon when shofars were blown at the temple and special sacrifices were made. By the first century, Jews were also enjoying several unofficial holidays, including Hanukkah, which commemorates the victories of Judas Maccabeus, and Purim, a celebration of the deliverance of the Jews by Esther and Mordecai. But the major celebrations each year were the three pilgrim feasts.

The pilgrim feasts were times when many faithful Jews traveled to Jerusalem to celebrate their religion, history, culture, and harvests with sacrifices and feasting.[2] Passover, held in conjunction with the Feast of Unleavened

Bread, was undeniably the most important and most popular of the pilgrim feasts. But there were two other major pilgrim feasts: Weeks (also called Pentecost) and Booths (also called Tabernacles). The feasts of Weeks and Booths are the subject of chapter 9.

The Gospel according to St. Luke tells of Jesus' parents going to Jerusalem for the Passover and that he went with them when he was twelve (Luke 2:41–42). This seems to have been the practice of most of the Jews living in Palestine. They attempted to travel to Jerusalem every year for Passover. Servants and perhaps a few family members stayed behind to keep watch over the farm and household and to tend to the young children. However, once the children reached the age of twelve or thirteen, they joined their families. Women were not required to make the pilgrimage to Jerusalem, but most of them did. Wives, mothers, and daughters were just as eager as the men were to escape the responsibilities of hearth and farm by joining the annual pilgrimage.

Large numbers of foreign Jews also traveled to Jerusalem for the feasts of Passover and Unleavened Bread. They came from all over the Mediterranean and Middle East: Rome, Greece, Egypt, Syria, and Babylon. Whether they walked, rode donkeys, or traveled in boats, almost all the Passover pilgrims traveled in large groups or caravans. This provided both safety on the road and companionship. In many ways, the celebration began while traveling. Much like Chaucer's *Canterbury Tales*, which many of us read in high school, those first-century pilgrims told stories, sang psalms, ate special meals together in the evening, and drank a little more wine than was their usual custom. Often the friendships forged on these trips endured for years, or even lifetimes. Families that traveled together might also lodge near each other and share the Passover feast with each other. Groups from Galilee, Samaria, and Alexandria in Egypt tended to stay in certain sections of the town or camped in large communities. We can suspect that, because of the large numbers who attended Passover, many of the small farming communities all but emptied as they traveled together to Jerusalem.

Unless they were quite wealthy, the Jews who lived the farthest from Jerusalem could not afford an annual journey to Jerusalem and did not participate in Passover. For many, the trip must have been similar to a Muslim's pilgrimage to Mecca. It was likely a once-in-a-lifetime experience. Families saved part of their profits for many years before they could afford the expense of travel and the time of extravagant spending in Jerusalem.

Like New Orleans during Mardi Gras or Time Square on New Year's Eve, Jerusalem became pandemonium as all the pilgrims arrived. Tens of thousands of Jews from all over the Mediterranean world and from Babylon streamed into Jerusalem to celebrate these feasts. During festival times the population of Jerusalem would mushroom from somewhere between twenty-five and fifty thousand to more than a hundred thousand, and maybe as many as twice that number.[3] One could correctly argue that, with the presence of the temple and the large number of pilgrims visiting each year, religious tourism was the primary industry of first-century Jerusalem.

Many people arrived a week early so they could participate in a ritual cleansing and make neglected sacrifices before going into the temple for Passover. There were many reasons why a person might be considered unclean; the most common was "corpse impurity." Exposure to a dead person or animal caused this impurity and included such common activities as killing and cleaning a fish or a chicken for dinner. Some pilgrims visited the local priest for the seven-day ritual of purification before leaving on the journey, but most waited until they arrived in Jerusalem for the ritual, which included a water bath or baptism. Many people also lingered after Passover for the week-long festival of unleavened bread.

Where did all these pilgrims stay? After all, if Jerusalem had to accommodate an influx of an extra hundred thousand people or more, then large numbers of pilgrims must have been competing for a very finite number of available rooms within the city. Some stayed with friends or with other members of a religious group or sect. Many Jewish Christians that continued to travel to Jerusalem for the Passover feast must have stayed with members of the local Christian community. Some people were lucky enough to get a room at one of the inns within the city. Others stayed with families that opened their homes to visiting families or at a room in one of Jerusalem's many synagogues. Still others, like Jesus and his disciples, stayed in rooms and houses in the nearby communities of Bethphage or Bethany and walked to Jerusalem for the daily festivities:

> Then [Jesus] entered Jerusalem and went into the temple; and when he had looked around at everything, as it was already late, he went out to Bethany with the twelve. (Mark 11:11, also see Matthew 21:17)

Instead of charging rent, most residents and innkeepers asked that they receive the skins of the unblemished Passover lambs in exchange for the room. These skins were quite valuable and were later sold at the marketplace.

Many of the wealthiest Jews had second homes in the city for use during the festival seasons. These families, along with their household servants, moved into the city from their first-century equivalent of a manor house in the country. But the majority of pilgrims carried tents with them and camped outside the city walls. There was a large flat place in the area of the present Damascus gate where many of the pilgrims camped.[4]

Despite the festive atmosphere, or maybe because of it, Passover was a time of political and social tension. Thieves and pickpockets were attracted to the large crowds of tourists. So were zealots and revolutionaries. The Roman procurator and a sizable body of soldiers arrived from Caesarea each year at Passover to prevent riots or other problems. They were not always successful. The Passover sacrifices were stopped in the year 4 CE when Passover pilgrims used the festival as an opportunity to protest the execution of two rabbis. A cohort of troops was sent to the temple only to be driven away. More troops were sent and about 3,000 Jews were killed.[5] There were other years after the death of Jesus when riots and bloodshed interrupted the Passover sacrifice. Tensions continued to worsen at the Passover festival throughout the first century. Escalating social and economic problems resulted in the development of a radical nationalism with more young Israelites turning to mob and revolutionary violence. The nation-forming themes of Passover only exacerbated nationalistic feelings.

Very few pilgrims brought food and kitchen supplies with them, choosing to purchase what they needed for the Passover feast at the Jerusalem marketplaces. The vast majority of the visitors had just sold part of their recently harvested barley crop—the festivities were in part a harvest celebration with a special harvest ceremony at the temple—or maybe surplus wine or olives from the preceding fall, and they had extra money for the feast. In expectation of the massive crowds, merchants flooded the markets with all the items necessary for Passover, including fruits, vegetables, nuts, legumes, and thousands of unblemished lambs.

A law in the Book of Deuteronomy required that Israelites set aside a tithe of their harvest for a celebration (Deuteronomy 14:22–27). Can you imagine a modern law requiring that we use a certain percentage of our income for vacations and feasts? Apparently most Jews took this seriously. Not only did they eat and drink much more than usual, but they used the feast as an opportunity to purchase special clothing, luxury items, and household wares to take home with them. Women bought new dresses, perfumes, and jewelry for the feast. Children were given almonds and other treats to eat. Some pilgrims gave money to caterers and street cooks who then prepared their meals for the rest of their stay in Jerusalem. Of course the ingredients for the Passover also were purchased: the unblemished lamb, bitter herbs, unleavened bread, fruit and nuts for the charoset, wine, and all the spices and ingredients needed to prepare the special feast.

A site for the feast was acquired. Arrangements with friends and relatives who shared the feast were made. Ideally, the Passover feast was held within the precinct of the temple. But as populations grew, families were allowed to celebrate the feast at other locations in Jerusalem and even as far away as the suburb of Bethphage. The location had to have adequate kitchen facilities to prepare the feast and a dining area large enough to hold a group of at least ten people.

The Sacrifice

Finally all the ingredients for the feast were purchased and the women were busily preparing the food. The men who were taking the lamb to the temple had participated in the required rituals for purification. There were new clothes and jewelry. The entire city was electric with excitement. Then tens of thousands of men from all over Jerusalem and the suburbs made their way to the temple with their unblemished lambs. Between five and ten thousand priests were on duty to help with the sacrifices. All the while a large chorus of the Levites and musicians playing their instruments occupied a corner of the courtyard adding to the tumult by performing the Hallel psalms—psalms 113 through 118. The Hallel psalms are so called because they begin with the word *hallelujah*. These are songs that are both celebratory and nationalistic, recalling the theme of deliverance.

The sacrifices were likely considered as important an aspect of Passover as the meal itself. They began at 4:00 PM and lasted two hours. Records written hundreds of years after the destruction of the temple state that the lambs were sacrificed together in three very large groups. Archaeologists and scholars tell us, however, that more likely long lines of pilgrims made their way to one of the thousands of priests. A male in the family killed the lamb by cutting its throat and a priest helped by collecting the blood in a basin made of gold or silver. Another priest took the basin and threw it on the altar as an offering to God. The priest then took the lamb to a hook on the temple wall where it was skinned and the fat removed. Like the basin of blood, the fat was taken to the altar. The skin and animal were returned to the pilgrim. The entire process of sacrifice lasted only about ten minutes.

For most of us, the visual image conjured by the killing of a lamb in the temple and the freshly skinned animal being carried back home is likely repulsive. It is difficult to grasp the festive aspect of the sacrifice. We live in a sterilized world where we are accustomed to seeing our meat already nestled in a Styrofoam container nicely wrapped in cellophane. Yet it was not that many generations ago when one of the highlights of the year for a farm family was the butchering of a hog each fall. It was an event in which the entire family was involved and for which there was great celebration. All in all, that holiday attitude was much more consistent with that of the first-century family.

After the sacrifice, the lamb was immediately taken home and roasted whole. A spit was constructed for roasting the lamb using pomegranate branches. In this way a hint of pomegranate flavor was added to the taste of the meat. Because the Passover required that all the meat was to be eaten that night and because of the expense of buying a lamb, families usually joined together with other groups to make a party of at least ten people. If the group was so large that it required more than one lamb, then another type of sacrifice, such as a *Todah* or Thanksgiving sacrifice, was offered a day or so before the Passover sacrifice and that meat was used to supplement the Passover lamb. It was a common practice for those who lived more than a day from Jerusalem to postpone a trip to the temple and then fulfill as many sacrificial obligations as possible once they arrived for Passover.

The Seder

Travel back to the year 30 CE, the year that many believe Jesus was killed, and join a Passover celebration in Jerusalem. There were a number of elements for the feast that were considered essential. In addition to the special foods and the four cups of wine described above, a special prayer was proclaimed that gave thanks for and sanctified both the day and the feast. That prayer is still called the *kiddush*. Equally important, the Hallel psalms were sung or recited and the story of the Exodus was told especially for the benefit of the children at the meal.

The feast doubled as a classroom. Teaching the children about the exodus from Egypt was an essential aspect of the feast (see Exodus 12:26). Children were encouraged to ask questions about the meal and what it meant. They heard the stories of their history within the context of roasted lamb and unleavened bread. In doing so, they began to experience their own history and culture. Because of this annual feast and the retelling of the story of the Exodus, the children of each generation participated in the event that formed their people and nation. They also heard the story of liberation from slavery at the very time when most Jews prayed to be liberated from the Romans. After their first seder feast, the children then relived the story of the Exodus year after year until they were the ones answering the questions and telling the stories.

On that special night, the entire family ate, drank, asked questions, heard stories about their history and heritage and celebrated. The past became for them a present reality because the story of the wonderful saving deeds of

God was once again told and appropriated. The salvation of their ancestors became *their* salvation. After all, had it not been for the Exodus, then would they not still be slaves in Egypt?

Not only was that night different than all others, the meal was different as well. Three foods were required: lamb, unleavened bread, and bitter herbs.[6] By the first century, a dip called charoset, made with fruit, nuts, and sweet wine, was also served, but was not considered a required element of the feast.

The Passover lamb was the primary food. Because meat was a luxury, it was typically used to supplement and add flavor to others foods. But at Passover, a large helping of roasted meat was the main course for everyone, rich and poor alike. Regulations even developed so that family members who fell asleep while eating the Passover feast could be awakened and begin eating lamb again. The lamb had to be roasted whole with none of its bones broken and all of its organs in place. After roasting, the internal organs were removed and eaten as appetizers before the beginning of the feast.

Lamb was the most important symbol for the Passover feast. The lamb was a sign of God's presence and redemptive purpose. After all, it was the animal that gave its life so that the last plague would pass over the people of Israel. In essence, the lambs died so that Israel's firstborn would live and the Hebrews could pass from slavery to freedom. At the first Passover, the lamb gave its life in sacrifice and its blood was painted on the door posts and lintels. By the first century, blood was no longer used to mark the house. Instead it was given as a gift to God, symbolically including God in both the sacrifice and the meal. The lifeblood of all creatures was a gift from God and, as such, it belonged to God and must be given back.

Lamb was not the only food. The rabbi Gamaliel at the end of the first century taught that unleavened bread and bitter herbs also had to be explained to the children present at the meal: "Unleavened bread' because our fathers were redeemed from Egypt . . . and bitter herbs, because the Egyptians made bitter the lives of our fathers. . . . In each and every generation one is obligated to see himself as if he went out of Egypt."[7]

Bitter herbs were dipped in salt water. We saw in an earlier chapter that bitter lettuces such as chicory and dandelion were commonly part of the diet. These lettuces and other herbs were eaten at Passover to remind the Jews of the bitterness of slavery in Egypt. They were dipped in salted water, a common condiment especially among the Romans, which reminded celebrants of the tears of their ancestors in Egypt. Charoset was another dip found on the table. It was made from dried fruit because the harvest of fresh fruit was months away. Charoset came to symbolize the mortar used by the Israelites when they were slaves. Additional appetizers might have included foods such as almonds, figs, and the intestines from the lamb.

Unleavened bread was another essential element of the feast. Along with the lamb, it was a part of the meal that was required by scripture and tradition. It was the bread of people that did not have the luxury of the time or means to let their bread rise. Bedouins, nomads, shepherds, and other ancient people who were constantly moving had historically eaten unleavened bread. The leavening of bread takes many hours, especially in days before *instant rise* yeast. The same was true of the Israelites during their time in the wilderness. Eating unleavened bread at Passover was a symbol that the Jews were a people who were unexpectedly leaving their homes to travel through the wilderness with no time to let their bread rise.

Everyone was required to stop eating regular leavened bread at noon before the Passover sacrifices. Earlier that day all the leavened foods in the house were hidden. Forty years later Jews began the practice of destroying all leavened foods, searching the house for breadcrumbs and even scouring warehouses and workshops for loaves of leavened bread. All the leavened foods were then burned in a public place or sold and given to the Gentiles. But this was not the practice during the life of Jesus. Most people simply removed leavened foods from their homes and retrieved them again after the festival. The unleavened bread was dipped in the salt water, charoset, and possibly a dip made with vinegar and herbs.

There were the requisite four glasses of wine. It was said that even the most destitute members of the community ate as much meat as they wanted and drank the four glasses of wine. Regulations were developed that required water and wine to be mixed at a ratio that the resulting drink was still wine. Apparently, at some point in time, unscrupulous vendors and hosts had diluted the wine for the poor to the extent that it looked and tasted more like water. Even the volume of wine was regulated. Each of the four ceremonial servings must contain one-fourth "log," the same volume as one and one-half eggs.[8] Guests drank additional servings of wine with their dinner, but could only drink the remaining ceremonial glasses once the meal was finished.

Other items likely were found on the table at a Passover feast. Spring vegetables, olives, and additional dried fruits and nuts were probably added to the table along with the bitter herbs. Hard-boiled eggs eventually became a standard element of the Passover feast and certainly could have been eaten at the time of Jesus. Eggs were a common food at that time and tasted good dipped in salt water or vinegar. Parsley is another modern

Passover standard that grew in the spring and could have been part of any first-century feast, including Passover.

The guests arrived for the feast. Their feet were washed and they were anointed with perfumed oil. Lamps were lit and hands were washed. Everyone reclined on special couches. The posture of reclining was one of luxury and honor, usually reserved for special banquets. It was also the posture of a free person. Slaves and servants were not allowed to recline. By eating while reclining, those at the feast were again reminded that, because of God, they were delivered from slavery.

The host prayed the blessing, giving thanks for the Passover, and then the first cup of wine was blessed. First the appetizers were served. At this point in the evening, an additional prayer was probably offered for the food by blessing the unleavened bread. Then the lamb and all the other foods were presented to the guests.

The second cup of wine was blessed and consumed before the questions and answers. The children who were present were usually twelve or thirteen years old, though sometimes families took their younger children to Jerusalem for the celebration. They were encouraged to ask questions about the entire experience of Passover. This gave the adults at the table the opportunity to retell and relive the Exodus stories about the liberation of their ancestors. These stories also offered hope to people whose country was occupied by the Romans that someday God would deliver them again. Unlike a modern Passover feast, where a set of formalized questions are asked and answered before the meal is served, first-century children asked questions and were told stories throughout the evening. Some of the questions asked by the children may have been standardized, such as "Why is this night different from all others?" Most of the questions were less formal than the ones in the modern seder and were likely based on the food that was served and the experience of participating in the feast: "Why are we eating lamb tonight and eating it roasted instead of boiled or in a stew?" "Why do we have two dips and we usually have just one?" "Why do we get to recline while we eat?" "Why are we eating unleavened bread tonight?" An adult may have prompted the first several questions. But once asked and answered, the children probably asked many more.

After the meal, a third cup of wine was blessed. Then a benediction, a concluding prayer of thanksgiving, was said for the feast. Usually desserts such as sweet breads, fruits, and salty foods were served at this point in a feast or banquet, but not at the Passover. The flavor of the Passover lamb was to be the last taste all Jews had in their mouths when the feast ended. At this point in the evening, the celebrants began singing songs and psalms, likely to include the Hallel psalms. Again the rabbis argued whether to sing to the end of Psalm 113 or to the end of Psalm 114 before the blessing of the fourth cup of wine. Regardless, the rest of the Hallel psalms were sung after the last glass of wine and a final blessing was prayed for the songs that were sung.[9]

The Israelites were instructed not to wander from party to party, eating lamb and drinking wine. Even with its nationalistic and community themes, the Passover was still first and foremost a family feast, to be enjoyed with friends and relatives. Besides, after eating a large amount of meat for the first time in months and drinking a minimum of four glasses of wine, most of the people in Jerusalem were probably ready for a good night's rest. Could this be one of the reasons why Jesus' disciples kept falling asleep in the Garden of Gethsemane?

The Feast of Unleavened Bread

By the time of Jesus, the Feast of Unleavened Bread was, to some degree, a continuation of the celebration of Passover. Many celebrants remained in and around Jerusalem to shop, eat, and drink. Scholars believe that this weeklong celebration began strictly as a celebration of the barley harvest. And certainly that aspect continued down to the first century. On the fifth day of the Festival of Unleavened Bread, sheaves of barley were presented in the temple as a symbol of their thankfulness for the new barley harvest. The ritual acknowledged that God was truly the owner of the land and the source of its fruitfulness. This ceremony of the sheaf was called a *wave offering* because the offering was not actually burned on the altar but presented to God by *waving* it in front of the altar and then giving it to the temple priests.

After the wave offering of the barley sheaves, the markets were filled with fresh and parched grain. People flooded to the market to buy the fresh barley for their bread, soups, and stews. The parched grains, like our bulgur, could then be made into salads, steamed like rice or added to soups and stews. Those who were unable to travel to Jerusalem for Passover waited until noon to begin eating from the new harvest because the wave offering of the barley sheaves was timed to take place at noon. In that way Jews all over the known world celebrated the harvest together by enjoying the fruits of the new harvest at the same time.

The First-Century Seder and the Twenty-First-Century Seder

Readers who have participated in a modern seder will notice a number of differences between the feast described above and the ones they have enjoyed. As one might expect, many elements of the Passover feast were added gradually over the centuries and became established traditions. The destruction of the temple in the year 70 CE was perhaps the single event that had the most profound change on the seder. Seven hundred years of tradition mandated that Jews travel to Jerusalem so the Passover lamb could be sacrificed in the temple. Then there was no temple and no Passover lamb. Foods like the bitter herbs and the unleavened bread began to receive a more prominent role at the feast. Other foods, such as eggs and lamb shank bones, symbolically represented the absent paschal lamb. Eggs were eaten instead of meat. The bone was present simply as a reminder of the importance of the Passover lamb in Egypt.

A lot of what we know about the actual structure of the ancient feast comes from the Mishnah, a collection of documents recorded several hundred years after the death of Jesus. The Mishnah is a written record of the oral teachings of the important rabbis from the first several centuries of the Common Era. This ancient document contains a section that describes the shape and traditions of the Passover feast. But by the time that the Mishnah was put together, the texts were already reflecting changes in attitude and belief caused by the destruction of the temple. The function and theology of the temple priesthood had long ended and the description of Passover in the Mishnah has an overlay of the rabbinical schools that had begun to flourish. Still, for our own Passover haggadah that follows in the supplement to this chapter, we use some of this material, including rabbinical style prayers, because early first-century material simply is not available to us.

By the third century, more changes to the Passover seder were occurring. The questions and explanation of Passover were moved so that they took place before the meal instead of during and after. No longer were the questions a response to what the children were experiencing, but were a pre-meal ritual that initiated a teaching opportunity for the family. The food was then served after the questions were answered.

Other traditions were added during the Middle Ages and closely track similar changes within Christianity. For example, at the end of the first millennium, many Christians began to expect that the second coming of Jesus was imminent. Likewise, many Jewish communities were looking for the arrival of the Jewish messiah. Medieval Jews had just experienced a period of intense persecution. This, along with the approach of the year 1,000 CE, fueled the expectation of the Messiah. It was also a common belief that Elijah would appear first, to announce the new Messiah. Many in the medieval Jewish community expected Elijah's initial appearance at a Passover seder. From this expectation, the practice of setting a place at table for Elijah and looking for his arrival became a common element of the Passover feast. Hymns like the "Denayou" were added about the same time as was the tradition of breaking the unleavened bread, now called the afikoman, and hiding a portion of it for the children to find were finding their place in the seder ritual.[10]

Was the Last Supper a Seder Feast?
If only we knew the answer! The first inclination is to say, "yes, of course it was." After all the gospels clearly state that Jesus' last supper with his disciples was a Passover meal, do they not? Well, yes and no. It is true that the gospels of Matthew, Mark, and Luke state that it was a Passover meal:

> On the first day of Unleavened Bread the disciples came to Jesus, saying, "Where do you want us to make the preparations for you to eat the Passover?" He said, "Go into the city to a certain man, and say to him, 'The Teacher says, My time is near; I will keep the Passover at your house with my disciples.'" So the disciples did as Jesus had directed them, and they prepared the Passover meal. (Matthew 26:17–19; also see Mark 14:12–16, Luke 22:3–6)

But then there is John's gospel. As is so often the case, with its stately language and powerful symbols, this gospel text gives a different point of view, or in this case, a different timetable. Instead of a Passover feast, their last meal together was a special meal the night before Passover. John states three times that the crucifixion took place on the day of the preparation for Passover. In the first reference, Pilate was handing Jesus over to be crucified at about noon, just as the men in Jerusalem were beginning to make their way to the temple with their unblemished lambs for the sacrifice (John 19:14). The second time John made reference, Jesus had just died: "Since it was the day of Preparation, the Jews did not want the bodies left on the cross" (John 19:31). The author wanted us to know that Jesus died at about the same time the lambs were being sacrificed in the temple, showing us the parallel between the deaths: the shedding of blood by both Jesus and the Passover lambs; concluding that Jesus' death fulfilled Passover. The third reference is in the last verse of the chapter. Jesus was laid in a tomb that was nearby, because the Passover Sabbath started at sunset and the Jews could do no more work, like carrying a body and opening and closing a tomb (John 19:42).

Some scholars believe that all four gospels actually point to the same day, that some sects within Judaism used a different calendar and celebrated Passover a day earlier. In this way Jesus could have eaten the Passover feast with his disciples and stilled died with the Passover lambs the next day. Others point out that John never claimed that the last supper was a Passover seder. They even suggest that the meal in the other gospels is suspect because they fail to mention the Passover lamb, the four glasses of wine or any of the other common characteristics of the Passover feast.

In the final analysis, we cannot say with absolute certainty whether or not the Last Supper was a Passover meal. What we can say was that the Passover provided the *theme and setting* for their final dinner together. The meal took place in Jerusalem, in the midst of pilgrims from all over the known world who were there to celebrate the Passover. Everyone was preparing for the big night, by cleaning, buying food, and cooking. There is no doubt that the festive atmosphere of the feast was in the air. If not a Passover feast, then it was certainly a large meal with friends on the eve of the Passover. Like a modern dinner on Christmas Eve, everything about the meal would have focused on the next day. The prayers would have had Passover themes, likely giving thanks for the Exodus. The songs that were sung would have been the Hallel psalms. The form of the meal would have been quite similar to the banquet described in chapter 4. There would have been a blessing of bread at the first of the meal and a blessing of the wine after the tables were cleared, before the questions from the disciples and teaching by Jesus.

So which was it? The authors do not know and have to say that the limitations of this book make it impossible to answer. We even wonder if the question truly can be answered. Rather, our purpose is to say that the themes and meaning of the Passover feast greatly inspired all four gospel writers and influenced the early church's understanding of the death and resurrection of Jesus. It continues to shape our understanding as well. Jesus celebrated the Passover seder in Jerusalem every year, and enjoyed at least one and likely more of these meals with his disciples. For these reasons alone, Christians should join this feast and ask, "Why is this night different from all others?"

Menu for a Passover Feast

Passover is such an important feast that we have placed instructions in a supplement to this chapter. The supplemental section follows this chapter.

- Unleavened Bread*
- Bitter Herbs and Salt Water*
- Vinegar Dip*
- Spring vegetables for dipping: parsley, green onions, radishes (from your market)
- Brined Olives* (chapter 4 or from your market)
- Charoset*
- Hard-Boiled Eggs* (chapter 6)
- Bulgur and Chard*
- Lentil Pottage*
- Roasted Leg of Lamb*

The Recipes

Unleavened Bread

This also makes a great flat bread for an elegant twenty-first century reception.

> 2 cups unbleached all purpose flour
> 1 cup whole wheat flour
> ½ tablespoon salt
> 1 tablespoon honey
> 1 tablespoon olive oil
> 1 cup water

Place all ingredients in food processor and process until it forms a ball. Remove and place on floured surface. Knead until smooth. Wrap in plastic wrap and let rest for 30 minutes. Preheat oven to 350°. Divide dough into eight sections.

Dust with flour and flatten each section. Then continue to flatten with pasta roller or rolling pin. If using a pasta roller, roll through level one 3 times, then through each subsequent level once, stopping with level five. If using a rolling pin, roll to ⅛ to ¼ inch thickness. Lightly dust with flour as necessary to keep from sticking to pasta rollers or to rolling pin. Cut in half when too long to continue rolling as one piece.

Place pieces on baking sheets and immediately place in the oven. Breads will stick to the pan while cooking if they are left there too long. Cook for 6 minutes, turn and cook for another 3–5 minutes. Cooking time may take longer if breads are thicker. Remove from the pan and cool on a rack. Makes 16 pieces of bread.

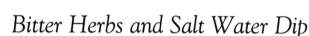

Bitter Herbs and Salt Water Dip

2 cups water
2 tablespoons salt
Spring lettuce mix

Place the water and salt in a saucepan and heat until the salt dissolves. Cool to room temperature. Use as a dip for the lettuce, boiled eggs, and the unleavened bread at a Passover seder.

Vinegar Dip

Can you get any simpler, or more authentic? Vinegar was a popular first-century dip. Add a teaspoon of honey to balance the bitterness of the vinegar or use a different herb if you'd like.

⅓ cup red wine vinegar
1 teaspoon thyme

Mix and use as a dip for vegetables, hard-boiled eggs, or bread.

Charoset

¼ pound raisins
¼ pound dried apricots, cut in half
¼ pound dried figs, stems removed
  and cut in half
2 tablespoons honey

1 teaspoon cinnamon
2 teaspoons Madeira or dry sherry
¾ cup sliced almonds, lightly
  roasted

Cover the dried fruit with water and soak for at least 4 hours or overnight. Drain and place in a food processor. Add the honey, cinnamon, and wine. Process until roughly chopped. Remove and stir in the almonds before serving. Serves 8 to 12 at a seder

Bulgur and Chard

This recipe is similar to the bulgur pilaf in chapter 5. Instead of chard, you can use spinach, very similar to ancient mallow.

1 head Swiss chard
1 cup bulgur, larger cut #2 or #3
⅓ cup olive oil (divided use)
½ medium onion, chopped
1 garlic clove, minced

1 cup chicken stock or water
¼ teaspoon ground cumin
1 teaspoon salt
¼ teaspoon ground black pepper
Roasted pine nuts for garnish

Remove the thick stems and ribs from the Swiss chard leaves, then rinse, dry, and chop the leaves. Using a fine mesh strainer, quickly rinse and dry the bulgur. Heat a saucepan over medium heat and add oil. Add onions and sauté until they turn translucent. Add garlic and continue to cook until it turns translucent. Add the bulgur and stir until it begins to toast. Add the stock (or water), cumin, salt, and pepper. Bring to a boil, reduce to a simmer and cover. Let it cook for approximately 10 minutes and then stir in the chard. Cover and cook for another 10 minutes or until the chard is wilted.

After the bulgur finishes cooking, remove the lid and stir with a fork to separate. Spoon the bulgur into a serving dish and garnish with roasted pine nuts. Serves 6.

Lentil Pottage

This may be the very dish that Jacob traded for his brother Esau's birthright. Hard to blame Esau!

2 tablespoons olive oil
1 onion, chopped
2 garlic cloves, minced
2 cups lentils
4 cups water or 2 cups water and 2
    cups chicken stock

1 teaspoon cumin
1 teaspoon dry mustard
1 bay leaf
1 teaspoon salt, or to taste
½ teaspoon pepper, or to taste

Heat a medium saucepan over medium heat. Add the oil and then cook the onion until translucent; add the minced garlic and cook until it is translucent. Add the lentils, liquid, and the rest of the ingredients. Cook uncovered for 40 to 45 minutes. Adjust the seasoning with additional salt and pepper and stir an additional tablespoon of olive oil into the lentils. Remove the bay leaf before serving. Serves 8.

Roasted Leg of Lamb

This recipe will work with boneless, bone-in, and partially bone-in legs of lamb. Should you choose, you may have your butcher remove the bone and trim. This is perfect for Passover or any other special occasion. The cooking time will depend on the weight of the leg, the presence of the bone, and the accuracy of your oven thermostat.

1 leg of lamb
2 tablespoon dried rosemary or 3
    tablespoons fresh rosemary, finely
    minced
Zest from one lemon, finely minced

3–4 cloves garlic, finely minced
¼ cup plus 1 tablespoon olive oil
1 tablespoon salt, or to taste
1 teaspoon pepper, or to taste

Trim the fat and silver skin from the outside of the lamb. In addition there is a large fatty gland within the muscle that should be removed. Make a number of slits, ½ inch long and ½ inch deep.

In a small bowl, mix the rosemary, lemon zest and garlic. Add a table-spoon of oil and stir so it makes a paste. Rub the lamb with olive oil then cover it with the paste, rubbing into the slits. Season with salt and pepper. Cover with plastic wrap and let marinate for 1 hour.

Preheat the oven to 350°. Place the lamb in a roasting pan. Add ¼ cup of water to the pan and place in the oven. Add additional water before the juices burn to the pan. Use a meat thermometer and roast until the internal temperature in the thickest section reaches 130° for medium rare, approxi-mately 1½ hours. It will continue to cook after it is taken from the oven and will reach 140°. The lamb should rest for at least 15 minutes before carving. Serves 8–10, according to the size of the leg of lamb.

A butterflied leg of lamb prepared this way is excellent cooked on the grill.

A First-Century Passover Haggadah

There are seven solo spoken parts in the script as well as parts for all who are present: Narrator; Family Leader; Female Member of the Family; Adults One, Two, and Three; and the Youngest Child. Short prayers are provided in English and with Hebrew transliteration. Feel free to skip the Hebrew if you wish. For the feast you will need to provide at least the bitter herbs (young spring lettuces), parsley, spring onions, saltwater dip, charoset, unleavened bread, roasted lamb, two side dishes and wine. Additional foods like hard-boiled eggs, nuts, olives, and other dips are certainly appropriate. If possible, eat and drink while reclining on cushions and pillows and serve the meal on trays or a coffee table. Instructions for the feast are given in brackets. You will also need candles, a pitcher of water, a basin, and towels.

The Seder

Narrator: We have gathered this evening for a Passover feast, or seder. The word *seder* literally means "order" and refers to the ordered ritual of the feast. If you have ever been to a Passover seder, then you will notice that this one is different. The teaching, or *haggadah*, for this celebration is an attempt to recreate a first-century Passover feast. Even though there are a number of similarities, there are also a number of differences between ancient and modern celebrations. As one might expect, many elements have been added to the traditions of Passover over the centuries. In fact, the tradition of using a written haggadah appears to have started during early medieval times, meaning that Jews celebrated Passover for several thousand years before using a written script.

There were some changes that took place a very long time ago. One big change took place after the destruction of the temple in the year 70 of the Common Era. Up until that time, all Passover lambs were sacrificed at the temple. With no temple, the Jews stopped sacrificing and eating lamb at Passover. Instead, eggs were eaten and a lamb shank bone was present at the table to remind the participants of the importance of the Paschal lamb. Because of the absence of lamb, the symbolic role of other foods, like the charoset (a dip made of fruit and nuts), wine, saltwater dip and especially the unleavened bread, became even more important to the celebration.

Another change from the first century was that the Passover feast was only celebrated in and around Jerusalem. This meant that people began preparing for Passover by first traveling to Jerusalem. It was a several-day walk for most Jews, though many had to travel across the Mediterranean Sea or in caravans for a week or more to reach the holy city. Families started eating the Passover feast in their homes only after the destruction of the temple.

Modern Jewish families prepare for the feast by searching for and disposing of all the leaven in their houses. This includes all food and drink products that include any grains and yeast. In ancient times, leavened foods were simply taken from the house to be returned later or they were sold to nearby Gentiles. Later in history, the community burned all the leavened bread. To-day, Jewish children from traditional families assist by using candles, feathers, and spoons to find and dispose of any stray breadcrumbs found in the house. The end result is that the house is thoroughly cleaned for Passover.

So here we are. The room is clean, though I must say that we did not use feathers, candles, and spoons. And most of us traveled here in cars, not on foot or on the back of a donkey.

We will begin by lighting candles. Two thousand years ago, these lights were oil lamps. A woman in the household lit the lamps before sunset because the Sabbath starts when the sun goes down and lighting candles is considered work. Along with providing light for the feast, this ceremony marks the beginning of the new day. And now for the prayer for lighting candles:

Female Member of Family: Barukh atah Adonai, Elohaynu melekh ha-olam asher kid' shanu bidevaro uvishmo anakhnu madlikim haneyrot shel yom tov. Blessed are you, Lord, our God, Ruler of the Universe, who sanctifies us with his word, and in whose name we light festival lights. Amen.

[Light the candles.]

Narrator: It was common for first century Jews to have their hands washed before a feast or banquet. In fact, because they ate with their hands, they usually washed several additional times during and after the meal.

Family Leader: Barukh atah Adonai, Elohaynu, melekh ha-olam, asher kid' shanu b'mitzvo tav v'tzi-va-nu al n' ti-lat ya da yim. Blessed are you, Lord, our God, King of the Universe, who sanctifies us with his commandments, and commands us concerning washing of hands. Amen

[Pour water over each person's hands using a pitcher and basin and use the towels for drying.]

The First Glass of Wine

Narrator: Now the meal begins with a special prayer that sanctifies the day. This prayer is called the kiddush. The blessing for the first serving of wine follows the kiddush.

[Begin with this reading if the Passover is on the Sabbath.]

Adult 1: God saw everything that he had made, and indeed, it was very good. And there was evening and there was morning, the sixth day. Thus the heavens and the earth were finished, and all their multitude. And on the seventh day God finished the work that he had done, and he rested on the seventh day from all the work that he had done. So God blessed the seventh day and hallowed it, because on it God rested from all the work that he had done in creation. (Genesis 1:31–2:3).

[Add the bracketed sections of the following prayer only on the Sabbath]

Family Leader: Let us pray: Blessed are you, Lord, our God, King of the Universe, who has chosen and exalted us from among all the peoples of the earth and sanctified us with your commandments. Oh Lord our God, you have lovingly given us [Sabbaths for rest,] festivals for rejoicing, holidays for gladness, feasts and seasons of joy, and this feast of the Unleavened Bread. It is a time of rejoicing, a season of freedom, and a sacred gathering in memory of the Exodus from Egypt. For you have chosen us and set us apart from all peoples, and you have granted us this holy festival as a heritage, in gladness and joy. Blessed are you, Lord, Who sanctifies [the Sabbath,] your people Israel and this festive season.

Everyone: Blessed are you, Lord, our God, King of the Universe, who has kept us alive, sustained us, and brought us to this season. AMEN.

[All present raise their glass of wine]

Family Leader: Baruch a-tah Adonai Elohaynu, me-lech ha-olam bo-rey p'ri ha-ga-fen. Blessed are you, Eternal God, Ruler of the Universe, who creates the fruit of the vine. Amen

[Everyone drinks the wine.]

Narrator: At this point, appetizers are served. They include bitter herbs, or young bitter lettuces. Other spring vegetables, such as parsley and green onions, were also served. The vegetables were dipped in salt water and other dips made from vinegar, wine, or olive oil. Because the Passover feast started so late in the evening, after sundown, additional snacks were on the table, especially for the children. These included nuts like pistachios or almonds and pieces of dried fruit. The intestines from the Paschal Lamb were also a favorite Passover appetizer in the first century.

[Eat the appetizers. While everyone is eating, the narrator continues:]

Narrator: The average person in the first century only ate meat three or four times a year. Lamb and goat were the most common meats eaten. For many families, the Passover was their first opportunity to have meat since the last feast, five or six months earlier. So, aside from being an important religious celebration, the Passover feast was a special meal because they finally could eat large amounts of roasted lamb or goat.

[After eating the appetizers, serve the unleavened bread, charoset, lamb, and other side dishes, but do not begin eating until after the blessing of the bread.]

Narrator: Now the main course of the feast is served. The charoset is a fruit dip that is eaten with the unleavened bread. It is traditional to have two warm side dishes served with the lamb.

The Rabbi Hillel, who lived during the time of Herod the Great, ate some of the Passover feast in this way: he would take some of the bitter herbs, charoset, and lamb, and eat it on a piece of unleavened bread, thus creating a sandwich, maybe even the first sandwich. Please try this with some of your dinner.

[The family leader lifts a piece of unleavened bread.]

Family Leader: Baruch atah Adonai, Eloheynu melech ha-olam mo-tzi le-chem min ha-a-retz. Blessed are you, Eternal God, Ruler of the Universe, who brings forth bread from the earth.

Baruch atah Adonai Eloheynu melech ha-olam asher kid'sha-nu b'mitz-vo-tov v'tzi-va-nu al a-chi-lat matzah. Blessed are you, Eternal God, Ruler of the Universe, who has sanctified us with laws and commanded us to eat matzah. Amen.

[The bread is broken and the meal begins. Allow everyone to eat some of the meal before proceeding.]

The Second Glass of Wine
Narrator: Now it is time for the second glass of wine.

[Everyone present raises their cup of wine]

Family Leader: Baruch a-tah Adonai Elohaynu, me-lech ha-olam bo-rey p'ri ha-ga-fen. Blessed are you, Eternal God, Ruler of the Universe, who creates the fruit of the vine. Amen

[Everyone drinks the wine and continues to eat the dinner.]

Narrator: One of the important purposes of the Passover feast was to teach the story of the Passover and Exodus to the children. With modern haggadahs, the questions from the children occur before the meal is served. However, two thousand years ago, the meal came first. The questions were based, not only on tradition, but also on the child's experience of the evening. This was a feast unlike any other during the year. So they were encouraged to ask lots of questions. These questions became formalized over the centuries and evolved into the four questions that have been asked for thousands of years.

The youngest child typically asks the questions. If the child is quite young, then an adult helps. One of the adults asks the questions if no children are present.

Child: How is this night different from all other nights? For on all other nights we dip once, this night twice? For on all other nights we eat leavened and unleavened bread, this night we eat only unleavened? For on all the other nights we eat meat roasted, steamed, or cooked in liquid, this night only roasted?

[Various adults are assigned answers to the questions. It should be similar to a modern dinner discussion, where one comment provokes additional comments from others present at the table]

Adult 1: A wandering Aramean was our ancestor (Deuteronomy 26:5b). Our ancestors went into Egypt during a very difficult time and continued to live there as aliens. We started out few in number but grew to be a great nation, mighty with many people. When the Egyptians treat us harshly and afflicted us, by imposing hard labor on us, we cry out to the Lord, the God of our ancestors. God hears our voice and sees our affliction, our toil and our oppression.

Adult 2: That is when the Lord our God brings us up out of Egypt, with a mighty hand and an outstretched arm.

Adult 3: The display of God's powerful is terrifying, such signs and wonders.

Adult 2: God chooses Moses to lead us out of Egypt into a land of milk and honey, a great and fertile land . . . this land, where we live today. And he appoints Aaron, Moses' brother to speak for him and for God. But the Pharaoh does not listen. His heart is hardened against us.

Adult 1: Then there are the plagues that the Egyptians suffered. Do you remember what the plagues are?

All Children: [Children present recite in unison] Blood, frogs, lice, wild beasts, cattle disease, boils on their skin, hail storms, locusts, and darkness during the day.

Family Leader: Good for you. But still the Pharaoh's heart is hardened. He will not listen. And then, and only then, is there the last plague, the most terrifying of all. God told Moses that death will visit Egypt. The firstborn of every family, even the firstborn of all the livestock, they will all die. But death passes over us. What we have to do is to sacrifice a lamb and put its blood on the doorposts and the lintel of each house. And because that lamb died, death passes over us and we have our freedom.

Adult 2: This night, just like that night, the lamb is cooked whole, with all its inner organs. All the meat has to be eaten tonight, because we will not be able to take leftover meat with us when we leave Egypt and begin our journey to the Promised Land.

Adult 3: It has to be an unblemished lamb and none of its bones can be broken, and it is roasted, not boiled or cooked any other way.

Family Leader: The blood is a sign on the houses where we live. When God sees the sign, then death and all other plagues pass over us. Then and only then can we leave Egypt.

Narrator: At the end of the first century of the Common Era, the famous and honorable Rabbi Gamaliel said: "Whoever does not say these three things on Passover does not fulfill the obligation: Pesah (paschal lamb), matzoh (unleavened bread) and meror (bitter herbs). The Paschal Lamb because the All Powerful God skipped over the houses of our ancestors in Egypt; bitter herbs because the Egyptians embittered the lives of our ancestors in Egypt; and unleavened bread because they were redeemed." So these three foods are required at Passover: lamb, bitter herbs, and unleavened bread. Charoset was also a standard dip at first-century Passovers, but scriptures do not require it.

Family Leader: And so that is why we eat lamb and eat it roasted. Because of the sacrifice of the lamb, we were spared death and delivered from slavery to freedom. The bonds of slavery and oppression are broken.

[Adult 1 holds a piece of unleavened bread for all to see]

Adult 1: Matzah is called the bread of affliction. It is the bread of haste, because once we left Egypt, we had little time to prepare dough. It takes many hours for leavened bread to rise before baking and we have very little time to prepare for the journey. So unleavened bread is the bread of haste and necessity, but for us, it is also the bread of divine assistance.

[Adult 2 holds pieces of bitter herb for all to see]

Adult 2: Tonight we also eat bitter herbs. They remind us of the bitterness of slavery and oppression. The scriptures say, "The Egyptians became ruthless in imposing tasks on the Israelites, and made their lives bitter with hard service in mortar and brick and in every kind of field labor. They were ruthless in all the tasks that they imposed on them" (Exodus 1:13–14). We dip them in salt water that reminds us of the tears we cried in Egypt.

Adult 3: And we dip the matzah, the unleavened bread, and the bitter herbs in the salt water. The salt water is the tears of oppression and suffering that we shed in Egypt while longing for our freedom. On this night we dip twice. We also dip in charoset, a dip made with fruit and nuts. The charoset reminds us of the mortar used to cement one brick or stone to another. We made mortar and used it to build monuments for Pharaoh.

Narrator: With the Passover feast, the past becomes present. Through food and symbols, the salvation and freedom of the Exodus becomes reality for those who eat the feast and tell the stories. For that reason, the story is always told in present tense, as though the storytellers personally experienced the Exodus and came out of Egypt. Scripture says: "You shall tell your child on that day, 'It is because of what the Lord did for me when I came out of Egypt. It shall serve for you as a sign on your hand and as a reminder on your forehead, so that the teaching of the Lord may be on your lips; for with a strong hand the Lord brought you out of Egypt.'" (Exodus 13:8–9) After all, if it had not been for the Lord, we would still be slaves to this day.

   Additional wine can be consumed during the meal. However, from this time on, we will drink only the wine that is blessed. The ancient and traditional four-part benediction follows the blessing of the third glass of wine. But first we will pause and answer additional question from the children.

[Pause the seder at this point so the adults can answer additional questions posed by the children.]

The Third Glass of Wine
Family Leader: It is time to bless the third cup of wine.

[All present raise their glass of wine]

Family Leader: Baruch atah Adonai Elohaynu, me-lech ha-olam bo-rey p'ri ha-ga-fen.
   Blessed are you, Eternal God, Ruler of the Universe, who creates the fruit of the vine. Amen

[Everyone drinks the wine.]

Family Leader: Come let us now pray the benediction for the feast.

Everyone: May the name of the Lord be blessed, now and forever.

Family Leader: Blessed are you, Lord, our God, King of the Universe. You nourish the entire world, in your goodness, with grace, with loving kindness, and with mercy. You give nourishment to all flesh. And through great goodness, nourishment was never lacking to us and may it never be lacking. Because you are the God who nourishes and sustains all, and benefits all, and prepares food for all creatures you created.

Everyone: Blessed are you, Lord, who nourishes all.

Family Leader: We thank you, Lord our God, because you have given to our ancestors as a heritage, as desirable, good and spacious land. Because you took us from the land of Egypt and you redeemed us from the house of bondage; for your covenant which you have given us; for your Law which you taught us and for your statutes which you have made known to us; for life, grace, and loving kindness which you granted us; and for the food with which you nourish and sustain us.

Everyone: For all, Lord our God, we thank you and bless you.

Family Leader: Have mercy, Lord our God, on your people Israel, on your city Jerusalem, the resting place of your glory, on the House of David, your anointed, and on the great and holy house where your name is called. Tend us, nourish us, sustain us, support us, relieve us and grant us a speedy relief from our troubles.

Everyone: Have mercy, Lord our God, on your people.

Family Leader: Blessed are you, Lord our God, King of the Universe, the Almighty, our King, our Creator, our Redeemer, our Maker, our Holy One, the Holy One of Jacob, our Shepherd, the Shepherd of Israel, who has done good to us, does good to us, and will do good to us. God who has bestowed, does bestow, and will always bestow on us grace, loving kindness, mercy and relief, rescue, success, blessing, salvation, consolation, sustenance and maintenance, mercy, life, peace and all good and everything good, may we never lack.

Everyone: Blessed are you, Lord our God, for everything good.

Family Leader: Amen.

Everyone: Amen.

Narrator: It was the custom that the Passover feast did not include dessert. In that way, the flavor of the paschal lamb is the last taste of food in our mouths. And now the Hallel, or Hallelujah psalms are sung or said.

Family Leader: It is that time in the evening when we bless and praise the Lord our God, King of the Universe, with songs and psalms.

Psalm 111

Family Leader:
Hallelujah!
I will give thanks to the Lord with my whole heart,
In the assembly of the upright, in the congregation.

Everyone:
Great are the deeds of the Lord!
They are studied by all who delight in them.

His work is full of majesty and splendor,
And his righteousness endures for ever.

He makes his marvelous works to be remembered;
The Lord is gracious and full of compassion.

He gives food to those who fear him;
He is ever mindful of his covenant.

He has shown his people the power of his works
In giving them the lands of the nations.

The works of his hands are faithfulness and justice;
All his commandments are sure.

They stand fast for ever and ever,
Because they are done in truth and equity.

He sent redemption to his people;
He commanded his covenant for ever;
Holy and awesome is his Name.

The fear of the Lord is the beginning of wisdom;
Those who act accordingly have a good understanding;
His praise endures for ever.

Psalm 112

Adult 1:
Hallelujah!
Happy are they who fear the Lord
And have great delight in his commandments!

Everyone:
Their descendants will be mighty in the land;
The generation of the upright will be blessed.

Wealth and riches will be in their house,
And their righteousness will last for ever.

Light shines in the darkness for the upright;
The righteous are merciful and full of compassion.

It is good for them to be generous in lending
And to manage their affairs with justice.

For they will never be shaken;
The righteous will be kept in everlasting remembrance.

They will not be afraid of any evil rumors;
Their heart is right;
They put their trust in the Lord.

Their heart is established and will not shrink,
Until they see their desire upon their enemies.

They have given freely to the poor,
And their righteousness stands fast for ever;
They will hold up their head with honor.

The wicked will see it and be angry;
They will gnash their teeth and pine away;
The desires of the wicked will perish.

Psalm 113

Adult 2:
Hallelujah!
Give praise, you servants of the Lord;
Praise the Name of the Lord.

Everyone:
Let the Name of the Lord be blessed,
From this time forth for evermore.

From the rising of the sun to its going down
Let the Name of the Lord be praised.

The Lord is high above all nations,
And his glory above the heavens.

Who is like the Lord our God, who sits enthroned on high,
But stoops to behold the heavens and the earth?

He takes up the weak out of the dust
And lifts up the poor from the ashes.

He sets them with the princes,
With the princes of his people.

He makes the woman of a childless house
To be a joyful mother of children

The Fourth Glass of Wine

Family Leader: Now it is time to bless the fourth cup of wine.

[All present raise their glass of wine]

Family Leader: *Baruch atah Adonai Elohaynu, me-lech ha-olam bo-rey p'ri ha-ga-fen.* Blessed are you, Eternal God, Ruler of the Universe, who creates the fruit of the vine. Amen

[Everyone drinks the wine.]

Psalm 114

Adult 3:
Hallelujah!
When Israel came out of Egypt,
The house of Jacob from a people of strange speech,

Everyone: Judah became God's sanctuary
And Israel his dominion.

The sea beheld it and fled;
Jordan turned and went back.

The mountains skipped like rams,
And the little hills like young sheep.

What ailed you, O sea, that you fled?
O Jordan, that you turned back?

You mountains, that you skipped like rams?
You little hills like young sheep?

Tremble, O earth, at the presence of the Lord,
At the presence of the God of Jacob,

Who turned the hard rock into a pool of water,
And flint-stone into a flowing spring.

[It is appropriate to end the Passover feast by singing additional religious songs and hymns.]

Narrator: Two thousand years ago, the feast ended when all the meat was eaten. And the meat had to be eaten that night. Just like their ancestors, they ate as though they were about to start on a forty-year journey. Any leftover meat was destroyed. We, on the other hand, have and will use the benefits of refrigeration should we choose, which were unavailable to the first-century Jew, so we can end the meal now. As we leave this feast, I pray that all here gathered have been blessed by the Eternal Lord and by this Paschal Feast. Go into the world living and sharing God's blessing. AMEN.

CHAPTER NINE

The Harvest Feast

You cause the grass to grow for the cattle, and plants for people to use,
to bring forth food from the earth and wine to gladden the human heart,
oil to make the face shine, and bread to strengthen the human heart.
(Psalm 104:14–15)

Most of us have only a peripheral understanding of crops and harvests. Maybe we hear on the evening news that a late frost or flooding has impacted the supply of oranges or asparagus, so the price of these commodities will substantially increase. But when are oranges and asparagus harvested anyway, and what is involved in bringing these products to market? Do we even know the state or country of origin for the fruit and vegetables at our markets? Because the vast majority of us are so separated from the process of growing our food, we have also lost the sense of joy and relief that comes with the successful completion of the harvest.

During ancient times, and actually until quite recent history, most communities were involved and impacted by the harvest of local produce. Wives, children, aunts, and uncles joined husbands and fathers in the fields and orchards to *bring in* the crop. Some years the harvest was hurried, with everyone working intensely for long hours because of the threat of inclement weather. In better years, the timing of the harvest was only slightly more relaxed because there was still ripe produce that must be gathered before it began to spoil. The harvest was hard work, but with an overarching air of excitement and celebration. Once the ingathering was completed, the celebration started in earnest.

Our next banquets are harvest celebrations. The Mediterranean world at the time of Jesus was familiar with a number of different festivities that focused on the harvest of local crops. Passover was the first and is described in chapter 8. The Jewish festivals of Weeks (Pentecost) and Booths (Tabernacles) were both harvest-time celebrations and occasions for important religious rituals. The festival of Weeks was also a large annual religious festival and was enjoyed each spring at the completion of the wheat harvest. Even at the time of Jesus, it was a very ancient holiday rich in both history and tradition. The festival of Tabernacles was the other large festival and was observed in the fall after the grape harvest. It was a popular pilgrimage festival with tens of thousands of Jews traveling to Jerusalem to participate in religious services, temple dances, and splendid feasts.

The chapter ends with a look at the use of grains in ancient food preparation. Grains were prepared and eaten in a variety of ways even though much of the harvested wheat and barley was ground and made into bread. There was a direct connection between the harvest of wheat and barley with the celebrations of Passover and Weeks, and grain dishes would have been present at the Tabernacle feasts even though the emphasis was on grapes and wine.

Bringing in the Harvest

Two months of ingathering
Two months of spring growth
Month of pulling flax
Month of barley harvest
Month when everything else is harvested.
Two months of pruning vines
Month of summer fruit[1]

This text is from an ancient Hebrew tablet called the *Gezer Calendar*. Scholars argue about the date of the artifact but agree that it was written somewhere between the eleventh to the sixth century BCE, or six hundred to eleven hundred years before Jesus was born. Despite its age, this Hebrew calendar continued to accurately describe the lives of the Middle Eastern farmer up until very recent times.

Try to imagine what it was like to live that life. The lion's share of farmers in Palestine practiced what is known as *mixed farming*. They grew several different types of crops and also kept vineyards and groves of olive and fruit trees. First and foremost they grew grains. There are certainly flat areas in Israel's terrain where large amounts of wheat and barley were grown. The Plain of Esdraelon that divides Galilee and Samaria is an example. But numerous places, and certainly most of Galilee, are hilly or mountainous. Grains were typically grown in the valleys. Between one thousand and fifteen hundred years before the time of Jesus (1000 to 1500 BCE), farmers terraced many of those hills so crops could be grown on the slopes without fear of soil erosion. These same terraces were still used in the first century and are still in place today. Olive and fruit trees, vineyards, and some vegetable crops were planted on terraced hillsides. In addition, a large garden usually grew near the house to provide families with fresh vegetables for their dinner tables.

Mixed farming also included livestock. The average first-century farmer kept a small herd of sheep and goats and maybe a donkey or two and, if fortunate, a few cattle that served as beasts of burden. The typical farmer did not own or use horses. In the first century only military officers and the very rich and powerful could afford a horse. Because most of the herds were small, in many of the farming towns, one or more of the men or older boys were hired to look after everyone's sheep and goats. Family members or hired hands served as the shepherd for larger herds. We can imagine that Jesus' comments regarding shepherds that were hired hands must have resonated with his audience. The shepherd certainly came to know the sheep in the flock very well, easily distinguishing which animals belonged to each farmer. But would the shepherd risk life and limb to protect a herd that he did now own? No doubt the shepherd who watched his own goats and sheep gave them better care (John 10:1–18). Usually the animals were quartered near or in the house. Small herds spent the night in the courtyard or in a pen made from branches of thorn. Thorn shrubs serving as a gate were pulled across the opening once the herd was inside. In the field, the shepherd himself served as the gate by sleeping in the entryway of a pen made from brambles.

Except for the winter, at almost any given time during the year some crop was being planted or harvested. Flax was the first plant harvested in early spring. Flax was used to make linen for clothing. Barley was the first major food crop, usually harvested in April and early May, followed by wheat during May and early June. Different fruits, especially figs and pomegranates, ripened and were picked during the summer, and honey was collected if the farmer kept bees. Vegetables for the kitchen table were planted in the spring and harvested throughout the summer. In late August or early September grapes were picked and made into wine or dried as raisins. Olives were the last crop to be harvested before winter, being gathered from the middle of

October until the first of November. After gathering olives and pressing olive oil, it was time to sow flax, wheat, and barley seeds and begin the cycle over again.

The times for the harvests varied according to a number of factors, such as rainfall and temperature. Often harvests overlapped. A farmer and his family might be finishing the barley harvest when it was time to begin reaping the wheat. The grape and olive harvests also were prone to overlap. The olives had to be ripe to produce oil so they could be left on the trees until the grapes were pressed for wine or dried as raisins. In some locales, first century farmers used the same presses for their olive oil that they just finished using for their wine.

As with modern agriculture, the weather patterns were extremely important to first-century farmers. Even though Israel is a small country, the climates are quite diverse. In Northern Galilee the temperatures are quite temperate and the area receives an average of thirty to thirty-five inches of rain per year. On the other hand, the Negev Desert south of Jerusalem has blistering hot summers and can receive as little as one inch of rain each year. Jerusalem typically received around fifteen inches per year. For most of the country, the weather is very similar to that in the Southwest region of the United States where most of the rain falls in the winter. In fact, in Israel, 70 percent of the rainfall occurs during the months of December, January, and February with 20 percent during November and March. Rarely is there any rain during the summer months. As one might imagine, activity on the farm slowed considerably during the wet winter season. Work continued, however. Grains were sowed right before the rains started so that the young plants could take full advantage of the moisture. Grapevines were pruned. Citrus, such as citrons and later lemons, was harvested during the winter. And the livestock still received daily attention. Animals were fed. Goats and sheep were still milked every day and cheese and yogurt made. Winter was also the time when farmers repaired or replaced their equipment.

The winter rains also curtailed travel by turning dirt trails and roads into deep mud. Most travel, especially to Jerusalem, was postponed until the spring and summer. This was not only true of the Holy Land, but for most of the Mediterranean countries. It is no coincidence that the major festivals and times for sacrifice occurred after the rain stopped.

All of the harvests were important, but the grain harvests were especially so. As described in an earlier chapter, grains and bread were dietary staples for everyone in the ancient world. These food products constituted over 50 percent of an average person's calorie intake. Lentils and legumes followed in importance, as did olives for olive oil and fruit such as figs and dates. Grapes and wine were a special product, not so much a necessity, but an everyday drink to add joy and ease the pain of lives defined by physical labor.

Laborers for the Harvest

The men of the family were typically the ones who worked the farm. Their jobs were diverse. They sowed seeds and then plowed the ground to bury them. Grapevines were pruned and weeds pulled away from plants. Trees were trimmed. Sheep were sheared for wool. The women in the family also had their roles on the farm. Only the wife of a quite prosperous farmer could spend the day in the house and kitchen. Farm women were likely responsible for the kitchen garden. Keeping the garden included planting, weeding, and harvesting vegetables for the table. Some vegetables were set aside for immediate use, and others were pickled or dried for the future.

But the entire household, including the women, children, servants, and all other relatives and trusted friends helped with the harvest. The book of Ruth tells the story of a young woman who joined the women of Boaz's household as they followed the reapers during the grain harvests:

> Then Boaz said to Ruth, "Now listen, my daughter, do not go to glean in another field or leave this one, but keep close to my young women. Keep your eyes on the field that is being reaped, and follow behind them." (Ruth 2:8–9a)

It was often the responsibility of the women to gather the stalks of grain that had been tied into sheaves and transported to a threshing floor. The owners of small farms typically used a threshing floor kept by the village, while wealthy landowners with large farms had threshing floors on their property. The first-century threshing floor could be dirt, solid bedrock, or paved with stones. The sheaves were loosened and laid on the floor where oxen trampled them to crack the hard chaff that encased the edible part of the grain. The grain was then winnowed; it was tossed into the wind with a basket or winnowing fork. The lighter chaff would blow while the berry or kernel of the grain fell at the winnower's feet. The chaff and stalks (straw) were then used as fodder for the livestock. It is likely that women also helped at the threshing floor. They could collect the grain and wet the chaff with water so it did not blow too far with the wind. Harvests by families with small farms in the Middle East still operate this way.[2]

The harvest of crops promoted a festive atmosphere among the entire family. Everyone helped with the harvest, including the children. The book of Ruth describes a dinner at the threshing floor where the laborers ate, drank, and slept, probably to keep the grain from being stolen. Ruth wore perfume and her best clothes to the dinner, leading us to believe that the dinner at the threshing floor was a harvest celebration and was at least one reason for her extravagance. The other was to attract her future husband (Ruth 3:1–3).

Grape harvests were especially celebratory. Laborers and family members cut bunches of grapes from the vines and stored them in baskets. And everyone helped transport the grapes to the wine press. The family watched over the baskets of grapes from the time they left the vineyard until they arrived at the wine press. The family patriarch supervised the pressing process to insure that the grapes and juice were not stolen. Other family members watched the grapes during transport. Still others guarded the grapes that were still on the vine. It was important that trusted family members supervised all aspects of a harvest.

Day laborers also were used for the harvest. The parable of the laborers in the vineyard told of a landowner that went to the marketplace to hire day laborers (Matthew 20:1–16). There is every reason to believe that Jesus' story accurately reflects the practices of the time. Most of his parables do, which was one of the reasons his teachings connected with those who heard them. Just as today, harvesting a crop requires significantly more people than any other aspect of farming. Day laborers supplemented the already large group of family, friends and servants that were required to complete the harvest in a timely manner. Because day laborers were poor and typically worked for enough money to provide dinner for their families, the Mosaic Law required that they were paid at the end of the day.

> You shall not withhold the wages of poor and needy laborers. . . . You shall pay them their wages daily before sunset, because they are poor and their livelihood depends on them; otherwise they might cry to the Lord against you, and you would incur guilt. (Deuteronomy 24: 14–15)

The Festival of Weeks: Pentecost

The Festival of Weeks or Pentecost was a one-day festival that celebrated the wheat harvest. The festival certainly speaks to the importance of the grain harvests in the ancient world. The celebration of Pentecost included two important themes: thanksgiving for the harvest's bounty and the resulting social responsibility that bounty brings. Eventually, Pentecost came to have significance for the infant Christian church as the occasion when the first Christians, filled with God's Spirit, began to preach the gospel (good news) that Jesus of Nazareth was the Messiah.

In many ways the Festival of Weeks was a completion of Passover and the Feast of Unleavened bread. Just as the Feast of Unleavened Bread marked the barley harvest, Weeks celebrated a successful wheat harvest. The fifty days leading to Pentecost were considered a sacred time when Israelites remembered that God was the source of fertile soil, rain, and all that made the harvest fruitful. This time culminated with the one-day celebration of the festival. Special animal sacrifices were made at the temple, and two loaves of leavened bread made from the newly harvested and milled wheat were presented at the altar as a wave offering. Along with the loaves, two lambs were presented, also as a wave offering. After presenting these gifts, the men who were present sang the Hallel psalms (psalms 113 through 118) and joined a joyful dance called the Altar Dance. After the ceremony in the temple, all that were present gathered with their families and neighbors for a communal feast.

The Festival of Weeks also marked the beginning of the summer-long season for offering first fruits that lasted until the Festival of Booths (or Tabernacles) in the fall. During that season, Jews from all over Palestine and beyond made their way to the temple in Jerusalem to bring voluntary offerings from their crops and herds. Many people took advantage of their presence in Jerusalem to combine the celebration of Weeks with their first fruit offering. Loaves of bread, containers of grains and flour, and young lambs and goats were presented at the temple as another *wave offering*. These were agricultural offerings brought to the temple in thanksgiving for bountiful harvests. Like other wave offerings, the gifts were not burned on the altar but instead were given to the priests to support their families. The worshiper solemnly presented his first fruits offering to the priests and recited his thanksgiving for the mighty acts of God that delivered Israel from slavery and gave them such a fruitful land.

Great food and feasts marked the celebration of Weeks, even for those who were unable to travel to Jerusalem. It was an ideal time for an outdoor meal. The rainy season was over and the beginning of the intense summer heat was still weeks away. Imagine the people in small farming communities and in the neighborhoods of larger towns working together to prepare the feast. The new wheat was ground to provide good quality flour for the bread. Long tables must have been erected so neighbors could share their food. Tables for the men and for the women and children were separated. Having participated in many potluck dinners, we can only imagine the family pride at stake as families arrived with their best-tasting fare.

Pentecost was not only a wonderful celebration of the harvest, but it also expressed the bond of communal responsibility that united everyone within the context of God's gift of covenant. The feasts were communal meals to which foreigners, Levites, and the poor in the community were invited. Day laborers and tenant farmers sat next to wealthy landowners. Widows joined with affluent wives who employed servants to bake their bread and make their beds. Those who had lost their farms and were unemployed ate and danced arm-in-arm with the rich and powerful. All reached in the same bowl to take a radish, eat a bite of lentils or take a piece of roasted lamb. The experience must have been almost sacramental, an outward sign of community and neighborly love within the context of a successful wheat harvest. After the destruction of the temple in the year 70 CE, as the livelihood of most Jews gradually became less centered on agriculture and more on commerce, the emphasis of the festival shifted to a celebration of God's gift of the law at Mount Sinai. Sections of the Torah, especially Exodus 19, were read in preparation for the festal meal. However, at the time of Jesus, the book of Ruth, with its emphasis on the harvest and helping the poor, was the book of the Bible that was traditionally connected to and read at the time of the festival.

The Festival of Booths: Tabernacles

Of the three great pilgrimage festivals, the festival of booths was likely the most fun. The celebration must have been both intense and exhausting. It lasted seven days and contained all the elements of a great party: travel, music, dancing, good food and wine, plus camping in unusual accommodations and peculiar religious rituals. And why not? The revelers and worshipers were celebrating the grape harvest. The ingathering was over, the grapes were pressed, and the juice was fermenting in large amphorae. Only the olive harvest remained before winter. So it was time to give thanks to God and enjoy a grand party.

Preparation for the feast began with the construction of a *booth* or *tabernacle*. The original concept was that the booth was similar to the small huts that farmers built in their vineyards to protect their crops. As described above, a farmer's fields and vineyards might be miles from his house. He would erect a temporary shelter on his land where his sons and he would spend the night to keep thieves from stealing the crop. In addition, the booths reminded the Israelites of the temporary shelters they used during their forty years in the wilderness, after the exodus from Egypt.[3]

All adult males were required to stay in a booth during the holiday season. In many cases, their families joined them. The residents of Jerusalem constructed their booths in courtyards and on the flat roofs of their homes.

Pilgrims built their booths in the flat areas outside the city gates. There were several rules concerning the design of the booth, primarily that it be temporary and not overly comfortable. It could not be over twenty cubits high, nor could someone simply spread a sheet over a four-poster bed and call it a booth. Living for a week in a tabernacle that was this size would be too comfortable and sleeping under a sheet would have been too much like a child's game and certainly too easy to build. Nor could the booth be thirty days old or older. A structure older than thirty days failed to represent the impermanence of a harvest booth or a dwelling in the wilderness.[4]

Preparation for the feast also meant constructing a *lulab*. The lulab was somewhat similar to a pennant or colored bandana waved at a sporting event, except it was used for a religious ceremony. It was made by tying together myrtle, willow, and palm branches with one citron. All the people that participated in the processions around the city and temple carried lulabs. Those Jews who were unable to attend the festival in Jerusalem celebrated Booths in their home village for one day and carried their lulabs throughout the celebration. The temple priests carried only willow branches, instead of the entire lulab, and waved them as they processed around the altar.

Each day of the celebration began with a water libation ceremony. On the first day, the temple priests and people processed to the Pool of Siloam where the priests filled a golden flask with water. The procession then proceeded back to the west gate of the temple. Accompanied by blasts on the shofar (ram's horn), the people sang the Hallel psalms and waved the lulabs when they sang the words, "O give thanks to the Lord, for he is good; his steadfast love endures forever!" (Psalm 118:1, 29). Meanwhile all the priests, waving their willow branches, processed round the altar, chanting, "Save us, we beseech you, O Lord! O Lord, we beseech you, give us success!" (Psalm 118:25). At another blast of the shofar, a priest carried the water up a ramp to two large silver bowls, one filled with water and one filled with wine. The people would repeatedly shout, "Lift up your hand," so they could witness the water being poured into the bowls. It is said that at one ceremony a priest poured the water on his feet instead of in the bowls, and at that the gathered crowd pelted him with the citrons from their lulabs.[5] Was this the birth of the ritual of throwing fruit at performers who make mistakes?

A second ritual was celebrated each day at dawn. The temple priests processed to the east gate of the temple accompanied by sustained and quavering tones played on the shofar. As the sun was rising, the priests said, "Our fathers who were in this place turned with their backs toward the Temple of the Lord and their faces toward the east, and they worshiped the sun toward the east." (based on Ezekiel 8:16) Then the people responded, "But as to us, our eyes are to the Lord." The Ezekiel passage was repeated and the response the second time was, "We belong to the Lord, our eyes are toward the Lord."[6] Many of the people in attendance came to this ceremony from the all-night feast and festivities in the temple court.

The third ritual was likely the one most enjoyed by the pilgrims. Four very large menorahs (seven-branch lamps of the shape that are still used to celebrate Hanukkah) were brought into the Court of the Women. The menorahs were so large that men had to climb ladders in order to fill the bowls of each menorah with oil. The priests used the cloth from their old robes and girdles to make wicks for the bowls. It is said that the light from the menorahs was so bright that every courtyard in Jerusalem was "lit up from the light."[7] The visitors then filled the courtyards of the temple with the men in one Courtyard of the Women and the women in another. Flute players provided dance music, and the Levites would play on their harps, drums, cymbals, and trumpets. The men would perform a torch dance, dancing with flaming torches in their hands. The party lasted throughout the night and ended with the Levites singing the Psalms of Ascent, psalms 120 through 134, one psalm for each of the stairs that separated the Court of the Women from the Court of the Israelites. All the revelers still awake then joined the procession to the east gate to participate in the ceremony of the rising sun. The Mishnah states that "anyone who has not seen the rejoicing of the *bet hashshoebah* (the celebration in the Courtyard of the Women) in his life has never seen rejoicing."[8]

This schedule of rituals and dancing continued for all seven days of the festival, punctuated by feasting and shopping. Those families that had not made the trip to Jerusalem for Passover had to spend their second tithe in Jerusalem, buying food and wine for the feasts, as well as jewelry, perfume, and special clothes for the celebrations and household items to take back home.

Our suspicion is that, after seven days of morning worship and all-night dancing, the walk home was not nearly as fun and joyful as the trip to Jerusalem before the festival. The pilgrimage for Booths was almost as popular as for Passover. Jews traveled to Jerusalem for the Festival of Booths from all over the Middle East, from Babylon and Egypt and from Jewish communities as far away as Greece and Rome. Like Passover, singing, storytelling, and camaraderie marked the trip to Jerusalem. But after a week of rich food, wine, and late nights, even the most stalwart pilgrims must have been exhausted. Walking the seventy miles back to Nazareth or even farther to North Galilee must have been a chore, but not bad enough to discourage repeating the experience the next year.

Grains in the Diet

Bread was certainly the most important food made with the grains grown in the first century. But grains were also used in many other foods. Historically, the development of cultivating grain closely parallels the progress of the civilization of humanity. Some twelve thousand years ago, sowing and harvesting grain allowed communities of hunter-gatherers to become farmers and stay in one place. No longer were they required to move, following the migration of large herds of wild animals for their food. Once they began to stay in one place, they were able to domesticate animals such as cattle, sheep, and goats. It is believed that large fields of barley and wheat attracted these animals. It became necessary to keep wild animals from eating the crop while making them easier to hunt. In time, they were captured and domesticated, thus ensuring the community a more reliable access to both meat and grain. These animals were also used for milk, wool, plowing, and for transport. Growing grains and herding animals also made it possible for residents of ancient communities to focus on specific vocations. No longer was it necessary for all men to hunt and women to gather produce. People were able to specialize, becoming potters, tool makers, scribes, artists, priests, and rulers. Such differentiation was not possible in a hunter-gatherer society, where everyone's time was required to find food.[9]

It just so happens that some of the earliest evidence of the cultivation of grains occurs in the eastern Mediterranean, Israel, Syria, along the Tigris and Euphrates rivers and into Turkey, areas that are also considered the biblical lands. This area is also known now as the Fertile Crescent. It is no coincidence that the Fertile Crescent was the earliest site for such developments as writing and large cities. Jericho of biblical fame happens to be one of the first locations for a number of food developments, including the cultivation of barley and wheat.

By the time of Jesus, in addition to barley, several varieties of wheat had been developed from their ancestors and were grown in the Middle East and Mediterranean region. Einkorn is an ancient wheat with hard berries that was especially appropriate for roasting or, if first ground, for making porridge or stews. Another ancient wheat, emmer, had softer berries and was excellent for bread. Spelt is an ancient hybrid wheat with a much tougher casing (chaff) around the berry and a nuttier flavor than emmer or einkorn. It was used as fodder for feeding livestock and was the wheat used most often by poorer people. Eventually another hybrid of emmer was to produce an even softer berry that produced vastly superior flour for making bread.

Cooking with Grains

Modern chefs are gradually rediscovering cooking with grains. Whole grains are tasty, healthy, and provide an excellent counterpoint to meat and fish. They offer an "out of the ordinary" alternative to potatoes and rice. In the first century, there were no potatoes and almost no rice in the Mediterranean and Middle East. So wheat and barley provided the foundation for most meals. Here is a review of a number of the methods used for cooking and eating grains.

To begin, wheat and barley were occasionally eaten raw. This was only possible while the kernel was still green. We suspect that the green berries were used as a snack, perhaps salted and served as a side dish to a meal. We do know that farmers and sometimes travelers walking near the crop ate the green kernels in the field. Jesus and his disciples received criticism for that very practice (Matthew 12:1, Mark 2:23, Luke 6:1).

The Old Testament also mentions roasted or "parched" grains. The laborers at the harvest simply held stalks of grain over a fire. The heat toasted the grain, softening the chaff and making the seed easier to open. The heat also converted some of the starch in the kernel to dextrin, giving it a sweeter flavor. Parched grains, mixed with olive oil and frankincense were offered in the temple as the grain offering of first fruits (Leviticus 2:14). Adding frankincense clearly made it an offering to God and not food for the dinner table! The harvesters in the book of Ruth roasted grains for dinner over an open fire and ate it with bread dipped in sour wine (Ruth 2:14). Ancient armies carried parched grain with them as part of their food supplies (1 Samuel 17:17, 2 Samuel 17:28). To produce a similar food product, wheat berries or pearled barley can be cooked in a hot skillet or placed on a jelly roll pan and baked in the oven until the color browns and grains become fragrant.[10]

Parboiling was another ancient process for preparing grains for cooking. Bulgur is a modern example of parboiled wheat. It is still made by soaking and cooking the kernel, drying it, and then removing part of the bran that surrounds the berry. The remaining kernel is cracked into smaller pieces. Its uses were and still are numerous: from salads to soups, breads to desserts. It was a nutritious extender, making the dish filling without using much meat, and it thickened both stews and soups. Bulgur will absorb twice its volume in water and can be used in place of rice in any recipe. Being already partially cooked, bulgur was convenient for cooks, since it could be soaked in water and quickly heated to be made edible.

Along with parching, grinding then boiling was an extremely ancient way to prepare grains. The ground grain was added to boiling water and then cooked to become porridge. Porridge made with either barley or wheat is still widely popular many thousands of years later. We eat porridges made from oats (oatmeal) and finely ground wheat (Cream of Wheat). Long before corn arrived in the Mediterranean region, barley was used to prepare a barley polenta. Ground barley was added to boiling and salted water and then stirred until it produced a thick polenta-style porridge. Barley polenta was a staple for the Middle East and throughout Greece and Rome. Grains were also made into pilafs. Dried, parched, or roasted, they were boiled first and then baked in the oven. Onions, garlic, herbs, spices, and other flavorings were added before baking.

The Symbolism of Wheat

Just as the dead are buried in the ground, so the wheat kernels are planted in the earth. It was a miracle, or a gift from God that a new plant emerged from the seemingly dead seed. For that reason, grains, and especially wheat, were symbols of resurrection. This was true for many ancient cultures, including both the Greeks and Egyptians. Early Christians adopted the symbol, and it was used by St. Paul in the New Testament's most extended discussion of the resurrection:

> But someone will ask, "How are the dead raised? With what kind of body do they come?" Fool! What you sow does not come to life unless it dies. And as for what you sow, you do not sow the body that is to be, but a bare seed, perhaps of wheat or of some other grain. (1 Corinthians 15:35–37)

Just as a grain of wheat was transformed from death and burial into a plant that bore new fruit, early Christians believed that the same would happen to them after their death.

Fertility, the mysteries of life, nourishment, and vitality were also represented by grains. The cultivation of cereals presented the opportunity for civilization to people and many ancient cultures believed that it must therefore be a gift from the gods. Because of the symbolic, nutritional, and cultural significance of grains, their harvest festivals were honored with special and even religious significance by all cultures.

Your Harvest Feast

The Festival of Weeks was a communal festival. Everyone was invited, including the poor and visitors in the community. It was likely enjoyed out of doors because of the large number of people sharing the feast. Because it was such an important festival, the celebration was made even more festive by the addition of meat to the menu. The Festival of Weeks also marked the end of the wheat harvest, so foods with grains and freshly baked wheat bread were a featured element of the feast.

The following menu was prepared as a celebration of the Festival of Weeks, or Pentecost. If you choose instead to celebrate Booths, then add grapes and other fresh fruits to the menu. We have included a honey lemon dipping sauce for dipping fresh fruit.

The Menu for a Harvest Festival

- Flat Bread (Pita)*
- Roasted Grains*
- Hummus* (chapter 3)
- Brined Olives* (chapter 4 or from the market)
- Bulgur and Parsley Salad*
- Spicy Split Peas*
- Lamb Shish Kebab*
- Fresh fruit with Honey Lemon Dip* (chapter 7) (for the celebration of Booths)
- Dried Fruit Pastries*

The Recipes

Flat Bread (Pita)

In some ways, pita bread breaks many of the rules. After baking, instead of cooling for several hours, it is stacked and wrapped in a kitchen towel so that some of the moisture remains in the bread. Bake in an oven with a glass window in the door so you can watch it form the pocket by puffing.

1 tablespoon yeast	1 teaspoon salt
1¾ cup water, approximately 110°	3 tablespoons olive oil
4⅔ cups all-purpose unbleached flour	

Place the yeast and warm water in the bowl of your mixer. Wait until yeast begins to activate, approximately 15 minutes. It will change color and begin to bubble. Add the flour to the yeast mixture. Then add the rest of the ingredients.

Mix with the dough hook for 5 minutes. Start on the slowest speed to keep the flour from splashing out of the bowl and then increase the speed to medium slow. Let the dough rest for 15 minutes and then mix for another 5 minutes. The dough should be slightly sticky and springy to the touch. Add flour 1 tablespoon at a time if the dough is too sticky or water if it is too dry.

Remove and place in a large bowl. Cover with a kitchen towel or plastic wrap and allow to rise until it doubles in size, approximately 1 hour. Punch down the dough, cover, and allow to rise a second time. After the second rise, turn out on a flowered surface and knead for approximately 20 seconds. Divide the dough into 10 to 12 balls and cover with the kitchen towel or greased plastic wrap. Allow until doubled, an additional hour.

Place a pizza stone, oven bricks, or a thick baking pan in the oven. Preheat to the highest temperature, usually 500°. Roll out each ball of dough on a floured surface until it is 7 or 8 inches in diameter. Using a pizza peal or the back of another baking sheet dusted with flour, slide several pitas onto the baking surface. In several minutes they will puff and then begin to brown. Take out of the oven and stack on a cloth kitchen towel. Fold the towel over the top of the pitas or cover with another towel so the bread continues to steam as it cools. Makes 10 to 12 pieces of flat bread.

Roasted Grains

This is an extremely ancient way to eat grains. They are addicting. Use a cast-iron or a heavy skillet or sauté pan that will hold all the grains on one level to roast. After cooking, you can coat with a small amount of olive oil and salt, though we like them just like this.

½ cup wheat berries or pearled barley, or any amount you choose

Heat the skillet and add the grain. Stir often as they brown. They are done when they turn a deep color of brown and pop like popcorn. Remove from the heat, pour in a bowl, and allow to cool to room temperature.

Bulgur and Parsley Salad

We love this salad! With the addition of tomatoes, it is very similar to tabbouleh.

½ cup finely cut bulgur (#1 bulgur)
8 green onions, chopped
4 cups parsley, finely chopped
½ cup mint, finely chopped

2 teaspoons salt, or to taste
¼ teaspoon pepper, or to taste
Lemon dressing

Place the bulgur in a bowl and cover with water to rinse. Drain the water from the bowl and squeeze out the water with your hands. Add the onions, parsley, mint, salt, and pepper. Just before serving, add the lemon dressing and toss. Serves 4 to 6.

Lemon Dressing: Place ¼ cup freshly squeezed lemon juice, ¼ cup olive oil and ¼ teaspoon cumin powder in a small bowl and whisk or stir to mix.

Spicy Split Peas

Spicy would not have meant "hot" in the first century. We believe the use of our regional spices mix gives these peas a very nice flavor. Try adding ¼ cup of chopped coriander (cilantro) after taking off the heat. Or pour a little extra virgin on top of the peas right before serving.

1 tablespoon olive oil
1 onion, chopped
2 garlic cloves, minced
1 cup dried split peas
1 cup each chicken stock and water
    or 2 cups water

1 tablespoon regional spices
    (chapter 7)
1 teaspoon salt, or to taste
¼ teaspoon pepper, or to taste

Heat a large saucepan and add the olive oil. Add the onion and sauté until translucent. Then add the garlic and sauté briefly, until translucent. Add the peas, stock, and water and bring to a boil. Turn down the heat until liquid simmers. Cook 1–1¼ hours. Fifteen minutes before peas are done, season with regional spices, salt and pepper. Serves 6

Lamb Shish Kebab

First-century Israelites used pomegranate sticks instead of bamboo skewers. So if you have a pomegranate tree in your back yard . . .

1 leg of lamb cut into approximately 32 1-inch pieces
3 tablespoons olive oil
1½ tablespoons minced fresh rosemary, or 2 teaspoons dried rosemary
2 garlic cloves, finely minced

2 tablespoons regional spices (chapter 7)
1 tablespoon salt, or to taste,
1 teaspoon pepper, or to taste
2 medium yellow onions, quartered and broken into pieces
Additional olive oil

Soak 8 bamboo skewers in water for at least 30 minutes. Place the lamb pieces in a large bowl. Add the olive oil and stir until lamb is coated. Then add the rosemary, garlic, regional spices, salt, and pepper. Stir again until the meat is coated with the herbs and spices. Cover with plastic wrap and refrigerate for 30 minutes.

Take skewers from the water and lamb from the refrigerator. Thread lamb onto the skewers, separating each piece of lamb with pieces of onion.

Preheat oven to 350°. Coat the bottom of a roasting pan with a thin layer of oil then set aside. Heat a 14-inch skillet or cast-iron griddle over medium-high heat. Add 1 tablespoon olive oil. Brown the shish kebabs several at a time and remove to the roasting pan. Place all the shish kebabs in a single layer in the roasting pan and then place in the oven. Roast for 25 minutes or until the lamb reaches the desired doneness. Serves 8.

These shish kebabs are excellent cooked on the grill, too. Both authors prefer lamb that is cooked medium rare. Lamb becomes dry and develops a distinctive aftertaste if it is cooked too long. Feel free to omit onions.

Dried Fruit Pastries

Use any dried fruit that you wish. As a timesaver, you can use pie dough from the freezer section of you market instead of this dough.

Crust

2½ cups unbleached all-purpose flour	5 tablespoons water
1 cup butter, cut into small pieces	1 egg
1 teaspoon salt	1 teaspoon white vinegar

Filling

1 cup dried apricots	4 teaspoons honey
1 cup dates	2 teaspoons Madeira wine

The Crust: In a mixing bowl, mix together the flour, butter, and salt, cutting in the butter with a fork. In a separate bowl, combine the water, egg, and vinegar, beating slightly with a fork. Add these ingredients to the flour and mix, kneading very briefly. You can cover and refrigerate the dough.

The Filling: One variety at a time, process the dried fruit in a food processor and place in separate bowls. Add half the honey and wine to each and stir to combine.

Preheat the oven to 350°. On a floured surface, roll out the dough. Cut with a biscuit cutter. Punch all over the rounds with a fork, then add 1–2 tablespoons of the filling; fold the dough over the rounds. Place on an oiled cookie sheet and bake in the oven for 15 to 20 minutes, or until beginning to brown. Cool before eating. Serves 6 to 8.

CHAPTER TEN

Eating with God—the Todah Feast

> This is the ritual of the sacrifice of the offering of well-being that one may offer to the Lord. If you offer it for thanksgiving, you shall offer with the thank offering unleavened cakes mixed with oil, unleavened wafers spread with oil, and cakes of choice flour well soaked in oil. With your thanksgiving sacrifice of well-being you shall bring your offering with cakes of leavened bread. From this you shall offer one cake from each offering, as a gift to the Lord; it shall belong to the priest who dashes the blood of the offering of well-being. And the flesh of your thanksgiving sacrifice of well-being shall be eaten on the day it is offered; you shall not leave any of it until morning. (Leviticus 7:11–15)

It is five years since completing chemotherapy and radiation for breast cancer. The doctor tells you that "all is still clear." Even though your car is destroyed, you walk away from the accident with only a few cuts and bruises. A tornado bears down on your house and then suddenly disappears back into the clouds. Your property, family, and you remain unscratched. Surgery is successful and the doctor tells you that your eleven-year-old daughter will fully recover and will feel better than she has in years. We can interpret all of these scenarios of deliverance from ruin or death as God's gracious blessing, and we respond by celebrating and giving thanks. Even more important, the experience can forever change our lives.

Some people might celebrate a life-altering event with a special trip. A friend recently observed the anniversary of her recovery from breast cancer by taking a Caribbean cruise with friends. Depending on the circumstances, others might buy or give special gifts, maybe by splurging on a new car or clothing, by making a donation to a charitable organization, or perhaps by purchasing something related to the recovery, such as a stationary bicycle or membership to a health club.

Almost all people, regardless of their faith or culture, include a special meal as a way of giving thanks. It might be a special dinner prepared by a spouse or friend or perhaps a gourmet affair at a five-star restaurant. Quite some time ago, a mutual friend of ours decided to cope with his mid-life crisis and rising blood pressure by competing in a triathlon. His training included almost a year of a rigorous exercise schedule and special diet. After finishing the event, his wife and he gave thanks with a movable feast. They rented a limousine and took their party of smoked salmon, caviar, and champagne to the homes of their friends all over Dallas. Everyone involved enjoyed the celebration and joined with our friend in giving thanks for his improved health and ability to successfully finish the race.

The human need to celebrate after a change of life experience is as ancient as civilization. So is the thanksgiving feast. In this chapter we will recreate a *Todah*, or thanksgiving feast. For the ancient Jews, the Todah included an offering and sacrifice in the temple and ended with a special feast with family and friends. Because the concept of sacrifice, especially animal sacrifice is so foreign to our twenty-first-century sensibilities, the chapter begins with an overview of temple sacrifices and offerings. We will also examine the place of meat at the Todah feast and in the first century diet.

Temple Sacrifices

The word "worship" will evoke a variety of images for our readers based on beliefs and background. We think of activities such as praying, singing, and listening to sacred scriptures being read and explained. For some of us, the ideal setting for worship is a Gothic style church with clergy in robes and a pipe organ playing centuries-old music. For others, it is an unadorned meeting room with ministers who wear casual clothes and a rock band playing contemporary praise songs. But in the ancient world, worship almost always included killing and butchering animals and then burning their fat and pouring their blood on an altar. Regardless of the religion or denomination, could there be an activity less associated with modern worship than animal sacrifice? Yet this was the most common understanding of worship and religious ritual in the ancient world.

There was a time in which any animal that was killed for food was first part of a sacrifice to God, so every meal with meat was also a religious celebration and feast. This was not entirely the case by the time of Jesus. The ritual sacrifice of all animals that were killed for the table became difficult once Jerusalem developed into the center of all Jewish cultic worship. The shepherd and his wife living in Galilee could no longer take a lamb or goat to the local priest operating an altar on the closest hill top. Worship at *high places*, shrines and altars other than the temple, was forbidden and all animal sacrifices had to be made in Jerusalem.

Other Mediterranean cultures and religions, like that of the Greeks, still required all animals to be killed in a temple as part of worship. In fact, most meat markets were conveniently located adjacent to the local temple. But by the first century, it was common for a wealthy Jew to eat lamb that was freshly butchered at home. Judaism allowed animals to be killed separate from a sacrifice and away from the temple, although, as we have seen, it was still a common experience for the average family to equate most meals that included meat with a festival that involved animal sacrifice. Like the harvest feasts in chapter 9 and the Passover seder described in chapter 8, many of the sacrifices were followed by a feast.

The temple in Jerusalem may have been a beautiful structure and the center of ancient Jewish religion, but it also functioned as a huge slaughterhouse with tens of thousands and possibly hundreds of thousands of animals butchered every year and approximately fifteen hundred priests on duty every week.[1] The altar was enormous, completely unlike the wooden tables at the front of liturgical churches that are usually called altars. The altar was a platform with a ramp leading to the top on which a large fire was built for burning the offerings. Cedar wood for the fire was transported from as far away as Lebanon.

There were both public and private sacrifices every day. Each day began and ended with the sacrifice of a lamb, with even more animals sacrificed on the Sabbath, special feast days, and days of atonement. These sacrifices were accompanied by drink and meal offerings; wine was poured around the altar and a mixture of flour and oil was burned with the lamb. The purpose of the sacrifice was one of general thankfulness for blessings of the day. In essence it was a banquet with God, a meal consisting of meat, cereal, olive oil, and wine. Pilgrims and people from the city crowded into the temple to witness these sacrifices, providing a general tone of celebration. The Levites played music and one of the priests, as the animal was carried up the ramp, pronounced the Aaronic blessing:

> The Lord bless you and keep you; the Lord make his face shine upon you, and be gracious to you; the Lord lift up his countenance upon you, and give you peace. (Numbers 6:24–26)

After the morning sacrifice, individuals began presenting sacrifices for a variety of reasons. For example, animals were brought as offerings for sin or guilt caused by a sin; for purification, especially after child birth; and just as a general gift to God. Most of the sacrifices were quadrupeds, that is, sheep, goats, and cattle. But doves, pigeons, flour, olive oil, and wine were also offered. In almost all cases, the priest assisting with the sacrifice retained a portion of the offering, typically one of the legs and half of the breast meat, one of the birds, or a portion of the flour or bread baked with the flour. If a man brought the offering, then he was the one that killed the animal, with two priests to help, one to catch the blood in a bowl and the other to skin and carve the animal. A woman gave her offering to a Levite, who worked at the temple as an assistant or musician, and he took it to a priest for sacrifice. She was able to watch from a balcony around the Court of the Women. Priests were not allowed to leave their court to assist women with their sacrifices and women were not allowed beyond their court.

It is worth noting that alternatives were available for people who could not afford to purchase a lamb or goat for sacrifice. For example, if a new mother's husband could not afford a lamb offering for the purification sacrifice, two birds could be offered instead. If they could not afford two birds, they could bring an offering of flour and oil. The Gospel of St. Luke tells us that for Mary's purification and the presentation of Jesus as the firstborn, Joseph and she offered two turtledoves or pigeons instead of a lamb (Luke 2:22–24).

With almost all the animal sacrifices, an important part was the laying of hands and confession. After handing over the animal, both men and women laid their hands on the victim's head and told the priest what kind of sacrifice they were making. The person then made a confession if it was a sin or guilt offering or told why he or she was making the sacrifice. After a prayer, the animal was then killed with a knife.

There were other types of offerings that have already been discussed in other chapters: tithes of first fruits, wave offerings of barley and wheat sheaves, and there was a temple tax of one-half shekel that every Jew in the world paid to provide for the costs of the public sacrifices and the upkeep of the temple.

The Todah Sacrifice

In very many ways, the Thanksgiving Sacrifice, or Todah, was different from other sacrifices, including other sacrificial meals like the Passover and Harvest Feasts.[2] *Shalom* was one of the primary purposes and the desired results of most sacrifices, and especially most meal offerings. *Shalom* is a Hebrew word usually translated as "peace" and it includes the idea of a general state of *well-being* and *right relationship* with God. Some of the Hebrew words for sacrifice mean such things as *to be lifted up* or to *come close*. By laying hands on the victim and identifying with it and giving its life to God, the person was also giving his or her own life to God as well. When the meat and fat from the victim was burned on the altar, the life blood poured around the altar, the person was *lifted up* symbolically, *coming close* and moving into right relationship with God.

The Todah was a celebration of thanksgiving for something that already happened. Through the sacrifice and the following meal, God was praised for having already saved and delivered the person from a life-threatening situation. The person might have recovered from illness, disease, or injury; or it might be someone rescued from death, saved from an attack, or from persecution that posed the threat of death. The person making the sacrifice and hosting the feast came to the temple already experiencing shalom, not seeking it.

Even the form of the sacrifice was different. The Todah was the only instance in which leavened bread was allowed to be offered. In fact, along with the animal, four different types of bread were offered in sacrifice: "unleavened cakes mixed with oil, unleavened wafers spread with oil, cakes of choice flour well soaked in oil, and cakes of leavened bread" (Leviticus 7:12-13). Leavened bread contained old dough, saved from the previous day. Because the dough was old and because it contained yeast, it was considered unclean and not appropriate as a gift to God. But the Todah sacrifice required both unleavened breads and a loaf of leavened bread. Because leavened bread was the common, everyday bread of all people, it likely represented the new life situation of the person making the sacrifice. Not only was it a gift to God for the act of salvation, it also honored the one who was rescued, who could start life over within the context of the sacred meal: "It represents through the sacrifice the basic human nourishment for the life of the one who has been rescued."[3]

As an essential element of the Todah meal, the host recited how God acted to deliver him or her from death. This was a song of salvation built upon the new foundation of the person's existence. It described the time when the issues faced death and then gave thanks for his or her salvation. This is another example of the difference of the Todah. In other religious feasts, the primary emphasis was on the community. For example, Passover celebrated the historically shared experience of an entire people passing from slavery to freedom. Pentecost was the community festival of the gift of the wheat harvest and a tribute to the community itself with an emphasis on their responsibility to the poorest members. Even sin offerings and sacrifices for atonement emphasized rejoining the community after separation caused by the sin. The Todah stressed the experience of an individual's salvation. The community was certainly involved in the celebration. But the experience was private, especially when compared to the rest of ancient Jewish religious life.

The Todah was worship where "word and meal and praise and sacrifice . . . constitute a unity."[4] It began at the temple. The person brought the animal and the four types of bread to the priest. The animal was sacrificed with the blood and the fat portions given to God and burned on the altar. Some of the unleavened breads were also offered by burning on the altar. As with other sacrifices, the priest kept the portion of the animal, traditionally one of the legs, the jowls and part of the breast. By the first century, the priest also kept one of the loaves of the leavened bread, though centuries earlier, it joined the other loaves on the altar.

The meat and bread from the sacrifice and the rest of the food were made ready for the feast after the temple ceremony. There might have been banqueting rooms available at the temple, but most likely the host rented space from someone living in Jerusalem or was staying in a tent outside the city gates. The Mishnah states that Todah meals were eaten throughout the city of Jerusalem and that the food, including the meat, could be cooked in any manner.[5] Tradition allowed the meat to be prepared in any number of methods: boiled or cooked in a stew were two common ways, but for Jews the most popular way to eat meat was roasted.

As with other feasts, bread, wine, and the meat played important roles. The bread served at the feast was the leavened bread of the sacrifice. It was *our daily bread* that represented not only basic human nourishment but also the life of the one who had been saved. The meat was also that which was offered in sacrifice. The animal at sacrifice represented life, life given by God to all creatures, but especially the life of the one making the sacrifice. For the Todah sacrifice and feast, it also represented the new life of the host, his or her life after the recovery from the near death experience. The wine was called the *cup of salvation* by at least one Old Testament source.[6]

Like the Passover feast, the meat had to be eaten on the same day that the sacrifice was made: "And the flesh of your thanksgiving sacrifice of well-being shall be eaten on the day it was offered; you shall not leave any of it until morning" (Leviticus 7:15). This regulation was a reminder that, without refrigeration, meat spoiled quickly. It also illustrated the importance of the occasion. The animal was killed for the purpose of the Todah, not so a family could eat leftovers for several days. The importance of the feast required that enough guests were invited to eat the entire animal.

Psalm 116 is one of the Todah psalms mostly likely used at Thanksgiving feasts. It illustrates many of the points we have discussed above. It begins with a short introduction by expressing both love and fidelity to the Lord for listening and responding to the petitioner's troubles. Then the psalm moves directly to a description of the threat and the Lord's response:

> The snares of death encompassed me;
>   the pangs of Sheol laid hold on me;
>   I suffered distress and anguish.
> Then I called on the name of the Lord:
>   "O Lord, I pray, save my life!" (vss. 2–4)
> . . .
> For you have delivered my soul from death,
>   My eyes from tears,
>   My feet from stumbling
> I walk before the Lord
>   In the land of the living.
> I kept my faith, even when I said,
>   "I am greatly afflicted";
> I said in my consternation,
>   "Everyone is a liar" (vss. 8–11)

The psalmist then explained what kind of response was made to a caring and gracious God:

> What shall I return to the Lord
>   For all his bounty to me?
> I will lift up the cup of salvation
>   And call upon the name of the Lord

> I will pay my vows to the Lord
> > In the presence of all his people . . .
> I will offer you a thanksgiving sacrifice
> > And call on the name of the Lord. (vss. 12–14,17)

The psalmist also described his or her new relationship with God because of the deliverance from the near death experience: "O Lord, I am your servant; I am your servant, the child of your serving-maid. You have loosed my bonds. Therefore I will call on him as long as I live" (Psalm 116:16, 2b).

The Todah was about a personal event that changed a person's life. Imagine the gratitude, relief, and thankfulness experienced by the person who had returned from the threshold of death. The host then shared the experience of deliverance and new life with a group of family and friends. On one hand, the Todah reflected something deeply personal. But the Todah also had a powerful communal aspect as well. Family and friends who knew and loved the host, joined with that person during their time of trial, to be thrilled at his or her deliverance. This was a community that would have been deeply impacted by the person's death and so were all the more joyful because of the recovery. But the Todah was also a public celebration at which both God and the people of Israel were symbolically present at the sacrifice and the following meal. The priest as a representative of the people took part in the celebration through his prayers at the sacrifice and joined in the feast by receiving a portion of the bread and meat. The sacrifice—the animal, unleavened bread, and leavened bread—all represented the basic human nourishment and thus the life of the one who had been rescued. God was believed to be present at the sacrifice by receiving the fat, blood, bread, the very *life* of the victim and the *new life* of the host. God was also present at the feast as the host sang the song of thanksgiving and told the story of redemption, and as the guests shared the sacrificial meat and bread and drank from the *cup of redemption.*

The Todah and Christian Theology

There are several possible touchstones between the celebration of the Todah and Christian theology. We do not know whether Jesus shared in a Todah feast on one of his many journeys to Jerusalem. But the themes of the Todah were and continue to be prevalent in Christian theology and practice and especially in the Christian understanding of worship.

Christianity has as one of its core belief that, through the person of Jesus, God has acted to deliver all people from death, especially from the *death of sin.* This salvation places people on a new foundation of existence. And as in the Todah, those who find that they have been rescued respond by giving thanks. One of the ways by which Christians give thanks for what they have experienced is by sharing the bread of life and the cup of salvation.

Of course, Christian belief is much more complex. Since New Testament times, Christians have disagreed as to exactly how the life and death of Jesus brings about deliverance and a new life. Christians have also given thanks in a wide variety of ways, including by sharing bread and wine. But Christians have also disagreed on exactly how to celebrate and what the bread and wine actually mean. At least some early Christian communities enjoyed a full meal with their Todah feast, while others ate and drank only bread and wine. In more recent centuries, some Christians have opted to stop eating and drinking anything and instead celebrate by singing songs of thanksgiving and listening to long lectures. Yet for most of the history of Christianity, worship was Todah. The host recited how God had delivered them from death, which gave them a new foundation of existence, and then they ate bread and drank wine that represented both themselves and God's saving presence.

Meat in the First Century

Some of us remember a popular advertising campaign from several decades ago that asked the question, "Where's the beef?" There is no doubt that meat is an important part of our North American diet. It is difficult for many to imagine an evening meal without some type of meat or poultry, whether it is beef, pork, or chicken. Even though meat and poultry were eaten a lot less frequently two thousand years ago, they were still an important part of the ancient menu. Meat was the special-occasion food of the first century. Fish or poultry might have sufficed for a special Sabbath dinner when the neighbors were invited over. But only meat was special enough for the big feast days. And feasts like Passover or Todah guaranteed meat on the table.

Food scholars believe that animals were domesticated not long after the development of agriculture. Around ten thousand years before the birth of Jesus, the barley and wheat fields of ancient farmers attracted animals like wild goats and sheep. Primitive farmers eventually realized the advantage of domesticating these animals. They provided a ready supply of milk and meat for the table and wool and skins for clothing. In fact, one might say that domesticated animals provided a means of storing grain and converting it to protein. The wool, hair, and hides were used for everything from clothing to wine skins and tents.

Civilization took another large step forward when people realized that their domesticated animals could help with work on the farm. Cows, donkeys and even goats were used as pack animals and could pull plows and carts. Fields were plowed and crops were transported to storage in a fraction of the time that it took without the help of animals. They were also used to tread the grain of the threshing floor and turn stone wheels that crushed olives, both time- and labor-saving advancements.

People who lived in the first century were especially fond of the cuts of meat that had the most fat. In fact, fat was a symbol for prosperity and blessing. Why would this be? We must remember, two thousand years ago, that the herd animals did not spend their lives in feed lots eating nothing but corn and other grains. They were what we now call *free-range* animals, resulting in meat that had significantly less fat. The cuts of meat with fat were much more tender and had better flavor. We do know that some animals were set aside specifically to fatten. The fatted calf that was mentioned in the parable of the prodigal son probably was a lamb or maybe a young calf set aside in a special pen to be fattened with grain. (Luke 15:11–32) People in the Mediterranean world used a similar technique to fatten geese and other birds and animals for a very special feast. But well-marbled meat was the exception, not the rule. First-century herd animals were leaner, leading to the preference for meat with fat.

This was especially true of ancient cattle. The cow of the Middle East, known as the Baladi ("village") cow, is a descendent of ancient livestock. They were only about one-fourth the size of a modern cow and produced less than one-tenth the amount of milk. These animals were used primarily as beasts of burden to pull wagons and plows or to turn the stone that ground wheat and barley. Even though small compared to modern cattle, they were still able to do significantly more work than a donkey or goat. This made them much more valuable. The price for a young calf was twenty denarii while a lamb was worth only one-fifth that amount. Because of their value and their work capacity, cows were rarely eaten, butchered only when the animal was advanced in age and no longer able to work as hard. Sometimes cows were butchered when a family had to feed an exceptionally large crowd, like a wedding party

Most first-century beef was very tough and stringy and had to be slowly cooked in a braise or stew in order to make it as tender as possible. Slow cooking an old, tough piece in a flavorful liquid eventually broke down the muscle fibers and produced a tender and flavor-filled piece of meat. It also gave the resulting broth a nice taste. The addition of vinegar, fruit juice, and peel from a citron to the broth helped tenderize the meat. The first-century cook also knew to stir in a mixture of flour and water or a beaten egg into the stew in order to thicken the broth after cooking the meat.

Sheep and goats were the primary herd animals of the Middle East and Mediterranean and were especially important in the ancient world. Because of their size and muscular structure they were pastured on hillsides and steep valleys, places that were not appropriate for cattle. Cows needed large amounts of relatively flat land that was covered with grass. Sheep and goats were not as picky about where and what they ate. By the first century, much of the traditional range land was used for growing crops. Large herds were more difficult to sustain on increasingly smaller tracts of pasture. Goats and sheep were kept in mountainous areas and in the woodlands where they would eat leaves and bark from the trees.

Both sheep and goats were valued for their wool for clothing, milk for drinking and making into cheese and yogurt, and for their meat. Long before the birth of Jesus, sheep were considered a sign of wealth and were used as a medium for exchange. People in the first century typically ate lamb or goat when they ate meat. A young lamb or goat would easily feed an average family without large amounts of leftovers requiring nonexistent refrigeration. The small amount of leftover meat from a special meal was added to the pot for soup or stew. The skins were tanned and used as we would use leather today. All the organs were eaten or were used for other purposes: for example, stomachs for storage or making cheese, intestines for sausages. The Jews raised a type of sheep that was famed for its large fatty tail, a first-century delicacy. This breed of sheep is still found in Israel today with some sporting tails that weigh as much as fifteen pounds! Ancient stories tell of prize sheep that pulled small carts behind them for the purpose of holding these mammoth treats.

First century farmers also kept poultry. The typical family had chickens, geese, doves, and pigeons. These birds had been domesticated for centuries and were used for a variety of purposes. Their eggs were an important part of the first-century menu and, like today, they were eaten in a variety of ways. The smaller birds, pigeons and doves, were kept in dovecotes in the courtyard or near the house. Their meat was added to enhance the flavor of soups and stews on occasions like the Sabbath. Chickens were relative newcomers to the Middle East by the time of Jesus, having arrived only several centuries earlier. These birds made their homes in the courtyards, nesting in out-of-the-way corners and providing the family with large eggs. They would have been eaten only for very special occasions. The same is true of the family geese. Their wings were clipped and they were kept in special pens in the courtyard or around the outside of the house. Domesticated geese were sometimes force-fed grain. Not only did this fatten the goose, but it also caused its liver to become quite enlarged. This method is still used today to produce *foie gras*.

First-century farmers hunted for pheasant and quail and used these birds for special meals. In the Mediterranean area, quail winter in Africa and migrate northward during the spring. They traveled in large flocks, and because of the great distances they traveled, were exhausted and easily caught when they landed. The book of Exodus tells of an extensive flock of quail that, having flown across the Red Sea, dropped exhausted into the Hebrew camp and provided them with meat for dinner. (Exodus 16:13; Numbers 11:31–32) Wealthier landowners also kept peacocks, beautiful but loud and messy birds that sometimes found their way onto the banquet tables. Apparently peacock meat was tough and stringy, but their tail feathers made beautiful presentations for important guests

Not all animals were considered fit to eat. Nor were Jews allowed to eat every part of the animal. First and foremost, Jews were not to eat blood:

> Only you shall not eat flesh with its life, that is, its blood. For your own life-blood I will surely require a reckoning: from every animal I will require it and from human beings, each one for the blood of another, I will require a reckoning for human life. (Genesis 9:4b–5)

It is fascinating that the biblical permission for formally vegetarian humans to eat meat and not eat blood occurs within a biblical discussion of prohibition against murder, for the passage continues, "Whoever sheds the blood of a human, by a human shall that person's blood be shed." (Genesis 9:6a) Blood was considered the vessel of life for all creatures and, as such, it belonged to God. And since life itself was a gift from God, humans were accountable for how that gift was used. They could eat meat but blood, the life force, had to be returned to God. It was easy enough if the animal was sacrificed in the temple. The blood was drained from the animal and poured around the altar. However, if the animal was killed away from the temple, as many certainly were, the blood had to be drained from its body and poured onto the ground. In this way the life force, its blood, was returned to the Creator. Following the same line of reasoning, Jews were not to eat an animal that had died of natural causes or one that had been killed by another creature. Any creature that was dead was considered unclean.

The prohibition from cooking meat in milk actually occurs three times in the Torah, or the first five books in the Bible: "You shall not boil a kid in its mother's milk" (Exodus 23:19; also Exodus 34:26 and Deuteronomy 14:21). Similar to the law regarding blood, this regulation reaches to the heart of

Hebraic understanding of God. Just as blood represents life, so milk is life for newborn animals, including humans. It must have seemed intrinsically wrong to use the very element that sustains the life of a young animal to cook it. Over many centuries this regulation was expanded so that meat and milk were not served at the same meal and the utensils and pans used to prepare meat and milk dishes were even segregated.

First-century Jews were well known in the Roman world for their avoidance of pork. Their refusal to eat pork often resulted in teasing and ridicule by non-Jews. Pork was not the only animal that Jews considered unclean. Animals, birds, water creatures, and insects all had their categories of clean and unclean creatures. Almost all insects were unclean. The only exceptions were locusts, grasshoppers, and crickets. Even in the first century, a person had to be quite hungry before resorting to insects for dinner. Water creatures that did not have scales or fins were unclean. Catfish, eels, water snakes, and all shellfish had to be avoided. Many birds were allowed, but all birds of prey and scavengers were unclean. That included eagles, hawks buzzards, ostriches, pelicans, herons, and bats. Mammals had to have cloven hooves and eat grass or grains, "chew the cud." (Leviticus 11:3–7) All animals that ate blood, all rodents, and reptiles were unclean.

Why is it that some creatures can be eaten while others must be avoided? An easy answer would be to say, "Because God required it." But even if this answer seems satisfactory to the reader, the question remains, "But why?" It is true that consuming some of the unclean animals can cause illness. Undercooked pork can transmit the parasitic disease called trichinosis. Both saltwater and freshwater shellfish grow in brackish water that was potentially polluted by sewage from a nearby village. It was probable that the towns around the Sea of Galilee caused some degree of pollution in the lake, especially after large winter rains washed sewage into the water. Because these creatures filter the water for food, they would become contaminated by any pollution. Many of the creatures on the unclean list are fish or animals that feed on carrion of one sort or another. Catfish are bottom feeders that eat refuse from the bottom of a lake. Most of the unclean birds such as vultures and buzzards are also scavengers. Almost without exception, the unclean animals are scavengers, rodents, or meat eaters that eat blood. Apparently, the regulation against eating blood was intended for all creation, not just humans! Even pigs are omnivores, eating both plants and meat.

So the prohibition against eating some creatures might have been for reasons of health or might have been for the sake of purity. Eating blood, eating something that had eaten blood, or eating something that was found already dead would certainly have violated the ancient Jewish sense of appropriateness, regardless of any perceived health risks. It would have des-ecrated their most basic understanding of the Jewish covenant relationship with God: life belongs to God.[7]

Preparing Meat, First-Century Style

The first-century cook had many of the same options for preparing meat or foul as the modern cook. Meats could be stewed or braised by cooking them in wine, stock, and other liquids. Boiling the meat in water or stock was a common method. The meat was cooked until it was tender and falling off the bone. It could then be used for other dishes and the resulting broth was used for soup or sauces. Casseroles with meat chunks or poultry were also popular and were cooked in the bread oven after the bread was baked.

A wide variety of spices and flavorings were used to flavor meat and poultry, especially if the meat was no longer fresh. Marinating the meat in vinegar, wine, and other acids was used to tenderize it. Sweet and sour foods were quite popular, so honey or a fruit juice was often added to the marinade while the dish was cooking.

Most Jewish families preferred roasted meats. For Passover, the lamb was cooked whole on a spit over an open fire. Bread ovens also provided an al-ternative for roasting. Families may have preferred their meat cooked in this manner, but out of economic necessity, meat and poultry were most often eaten as part of a stew or soup. Consider that at a modern restaurant, one pound of meat will probably feed one or maybe two people. At home, the same one-pound steak might feed an additional person or two, especially if the home cook serves a number of side dishes and serves the meat thinly sliced. The same piece of meat will feed even more people if the home cook cuts the meat into one-inch chunks and uses it in a stew. Finally, the cook can cut the meat even smaller and add it to a hearty barley and vegetable soup. With a lot of bread and dried fruit on the side, suddenly the same piece of meat might feed as many as ten or twelve people. Now, if the cook's fam-ily has a very limited income and twelve people to feed, which technique would they use?

Your Todah Feast at Home

The home cook need not have a near-death experience in order to celebrate a Todah feast with family and friends. Three elements should be included as part of the meal: unleavened bread, leavened bread, and red meat. Like other meals in this book, the meal should begin with the blessing, breaking, and sharing of bread. In addition, the meal should include a blessing of a cup of wine, the cup of salvation. Finally, the guests of the feast or the host should recite one of the Todah psalms from the Old Testament. A list of appropriate psalms is found in note 6. It would also be appropriate, if the meal does not have a specific theme of thanksgiving, for all the guests to share an element of their lives for which they are thankful.

The Menu for a Feast of Thanksgiving

- Leavened Bread* (any bread recipe in this book using yeast)
- Unleavened Bread* (chapter 8)
- Olive Oil and Thyme Dip* (chapter 5)
- Almond Dip* (chapter 7)
- Pistachios (from the market)
- Lentil and Parsley Salad*
- Lamb and Chickpea Stew*
- Fresh fruit (from the market)
- Stuffed Dates with Soft Cheese*

The Recipes

Lentil and Parsley Salad

This salad was always a great hit with Doug's catering customers, whether for a first-century feast or a salad luncheon.

Salad

1½ cup lentils	6 green onions, chopped
½ cup parsley, chopped	1 teaspoon salt, or to taste

Dressing

2 small lemons, juiced	½ teaspoon ground cumin
2 garlic cloves, finely minced	¾ teaspoon salt
½ teaspoon ground coriander	½ cup olive oil

Place lentils in a 3-quart pot. Cover with water 1 inch above the lentils. Bring water to a boil and then lower heat to a simmer. Allow lentils to simmer until they are tender but not mushy (approximately 30 minutes). Drain and cool.

To make the dressing: place all the ingredients except the oil in a small bowl. Pour the oil into the bowl while whisking with a wire whisk. Or place all the ingredients in a Mason jar. Put the top on the jar and shake vigorously.

Put the cooled lentils in a salad bowl. Add the chopped parsley and onions. Add some of the dressing and toss. Adjust the seasoning. Serves 8.

As an alternative, add ½ cup of bulgur to the salad before dressing. There should be left over dressing for another salad.

Lamb and Chickpea Stew

This is one of the first recipes we developed and is very good.

1 pound dried chickpeas or 2 (15 ounce) cans, rinsed	2 tablespoons olive oil
2 pounds of lamb shoulder or leg, cut into 1 inch cubes	2 medium onions, chopped
	4 garlic cloves, minced
1 tablespoon of regional spices	6 cups water or 3 cups beef stock and 3 cups water
2 teaspoons salt	
¾ teaspoon fresh ground pepper	1 bay leaf

Soak the dried chickpeas overnight and then drain. Season the lamb by rubbing with regional spices, salt, and pepper to taste. Heat a Dutch oven over medium heat and add a tablespoon of olive oil. Add the lamb and brown. Remove the lamb and add additional oil only if needed. Sauté the onions until just starting to turn brown. Add the garlic and continue to cook until the garlic turns translucent. Return the lamb to the pan and add the chickpeas, liquid, and bay leaf. Cover the Dutch oven and turn the heat down and simmer until the meat is almost tender, 1¼ to 1½ hours. If using canned chickpeas, add them to the Dutch oven for the last thirty minutes of cooking.

Stuffed Dates with Soft Cheese

These are a delicious treat whether preparing a first-century or a twenty-first century feast. If using cream cheese from the market, stir it first with a fork to soften. And you do not have to stop with 16 dates. Make as many as you want. Top with almond slivers.

16 dates
16 tablespoons of soft cheese from chapter 5, or Philadelphia cream
cheese

Slice each date lengthwise and remove the pit. Fill the cavity left from the pit with a tablespoon of cheese.

An ancient fishing boat. The drawing is modeled from the remains of a first-century fishing boat recently discovered in the mud near the Sea of Galilee.

CHAPTER ELEVEN

Picnic at the Beach

When they had gone ashore, they saw a charcoal fire there, with fish on it, and bread. Jesus said to them, "Bring some of the fish that you have just caught." So Simon Peter went aboard and hauled the net ashore, full of large fish, a hundred and fifty-three of them; and though there were so many, the net was not torn. Jesus said to them, "Come and have breakfast." Now none of the disciples dared to ask him, "Who are you?" because they knew it was the Lord. Jesus came and took the bread and gave it to them, and did the same with the fish. This was now the third time that Jesus appeared to the disciples after he was raised from the dead. (John 21:9–14)

It is a rare person who does not enjoy eating an occasional meal al fresco. The same was true for first-century Jews. They frequently enjoyed their dinners while sitting in the courtyard or on the roof, especially during the heat of the Palestinian summers. Every day of the week but the Sabbath, farmers and laborers stopped their work for a light meal and a drink of wine in the field with their colleagues. During the harvest, families and workers lived in the field and roasted their dinners over an open fire. Most of the pilgrims to Jerusalem during festival times stayed in large tents outside the city walls and probably cooked and ate their meals outside. Community feasts, like weddings and Pentecost, were likely enjoyed in the open air, if for no other reason than a small village did not have an indoor space large enough to hold all the celebrants. These meals were not exactly *picnics* or *cookouts* in the same

211

sense that we understand open-air dining. Still, we strongly suspect people in the first century enjoyed the change of venue when they ate outside.

The gospels of Jesus tell stories about several outdoor meals. The two most well known of his open-air banquets both called for fish as the main course. All four gospels have at least one account of a very large picnic, where thousands of people dined on bread and fish. (Matthew 14:15–21, 15:32–38; Mark 6:36–44; 8:1–9; Luke 9:12–17; John 6:5–14) But it is John's gospel that draws our attention. It ends with a curious story of the resurrected Christ using a fire to grill fish and bread for his disciples. The meal is breakfast and it occurs after a night of unsuccessful fishing followed by a miraculous catch. The result was a most unusual picnic on the beach. What a fascinating setting for John to end his account of the good news of Jesus. There are many elements of this story worth investigating, but it is the fish and fishing that we wish to explore in this chapter.

Commercial fishing played an important role in the life and economy of the people who lived in Galilee. Because their flesh deteriorates quickly, processing and storing the catch were large businesses. Fish from the Sea of Galilee were exported to communities all around the countries of the Eastern Mediterranean. This chapter will explore these aspects of fishing and will also look at salt. Salt actually is not a food at all, or at least not a food product derived from a plant or animal. Salt is a mineral, a rock. It was the only mineral used to season food and is needed by all known living creatures. It was also used as a preservative for a wide variety of foods, including fish. Therefore, access to salt supplies was essential, and wars were fought so cities and nations could season their food. The final section will help readers reconstruct their own first-century-style picnic.

The Life of a Fisherman

The world of fishing in the first century was not what we might think. For many of us the image of a fisherman, even a professional one, is quite idyllic. It was certainly hard work, but the fisherman, like the farmer, must have been his own boss. He and his family or partners were alone on the lake, controlling their own destiny with boat and nets. Nothing could be further from the truth. First-century fishermen had to contract for a license from a licensing broker in order to fish commercially on the Sea of Galilee. The licensing brokers received their fishing rights from the local ruler, Herod Antipas during the ministry of Jesus.

Most fishermen also received capitalization for their businesses from the same brokers, thus they were usually heavily indebted to the very person who sold the license. It is interesting that the Greek word for "broker" was *telōnai*, which was also the word for "tax collector" or "publican." It is certainly possible that Matthew (Levi) the tax collector was actually a fishing broker.[1] The broker had a booth or office at the docks where he was ready to receive his share of the fish or revenue as the boats arrived. In order to afford a license, and because there were a limited number of licenses, many of the fishermen became part of a partnership or a consortium that worked together. The Gospel of Mark described Zebedee as a fisherman who had two sons and additional hired laborers working as a team or partnership.

Fishing on the Sea of Galilee was a "highly regulated, taxed and hierarchical economy."[2] After the licensed fishermen caught the fish, they were sold to government-approved distributors who processed the fish for storage and transportation. The fish were then dried, salted, pickled, or cured in some manner. To accomplish this, the processors purchased a number of additional goods and services, all of which were taxed and regulated as well. In fact, the fishermen and processors were supported by an orchestra of businesses and craft people: vintners who sold wine for pickling the fish; merchants who provided salt and olive oil; potters who supplied clay vats and jars; and craftsmen who furnished lumber for building and repairing boats, flax for nets, sail linen, and stone anchors. The processed fish were then transported by a merchant, using roads that required tolls and taxes. Once the processed fish reach a market, the merchant paid rent for a stall and the customer paid sales tax. It is easy to understand why first-century tax collectors were so despised!

Now might be the appropriate time to say that the first-century world also had a thriving underground economy separate from the one that was regulated and taxed. Both farmers and fishermen engaged in bartering, where goods or services were traded for other goods or services. A fisherman might trade fish for a new sail or a processor give dried fish for new stone jars or a load of salt. Farmers did the same. An amphora of wine might be exchanged for a new plow blade or lumber to begin building a new room for the house. Using a barter system, farmers, fishermen, and trades people were able to buy and sell without supporting the hierarchy with tax money. We believe that this practice was widespread in Palestine and throughout the Mediterranean region.[3]

There were a number of ways to catch fish. First-century anglers had rods with metal hooks and flaxen line. This was a fun way to catch a fish or two and was a popular means of entertainment for kings and pharaohs, but it was not an effective method to make a living on the water. Harpoons and tridents were used by fishermen on the Mediterranean to catch very large fish, but again this was a method that was not used in Galilee. By far the most common method of fishing was with a net. Small handheld cast nets were thrown while wading along the shore or from a boat. These nets were fine for catching smaller fish or a few big fish, but larger nets were needed to catch the number of fish needed to pay bills and keep the license. On the other hand, cast nets were perfect for fishermen and unlicensed townspeople who wanted to poach a few fish for dinner. Dragnets and other types of large nets were the choice for the licensed fishermen on the Sea of Galilee. A large net was stretched between two boats, with one of the boats staying somewhat stationary and the second boat gradually circling back toward it. The fish were trapped and the net was either pulled into one of the boats or dragged to the shore.

First-century fishing involved much more than just catching fish. A fisherman had to be able to make nets, repair sails, and keep his boat in good shape. Each day ended by taking down the sail; turning over the fish to the processor; and then washing, drying, mending, and folding the nets and sails. The teams of fishermen also had to be willing to fish both during the day and at night. We know from the story of the picnic on the beach with the risen Lord that the disciples had been fishing unsuccessfully straight through the night. Unlike John's account, there are many times when fishing was much more productive in the dead of the night. An experienced angler also knows that the dawn can be a good time for finding fish.

We are fortunate that in 1986 an ancient fishing boat was found in the mud near the town of Magdala. The boat is well preserved and demonstrates how they were typically constructed. Further, this boat was carbon dated to have been built between 40 BCE and 70 CE and thus was used during the time being studied by this book. The boat is twenty-six and one-half feet long and seven and one-half feet at the widest. A boat this size required five crew: four oarsmen and one steering with a tiller. The boat also had a mast and sail and could accommodate up to two thousand pounds of crew and fish.[4] It was also just about the right size for a teacher and his twelve followers.

The Sea of Galilee is not a large body of water and is more accurately called a freshwater lake than a sea. It was also known as Lake Tiberias and Lake of Gennesaret. It is approximately thirteen miles long and between three and seven miles wide. In places, the hills and mountains of Galilee come down to the very shore of the lake with dramatic cliffs on the east side. On a clear day, a person standing on a small rise can easily see across the lake.[5] At approximately seven hundred feet below sea level, it is the lowest freshwater lake in the world, and only the Dead Sea sits further below sea level. The sea is quite deep, as much as two hundred feet in some places. Shoals and ridges in the lake provided excellent places for fish to feed. The

Sea of Galilee is purported to still be teaming with the same varieties of fish and wildlife as it did two thousand years ago.

As might be expected, the towns and cities around the Sea of Galilee were primarily fishing communities. Capernaum was on the Northwest side of the lake, situated on a small plain surrounded by mountains. It was a large town with a cosmopolitan flavor, and fishing was its primary industry. Two miles to the north was Chorazin, which sat on a major east-west highway that connected spice caravans to the Mediterranean Sea. Bethsaida, across the lake from Capernaum, literally means "the fishing place." Mary Magdalene was from the fishing community of Magdala, which was called Tarichaea by the Romans. This town was a center of fish preservation; in fact, the name Tarichaea has its root in the Greek word for "pickling" and "preserved fish." It would be like living in a community named Town Where We Preserve Fish.

Fishing for saltwater fish and shell fish in the Mediterranean Sea produced most of the seafood for Greece, Rome, and the rest of the Mediterranean Region. The coastline of Palestine had been the ancient seafaring country of Phoenicia that was known both for maritime trade and fishing. It contained coastline and harbors that were repaired and updated by Herod the Great and his son. Long before the first century, tuna was a much-sought-after fish by many of the people in the Mediterranean Region. Mediterranean fisherman targeted schools of tuna, herding them into nets and a labyrinth of net traps. Salting and storing tuna in olive oil was a favorite preparation, as it still is in Mediterranean countries. Other fish were also popular, including sea bream, mullet, turbot, grouper, and conger eels. The Greeks and Romans were also connoisseurs of shellfish such as clams, mussels, oysters, shrimp, and lobsters.

The large towns and cities all over the Mediterranean world had thriving fish markets. The large cities in Palestine were no exception. Some of the seafood made its way from the coast inward to cities like Sepphoris and Jerusalem, while the smaller communities remained content with the fish from the Sea of Galilee. Jerusalem had an entrance on the northern side of the city that was called the *fish gate*. A thriving fish market was located just inside the gate. We know that it included seafood merchants from the coastal city of Tyre, located on the Mediterranean in the region of modern Lebanon. Jerusalem was far enough from the Mediterranean Sea that all of the saltwater fish sold at market was first processed by drying or salting before transporting.

Rome was very different. The largest city in the world was located only fifteen miles from the sea, and it had a huge fish market. From the Red Sea to the Atlantic Ocean and all around the Mediterranean Sea, fish and other seafood were transported to the great city of Rome. The stalls were piled high with every product imaginable: salt- and freshwater fish, lobsters, sea turtles, crayfish, eels, shrimp, mussels, and oysters were only a sampling of what was available. There were freshwater fishponds and saltwater tanks for live fish and shellfish. The city's aqueducts supplied water for the ponds. Seawater was transported from the coast. Seafood was brought to the coast near Rome in special boats with saltwater containers and then carts carried the fish in large tanks of water, packed in bags and wet seaweed or even packed on ice. The wealthiest of the wealthy Romans imported ice from the Alps! They used their ice to cool their wine and ship their fish.

Jesus' Ministry and Fishermen

Much of Jesus' ministry was spent in the towns around the Sea of Galilee, and many of his friends and disciples came from that area. At some point in his adult life, Jesus moved from the small agricultural town of Nazareth to Capernaum where he had a home that he eventually used as a base for his teaching (Mark 2:1). It is likely that many of Jesus' acquaintances were connected to some aspect of the business of fishing, and it makes sense that his first disciples were fishermen. Simon Peter and Andrew, who both lived in Capernaum, were fishermen, as were the sons of Zebedee. The gospels give a glimpse of Jesus' ministry and life in the lake town, teaching in the synagogue, walking along the shore near the town, and describing the Kingdom of God while sitting in a fishing boat.

From time to time, fish and fishing worked its way into the teaching of Jesus. His parables and stories reflected the lives and work of his audience, thus making his lessons easier for common people to comprehend. He often used agricultural imagery but only occasionally spoke of fishing. In an example of the graciousness of God, Jesus asked, "Is there anyone among you who, if your child asks for bread, will give a stone? Or if a child asks for a fish, will give a snake?" (Matthew 7:9–10; also Luke 11:11). More important, Jesus depicted the mission of discipleship in terms of angling: "Follow me and I will make you fish for people"[6] (Mark 1:17). The gospels report that the fishermen who heard this call walked away from their valuable license and tackle to begin their journey with Jesus. However, because of the presence of boats, nets, and fish in later stories, we might assume that they continued with their work to some degree, or at least had access to fishing boats, until their mission took them away from the lake.

Several of the miracles described by the gospels also involved fish and fishing. The feeding of the multitudes was a feast of bread and dried fish that occurs six times in the gospels. Just as Jesus fed the crowds with his teachings, in these accounts they are also miraculously fed with a very small amount of bread and fish. We learn that in some circumstances farmers and laborers carried loaves of bread and pieces of salted or dried fish with them into the fields.

In one of the most unusual stories in the gospels, Jesus told Peter to pay his temple taxes by taking a coin from the mouth of a fish caught for that purpose (Matthew 17:24–27). Jesus used the occasion to teach Peter a lesson about freedom for the children of God's Kingdom and yet the need to pay taxes in order not to give offense. It was believed that the fish with the coin was a tilapia, and that variety is still called St. Peter's fish.

There are two accounts of a miraculous catch of fish, both occurring at significant points of understanding the call to follow Jesus. In Luke's gospel, a catch of fish provoked by Jesus was so great that it filled two boats to the point of almost sinking. This miracle provides the context for the call to discipleship, for immediately afterward, Jesus calls the fishermen to be disciples who will fish for people (Luke 5:1–11). The story of the miraculous catch from John's gospel has already been described above. This catch was also the setting for the breakfast of grilled fish and bread. After breakfast, Peter was asked by Jesus to follow him and "tend his sheep." (John 21:15–19) Even though the stories of the two catches are very similar, the one in John occurs after the resurrection of Jesus and provides the context for the beginning of the next phase of the disciples' ministry as apostles. Both this story and other gospel stories on the lake point to the necessity of the presence of Jesus for their mission's success:

> To row all night without Jesus is to get nowhere; to fish all night without Jesus is to catch nothing. But, of course, it is the leadership group of the disciples who are both rowing and fishing, and it is to them that Jesus' resurrectional assistance is forthcoming.[7]

Fish imagery was also used by the early church and was found in some of the most ancient of the Christian Roman catacombs. As mentioned above, the feast for the multitudes and the breakfast on the beach both included bread and fish. These two foods became a symbol for dining with the resurrected Christ and for the Eucharistic worship of the early Christian communities. The letters in the Greek word for fish, *ichthus*, are an acronym for the phrase "Jesus Christ, Son of God, Savior," a confessional statement regarding the identity of the risen Christ and so was an often used symbol down to present time.

The Fish That Peter Caught

The Sea of Galilee yielded several varieties of fish eaten by first-century Jews. One was tilapia, the fish that is now bred on farms and available in most grocery stores and fish markets in the United States. The tilapia was a favored species for eating and processing. Tilapia is still a principal fish caught in the lake. In addition, there were fish of the carp family called *barbels*. The smallest of the Galilean fish were freshwater sardines. The Sea of Galilee also had catfish, eels, and freshwater mussels, but these were considered unclean because they were water-dwelling creatures without scales, so they were not eaten by Jews: "everything in the waters that has fins and scales . . . such you may eat. But anything in the seas or the streams that does not have fins and scales . . . of their flesh you shall not eat, and their carcasses you shall regard as detestable" (Leviticus 11:9–12). Shellfish tend to live in brackish water near the shore and are extremely susceptible to pollution. Even two thousand years ago, the Sea of Galilee would have been subject to human pollution, especially after a large rain. Catfish were bottom feeders and eels probably looked too much like the snake that tempted the first family. The Jews may not have eaten catfish and other unclean fish and seafood, but there was no law against selling them if caught in the net with other fish. In fact, Jewish fishermen did sell these and other unclean fish, eels, and freshwater mussels to the surrounding Gentiles in the community.[8]

Only those who lived in villages or towns adjacent to a lake or river experienced the luxury of eating fresh fish. If fresh fish were transported around Galilee, they were usually wrapped in wet sacks or straw and only taken a short distance. However, most of the fish were preserved before they could be taken and sold at towns that were any distance away from the source. Fresh fish have a high water content, as much as 80 percent in some species. Ancient people discovered that if much of the water was extracted, bacteria were killed, making the fish edible for a much longer period of time and easier to store and transport. In fact, the presence of the salt kept new bacteria from growing and ruining the fish. One-half or more of the water is eliminated by drying and salting. Nutrients are also more condensed in fish when moisture is removed. One method for drying fish was to gut and hang them in the sun. Salt naturally draws moisture from any food product so salting fish was another commonly used method for drying fish. Small fish were dried whole after being gutted, while larger fish were first sliced into pieces. Sea salt or rock salt was used for the process. The salt was rubbed onto the fish and then the fish were layered, covered alternately by salt and reed mats. Another method of preserving fish involved storing the fish in brine for pickling. This brine consisted of a combination of salt and water or seawater that was concentrated by evaporation. Once preserved, the fish from Galilee were shipped all over the Middle East and as far away as Rome.

Fish were cooked in any number of ways. Dried and salted fish were prepared by first soaking in water to add moisture back to the flesh and to remove the salt. Dried fish was also used in soups and stews where it was reconstituted by the broth or stewing liquid. Like other animal flesh, fish was cooked by roasting and grilling. Smaller fish were skewered and grilled over an open fire. Whole fish or fillets were also wrapped in damp fig or grape leaves and cooked in the coals of a fire. Greeks came to prefer baked or roasted fish, but some Greek cooks and writers longed for the day when a piece of fish was placed in a fig leaf pocket and simply steamed on the coals.[9] Fish were also fried, either deep fried in a large amount of very hot oil, or pan fried. Fish were prepared with leeks or onions and often eaten with eggs or cheese. Unlike meat, Jewish cooks were allowed to cook and serve fish in milk.

Romans preferred fish baked or boiled and served with a sauce.[10] The sauces, even for families of more modest means, could be quite extravagant. Egg yolks and oil were whisked together to form a mayonnaise, and other flavorings, such as mashed anchovy fillets or fig syrup, were then added. The finished product was served with the boiled fish. Vinaigrettes made with herbs and spices were used as well. First-century vinaigrettes and sauces also included such ingredients as chopped hard-boiled eggs, raisin or date wine, and honey. Sometimes sauces were poured over the fish and then baked. Jews, and especially wealthy ones, also used sauces with their fish, but not with the same complexity or frequency as Romans and Greeks. Fish were also used as an ingredient in a sauce or a finished dish. For example, small fish, whether fresh, salted, or pickled, were cleaned and used in an omelet or egg pie. Lobsters, mussels, oysters, sea urchins, and eels, although not eaten by Jews, were staples for other Mediterranean cultures. Like fish, these fruits of the sea were prepared in a number of ways: grilled, broiled, baked, boiled, added to soups and stews, and served with sauces. They were also thinly sliced and added to sauces that were served on fish or with other foods.

Without a doubt, a sauce made with fish and salt, called *garum* or *liquamen*, was the most loved condiment in the Roman world. The production of this fish sauce was another method of preserving or using fish before they spoiled. First made by the Greeks, the Romans took it over as one of their favorite foods. It was made in many Mediterranean countries, including Palestine. Fish pieces layered in salt were placed in large barrels and left to ferment in the sun for two to three months. After pressing the remaining liquid from the fish and straining all the fish solids, the finished garum was placed in clean containers, leaving a salty and fishy-tasting liquid. Low-quality garum was made with the scrap pieces: heads, intestines, and tails. Whole, small fish like smelt, small mullet, anchovies, and sardines were used for a higher-quality sauce.

Flavorings were sometimes added to garum. Wine, vinegar, honey, oregano, grape or raisin syrup, and other seasonings were all added to the finished fish sauce. The Romans used garum on almost everything. It was a marinade for meats, poultry, and fish. It flavored vegetables, was used in sauces and soups, and was drizzled on top of finished dishes. First-century gourmands used it as often as they used salt.

We do not know exactly how garum tasted, but we have a good idea. It was probably very similar to *nuoc mam*, the fish sauce made in Vietnam and Thailand. The manufacturing methods were very similar. Worcestershire sauce is another modern fermented sauce made with anchovies and salt. We recommend that, for first-century cuisine, the modern cook use nuoc mam.

Salt of the Earth

Salt deserves our special consideration. Plutarch called it "the noblest of foods, the finest condiment of all."[11] But what exactly are we purchasing when we pick up a box of salt at the grocery? Usually it is in the same aisle with flour and sugar and is probably located under or next to the spices. Is it a spice? It certainly enhances the flavor of food and is in almost everything we eat, and many of the things that we drink. But is it more than simply something we use to make food taste good? So when Jesus said, "You are the salt of the earth" (Matthew 5:13), what was he talking about?

Salt actually is not derived from a plant and is not a spice. In its pure form, salt is a crystalline compound containing sodium and chloride, though it almost never occurs naturally in a pure form. Other chemicals, such as magnesium, potassium, and iodine are often found in salt, especially in sea salt. We consider salt an important seasoning for cooking; actually it is the most important seasoning. Unlike herbs and spices, it does not add fragrance to the food, but it does significantly enhance the other flavors. Unless the first-century family was overwhelmed by poverty, a bowl of salt would have had a prominent place in the kitchen and on the table.[12]

However, salt use was not limited to flavoring food. Because it also absorbs moisture, salt was used as a preservative. Foods were packed in salt and then stored. It was also used to help dry foods for storage. Simply leaving them in the sun dried many foods. For others, salt was used to expedite the drying process. Salt and water combined as brine became an essential ingredient for softening and storing tough, hard-to-digest foods. In chapter 4, we saw that green olives are an example of a food that became edible only when cured in brine.

Our bodies need salt. The average adult needs six to eight grams a salt per day, and even more in hot weather or when engaged in physical labor. Without salt we become dehydrated and can even die. But average contemporary adults eat almost twice as much as they need. We know that it greatly enhances the flavor of food. We also know that, when eaten in excess, salt causes a number of health problems, including hypertension. Over-salting home-cooked food is only a small part of the problem. Preprocessed foods, snack foods, pastries, carbonated drinks, even many medicines contain salt, and many have a lot of salt.

The situation was different two thousand years ago. Many of the major events in ancient history, including wars, were driven by the need to acquire salt. It is found all over and under the earth's surface and in the earth's seas. Yet, because of uneven distribution, acquiring salt remained difficult for some peoples and nations. For first-century Palestine, the Dead Sea and its environs was the primary source of salt. The Romans used a variety of natural resources for their salt, including seawater. One of the reasons Rome invaded Gaul (Modern France) was to have access to its salt deposits. One of the unfortunate practices of the Roman salt works was the use of large lead pans to process seawater for table salt. The pans were heated until the water evaporated, leaving behind a salt and lead residue. Because the lead in the salt gave the food a reportedly unpleasant aftertaste, Romans used even stronger seasonings, including more salt. Lead poisoning was a likely result.[13]

One can easily see, with the importance of salt in the ancient world, why it was also such an important symbol. People in the first century experienced salt as something of great value. It enhanced the flavor of almost all foods and made some foods edible. It also purified and protected food by its use for storing and drying. But most of all, salt was necessary for life itself. For these reasons, it was considered a gift of God, or of the gods, by most cultures. So salt became a symbol of all these things: life-giving, purifying, and protecting, and thus was a gift of great value.

Because of the rich symbolism attached to salt, it was used in both Jewish and Christian worship. In later Christianity it was sometimes used as part of a baptism service to represent purity and to symbolically protect candidates from the devil. For Jews, and for Romans, it was used to purify animals before sacrifice. When Jesus taught, "You are the salt of the world," he was speaking not just of a tasty spice, but of a product of great value, perhaps even a life giving value, to those that heard and followed his teachings.

Why was spilled salt thrown over one's shoulder? Salt was also considered a symbol of hospitality. The gracious first-century host and hostess shared two very valuable commodities with their guests, their bread and their salt. When sharing these foods, the family was symbolically promising that no harm would come to the guest while under their care. A bond of community and trust was established. Because salt was also considered a gift from God, it represented the same kind of bond between the Divine Host and earthly people. Spilled salt was considered a misuse of the gift and a breaking of the bond. The person spilling the salt suddenly was vulnerable to the advances of evil spirits waiting behind him or her. So protection was guaranteed by casting salt three times over one's shoulder.

Your Fish Picnic at the Beach

We include two recipes for tilapia, both to be cooked on the grill. It was common to prepare the fish by wrapping fillets in fig leaves and then setting the packets on the coals of the fire, allowing the fish to steam inside of the leaves. The fig leaves impart a nice flavor to the fish. We wonder if Jesus had a little olive oil available to pour on the fish, or a dash of salt and maybe a little spice, like ground cumin seed, to add before the fish fillets were sealed in the leaves. We hope so.

Don't eat the raw leaves, but cut the package open on your plate and serve with bread toasted over the fire.

Menu for a Picnic on the Beach

- Grilled Bread* (Mediterranean Grain or Flat Bread, chapter 3 or 7)
- Roasted Chickpeas*
- Goat Cheese Marinated in Olive Oil and Herbs* (chapter 4; Use the cheese to spread on the bread and the flavored olive oil as a dip)
- Grilled Tilapia with Pomegranate Marinade*
- Tilapia Cooked in Fig Leaves or Grape Leaves*
- Dried fruit* (from the market, or Raisins from chapter 7)
- Date or Fig Cake* (chapter 4)

The Recipes

Grilled Bread

1 loaf of the Mediterranean Grain Bread, sliced, or pita breads
olive oil for brushing

Start charcoal in grill. Brush bread slices with olive oil. Cook on the grill until toasted.

Roasted Chickpeas

This calls for cooked chickpeas. To cook, use the method found in the Lentil and Chickpea Soup recipe in chapter 3.

1½ cups cooked chickpeas or 1 (15 oz.) can, drained, rinsed, and dried
Preheat oven to 400 degrees.

Place chickpeas on a jelly roll pan or baking sheet. Bake in the oven for 20 to 30 minutes, stirring occasionally so they do not stick to the pan. When done, they should be somewhat crisp on the outside and soft in the middle. Cool on a kitchen towel. Keep covered until served. Serves 4 to 6 as an appetizer.

Grilled Tilapia with Pomegranate Marinade

If you do not have access to pomegranate molasses, use pomegranate juice and boil it until it is the consistency of a thin syrup. Instead of grilling, these tilapia fillets can be cooked using a cast iron or heavy weight skillet on the stove top or baked in the oven.

4 tilapia fillets	1½ teaspoons salt, or to taste
1 tablespoon olive oil	¼ teaspoon pepper

Pomegranate Marinade

¼ cup olive oil	2 teaspoons honey
¼ cup pomegranate molasses	1 garlic clove, minced

Mix the ingredients for the Pomegranate Marinade. Pour mixture over the fillets and marinate in your refrigerator for thirty minutes. Remove fish from the marinade and dry with paper towels. Reserve the remaining marinade.

Start a charcoal fire in a grill and heat until ash white and glowing. Meanwhile, rub the fillets with olive oil, then sprinkle with salt and pepper. Once the charcoal is ready, oil the grill grate. Place the fillets over a cooler section of the fire and cook for 2 to 3 minutes. While cooking, brush the fillets with additional pomegranate molasses. Very carefully turn the fillets with a large spatula. Tilapia is a fish that flakes very easily and tends to stick to the grill. Then cook for an additional 2 to 3 minutes, brushing the top of the fillets with additional marinade. To see if cooked, cut into one of the fillets; it should be white throughout and should easily flake. Serves 4 to 6

Tilapia Cooked in Fig Leaves or Grape Leaves

We were both lucky enough to live close to several people in Dallas who had beautiful fig trees. Fig leaves were traditionally used to cook fish. The leaves impart a delicious, delicate flavor to the fish. Realizing that most people do not have access to fig leaves, we suggest that you use canned grape leaves or aluminum foil as an alternative.

Fig or grape leaves	1 lemon
4 tilapia fillets	1½ teaspoons salt, or to taste
1 tablespoon olive	¼ teaspoon pepper

Wash and soak fig leaves in water for at least 1 hour or wash grape leaves and partially dry. Start a charcoal fire in a grill and heat until ash white and glowing.

Meanwhile, cut the fillets into 2 to 4 pieces, in sizes that will fit into leaves. Rub the fillets pieces with olive oil. Cut the lemon in half and squeeze the juice over the fillet pieces. Season with salt and pepper. Fig leaves are large so fish pieces can be wrapped in one or two overlapping leaves. Keep the leaves soaking in water until time to wrap. Fold corners over the fish and wrap the center around the pieces. Secure with a toothpick. Alternatively, wrap grape leaves around the fish and secure with a toothpick. With foil, oil the inside of the foil before wrapping around the fish.

The fish wrapped in fig leaves or foil can be placed directly on the coals. Cook for 2 to 3 minutes and the turn and cook for an additional 2 to 3 minutes, or until the fish flakes with a knife and is white throughout. Add another several minutes of cooking if using foil. Because the brined grape leaves are thinner, cook on an oiled grill over the charcoal for approximately 8 minutes, turning after 4 minutes. Serves 4 to 6.

CHAPTER TWELVE

What We Have Learned and
Why We Join the Feast

Cuisine is the very symbol of civilization and of culture. (Massimo Montanari, from *Food is Culture*)

For years, we made wine, cheese, and bread; we brined olives and stewed lentils. We studied ancient farming and cooking. Families and friends joined us for first-century banquets and Passover feasts. We roasted lamb and studied Jewish culture, history, and economics. We started researching and writing this book with the belief that we can learn about the history and culture of a very important time by studying food, food production, and feasting. We hoped that our studies would provide insights into the life and teaching of Jesus. We suspected that this cultural study would also help us understand our own culinary habits. Finally, we wanted to try cooking and eating food in a way similar to that of Jesus and his disciples.

Food and Diet

Along with our experiments with food production, we also spent time eating and living with a first-century diet. It was quite clear that our first-century meals were quite similar to the modern Mediterranean Diet, but without pasta, corn, and tomatoes. It was rich with whole grains, legumes, and fresh fruits and vegetables when they were in season, dried and pickled during the rest of the year. Herbs, spices, and sauces were available to give added flavor to whatever was in the pot. Fish and poultry were eaten once a week. Meats

227

were eaten very sparingly; roasted lamb, goat, or beef was a treat, certainly not part of the daily meal, not even part of a weekly diet. Even though wine was frequently consumed, it was at least 50 percent water and often flavored with honey and spices. Milk was also a frequent drink, and beer was consumed by the common people, except for Jews. In the Mediterranean area and Middle East, olive oil was the principal fat used for cooking. Even though many of the foods were salty because they were stored in brine or salted for preservation, the daily salt consumption was quite a bit less than that of most Americans.

All in all, the daily diet in the first century for many people was quite healthy. However, the daily diet for the poorest members of society was not. The only meal of the day most often consisted of just bread and legumes, with nothing to drink but watered-down vinegar. During bad times, even beans and lentils were a luxury, leaving the poorest families with a dinner of thick bread or barley porridge. The poor who lived in the country might have been able to grow vegetables and some fruit in a small garden. Those who lived in the city had only occasional access to fruit and vegetables. The disparity between the dining habits of the richest and the poorest members of society was vast. Living on the menu of the poor would be hard for almost all of us to comprehend.

What have we learned about the first-century Holy Land? Food was one of several ways that the Jews continued to differentiate themselves from surrounding cultures. Despite being conquered first by the Greeks and then the Romans, the Jewish people remained, for the most part, steadfast in their adherence to traditional foods, ignoring the "give-and-take" of culinary fads and tastes. There was significant pressure from the other Mediterranean countries, especially from Greece and Rome, to forsake their culinary heritage. And yet the vast majority of Jews continued to keep a kosher diet.

Feasts and fasts also served an important cultural function, and we will reflect on their role later in this chapter. There were certainly elements of the feast that Jews shared with surrounding cultures. The form for banquets was almost universal in the Mediterranean and Middle East. Weddings and harvest feasts also shared many cross-cultural characteristics. Yet Jewish feasts had strong historical, religious, and cultural characteristics that in part defined who they were.

Jesus and Those Who Produced Food

Food, feasting, food production, culture, and history are all intricately intertwined. By observing Jewish farm and food production, we found that the policies of Herod the Great and his descendents resulted in the loss of security and the ability to help the poor with the reduction of foods stored in warehouses. Scholars will sometimes blame the Romans and their emperor, and certainly Rome took its share of tax money to construct and protect roads, bridges, and other infrastructure elements. In addition, armies had to be paid and quartered. But actually, it was Herod and his structure of taxation that ultimately caused an economic crisis. Farmers lost their farms, resulting in increased unemployment that engendered discontent among the common people and eventually an open rebellion against Rome that also targeted the properties of large Jewish land holders. The Roman crackdown led finally to the sacking of Jerusalem and the destruction of the temple by Roman troops in the year 70 CE.

There is no denying that Jesus had a special affinity with the poorest members of society. He spoke often of the poor, calling them blessed and entreating the rich to sell their possessions and give to those in need. He compared himself to those who are hungry and thirsty and told followers that whoever helped the poor were actually helping him. Even Jesus' first sermon in his home town of Nazareth illustrates this aspect of his ministry. In it he quoted a passage from Isaiah:

> The Spirit of the Lord is upon me,
> because he has anointed me
> to bring good news to the poor.
> He has sent me to proclaim release to the captives
> and recovery of sight to the blind
> to let the oppressed go free.
> To proclaim the year of the Lord's favor.

Jesus then added, "Today this scripture has been fulfilled in our hearing" (Luke 4:18–20). Many biblical scholars argue that this passage is calling for a Jubilee year as it was described in Leviticus in chapters 25 and 27: a year in which all slaves were set free and all land returned to the original owners. The idea of a Jubilee year would have been radical by the first century and would have involved taking land away from Herod's family and allies and giving it back to people who were then tenant farmers and day laborers. It seems as though, from the beginning, Jesus understood that a significant part of his ministry was to and with the poor and dispossessed.

Somewhere between 80 and 90 percent of the people in Palestine were involved in food production. The rhythm of planting and harvesting, processing and storing food influenced all manner of life, including the life and teaching of Jesus. He often used landlords and tenant farmers, loan holders and day laborers as characters in his stories and parables. The gospels record accounts of Jesus as a guest at banquets, weddings, and Sabbath feasts hosted by the wealthier and more powerful members of rural Galilean society. But we know he also was the guest of much more common people, fed by the families of fishermen and farmers. We assume that sharing a pot of lentils, a piece of bread, and a glass of wine was a much more common experience for Jesus and his disciples than feasting on roasted lamb.

Food and Culture

As part of our research, we prepared first-century feasts for a wide variety of family, friends, and church and community groups. At the end of each meal, our guests shared perspectives on what they experienced. Their stories were consistent with the accounts from ancient feasts. What we learned was this. First and foremost, feasts foster a sense of community. At the same time, they can also define a community and separate it from other groups. Feasts and important meals celebrate and teach history and reinforce cultural norms, whether the group is a family unit, clan, nation, or racial group. Feasts are clearly opportunities for generosity and hospitality, where the object of bounty can be family, friends, neighbors, or a stranger or visitor. Finally, and perhaps most obviously, the feast is an occasion of celebrating a significant landmark in a relationship, in someone's life, or in the larger community.

First, as we suspected, food and feasts foster community. This was certainly the experience of the Israelites. Their annual feasts and banquets helped support their family units, as well as their local and regional communities. These feasts promoted a sense of nationalism and religious unity. They still do, whether the feast is a church potluck, a neighborhood barbeque, or a dinner party with friends. But in doing so, feasts encouraged differentiation from other communities and religions. Cultural differences were emphasized by the food and drink that was preferred and the manner of feasting. First-century Greeks mostly surely would have said, "We are the ones who like pork sausages and cabbage." Romans insisted that roasted meats were only for barbarians and preferred boiled meats with rich sauces. Jews passed on pork and loved roasted foods, but refused to eat cheese and meat at the same meal.[1]

The feast, both ancient and modern, is also an opportunity to teach history and culture. The Passover Feast was in large part a lesson in Jewish history and cultural identity taught within the context of a feast. Food takes on symbolic significance. Children are indoctrinated into the cultural identity of their people while, year after year, their elders are reminded of *who they are*. Many modern feasts take on the same character, for example, Thanksgiving Day dinners, wedding receptions, rehearsal dinners, and funeral wakes. National myths are taught. Family histories are repeated. Stories are shared.

The feast is an occasion of generosity and hospitality. For the people of the Mediterranean and Middle East hospitality was and still is considered an important virtue: "Do not neglect to show hospitality to strangers, for by doing that some have entertained angels without knowing it" (Hebrews 13:2). For at least some of the ancient feasts, especially Passover and Weeks (Pentecost), it was customary to invite the poor and foreigners. Even street people in the large cities ate meat and enjoyed four glasses of wine at the Passover feast. At the Festival of Weeks, everyone was included, poor and rich alike, to sit at the same table, eat from the same bowl, and enjoy the fruits of the harvest. The emphasis of this celebration was on the Book of Ruth and sharing the crop with those who were less fortunate. We tend to practice generosity by preparing and serving our favorite foods, made with the best ingredients and served with our favorite beverages. At times, our hospitality will reach beyond family and friends when we invite a new neighbor or coworker to share a special meal. Both authors were involved in a wedding in coastal Texas where a homeless man came into the church to avoid a bad rain storm. He enjoyed both the wedding and the reception before leaving.

Whether in the first century or the twenty-first century, the feast is a way to celebrate. The ancient wedding feast was a celebration of a couple beginning their life together. The Todah was a celebration of salvation from a near-death experience. Harvest feasts celebrated the gathering of life-sustaining crops. The banquet was a celebration of friendship. Likewise, we celebrate anniversaries, holidays, birthdays, promotions at work, buying new homes, and a myriad of other special events by sharing a special meal with special people. Today, we tend to celebrate with an extravagant meal at a special restaurant. Two thousand years ago, the celebration likely included a special sacrifice and then a feast lovingly prepared and shared with family and friends.

The authors find it fascinating that these characteristics of feasting are also traits of worship. The worship of almost all religions builds community even while it defines that community and differentiates it from others. It provides worshipers with a sense of their history in the telling of sacred stories from scriptures. Worship is also an opportunity for hospitality and generosity, where the stranger is welcomed as an angel. And last, worship is a celebration. Is it any wonder that for most of the history of humanity, worship included food and feasting? This was even true of the early Christian church.

Join the Feast

Reproducing a historical feast is always a bit problematic. At least some of the ingredients no longer exist. The few instructions we have from most periods of history are more guidelines than they are modern recipes, with no measurements or detailed, step-by-step directions. To some extent, we are guessing how the finished product tasted. Yet we believe that the modern cook can learn a lot about the history and culture of a people by cooking, eating, and studying food and feasting.

Perhaps it is time to separate ourselves from our fast-food culture. We must rediscover the wonder of preparing special food. The tradition of the Shabbat, a weekly feast for family and friends, should be recovered. In our introduction we challenged you the reader to join the feast. We hope you will specifically create a first-century feast. By doing so, we predict that you will experience something of the time when Jesus lived, taught, and ate. We encourage you to form groups at church or temple and in your neighborhoods. Suggest a chapter to read and then assign recipes for your friends to prepare. Then come together, eat, drink, and enjoy each other's company, setting aside at least part of the meal to discuss what you have read. Our hope is that our readers have the best-fed book clubs in the nation.

But ultimately, what we really desire is that you simply cook for your family and friends. We hope that you will use the best and freshest ingredients you can find and, with love and care, prepare your favorite foods to be enjoyed by good friends. The food for the feast does not have to be fancy. We learned that it does not even need to include meat. But it does need to be an offering of generosity and hospitality.

Join the feast. And in all things, remember the poor and those who have less than we do. Following the teachings and example of Jesus, we can even invite them to join us at the table.

Notes

Chapter 2

1. Winifred Walker, *All the Plants of the Bible* (New York: Harper and Bros., 1957), p. 90.

2. At least one author believes that Jonah's gourd was the fruit of the castor oil tree, the Hebrew name meaning "nauseous to the taste." Castor oil was sometimes used as fuel for lamps. Walker, *All the Plants of the Bible*, p. 94.

3. "And these are herbs through [eating of] which a person fulfills his obligation on Passover: lettuce, chicory, pepperwort, endives, and dandelion." Pesahim 2:6, Jacob Neusner (trans.), *The Mishnah: A New Translation* (New Haven, CT: Yale University Press, 1988), p. 232.

4. Maguelonne Toussaint-Samat, *A History of Food* (Oxford: Blackwell, 1992), p. 623.

5. Toussaint-Samat, *History of Food*, pp. 519–20.

6. See Joseph D. Vehling, *Apicius: Cookery and Dining in Imperial Rome* (New York: Dover, 1977).

Chapter 3

1. We use the commonly accepted acronyms of BCE for Before Common Era and CE for Common Era.

2. K. C. Hanson and Douglas E. Oakman, *Palestine in the Time of Jesus: Social Structures and Social Conflicts* (Minneapolis, MN: Fortress Press, 1998), pp. 104–5. In addition, as much as 65 to 70 percent of the land was used for agriculture, compared to 40 percent in Israel today.

3. Andrea M. Berlin, "What's for Dinner? The Answer Is in the Pot," *Biblical Archaeology Review* 25, no. 6 (November–December 1999).

4. Ketubot 5:5, Jacob Neusner (trans.), *The Mishnah: A New Translation* (New Haven, CT: Yale University Press, 1988), p. 388. Also, E. P. Sanders, *Judaism: Practice and Belief, 63 BCE–66 CE* (London: SCM Press, 1992), p. 122. The Mishnah is a collection of ancient oral rabbinical teachings that were recorded around the year 200 CE.

5. Maguelonne Toussaint-Samat, *A History of Food* (Oxford: Blackwell, 1992), pp. 203–4.

6. Ibid.

7. There is an exception. Both unleavened and leavened breads are offered at a sacrifice of thanksgiving. See chapter 10 for a more detailed description of the thanksgiving sacrifice and feast.

8. See Exodus 12 and chapter 8 in this book for a more detailed description of the Passover and the role of unleavened bread.

Chapter 4

1. S. Applebaum, "Economic Life in Palestine," in *The Jewish People in the First Century* (Amsterdam: Van Gorcum, 1976), p. 657.

2. Carey Ellen Walsh, *The Fruit of the Vine: Viticulture in Ancient Israel* (Winona Lake, IN: Eisenbrauns, 2000), p. 158.

3. Applebaum, "Economic Life in Palestine," pp. 659–60.

4. Miriam Vamosh, *Daily Life at the time of Jesus* (Herzlia, Israel: Palphot, 2007), p. 66. See also Applebaum, "Economic Life in Palestine."

5. It should be recognized that by the time of Jesus there were rabbis who interpreted "strangers" as those non-Jews who were proselytes, or gentiles that were converting to Judaism, thus restricting whom one had to legally help. See Joachim Jeremias, *Jerusalem in the Time of Jesus* (Philadelphia: Fortress Press, 1969), pp. 328–29.

6. The dowry from a provincial bride marrying a man from Jerusalem was said to be "her weight in gold," reflecting the high cost of city living. Joachim Jeremias, *Jerusalem in the Time of Jesus* (Philadelphia: Fortress Press, 1969). pp. 120–21.

7. See, e.g., Zerwick, *A Grammatical Analysis of the Greek New Testament*, vol. 1 (Rome: Biblical Institute Press, 1974), p. 16.

8. Josephus, *Antiquities*, Book 17.190. See *The Works of Josephus*, trans. William Whiston (Peabody, MA: Hendrickson Publishers, 1987), p. 464.

9. Maguelonne Toussaint-Samat, *History of Food* (Oxford: Blackwell, 1992), pp. 203–4.

10. Ibid., p. 205.

11. The Romans were an exception. They especially liked the more bitter flavor of olive oil made from green olives, so these were crushed and pressed.

12. Pliny, *Natural History* 13.19. See Pliny the Elder, *Natural History*, Book 13, trans. H. Rackham (Cambridge, MA: Harvard University Press, 1950, 1961).

13. Anointing with oil was part of the ancient ritual of baptism. See Hippolytus, *Apostolic Tradition*, in Geoffrey Cuming, *Hippolytus: A Text for Students* (Bramcote, UK: Grove Books, 1976), p. 20.

14. Ibid., p. 11.

Chapter 5

1. However, there were some ancient peoples that practiced a Sabbath style rest. For example, both the ancient Canaanites and Babylonians practiced a seventh-day cessation from agricultural work. The Hebrews were the first to tie the day to worship of God.

2. E. P. Sanders, *Judaism Practice and Belief, 63 BCE–66 CE* (London: SCM Press, 1992), p. 209.

3. Shabbat 14:2, Jacob Neusner (trans.), *The Mishnah: A New Translation* (New Haven, CT: Yale University Press, 1988), p. 197. We understand the desire to bring holiness into everyday life through prayer and practices like those described in the Mishnah and other ancient Jewish literature. They show how ancient Jews lived their relationship with God in even the most mundane aspects of life. However, for most modern readers, many of the regulations would seem burdensome or even humorous.

4. Shabbat 1:6, ibid., p. 180.

5. Sanders, *Judaism Practice and Belief*, p. 210.

6. Josef Jungmann, *The Early Liturgy* (Notre Dame, IN: Notre Dame University Press, 1959), p. 31.

Chapter 6

1. Dennis E. Smith, *From Symposium to Eucharist* (Minneapolis, MN: Fortress Press, 2003), p. 25.

2. Ibid., p. 137.

3. Paula Wolfert, *The Cooking of the Eastern Mediterranean* (New York: HarperCollins Publishers, 1994), p. 6.

4. Smith, *From Symposium to Eucharist*, p. 34.

5. Reay Tannahill, *Food in History* (New York: Three Rivers Press, 1988), p. 81.

6. Smith, *From Symposium to Eucharist*, p. 35.

7. Bikkurim 1:3 and 3:9, Jacob Neusner (trans.), *The Mishnah: A New Translation* (New Haven, CT: Yale University Press, 1988), p. 167, 174. See also Deuteronomy 8:7–9: "For the Lord your God is bringing you into a good land . . . a land of wheat and barley, of vines and fig trees and pomegranates, a land of olive trees and honey, and land where you may eat bread without scarcity, where you will lack nothing."

8. For example, see Deuteronomy 34:3, "the Negeb, and the Plain—that is, the valley of Jericho, the city of palm trees—as far as Zoar." Also see, Judges 1:16 and 2 Chronicles 28:15.

9. See Maguelonne Toussaint-Samat, *A History of Food* (New York: Three Rivers Press, 1988), p. 676.

10. Miriam Feinberg Vamosh, *Food at the Time of the Bible* (Herzilia, Israel: Palphot), p. 43.

11. Do be careful if eating or juicing a pomegranate for the first time. The red juice causes bright red stains that are difficult to remove. The authors learned this by experience.

Chapter 7

1. The average life span was only twenty-five years, but that average was greatly skewed by the high rate of infant mortality. The child who lived to age five could expect to live to age fifty. For additional information, see Tim Parkin, *Roman Demography and Society* (Baltimore: Johns Hopkins University Press), 1992.

2. Joachim Jeremias, *Jerusalem in the Time of Jesus* (Philadelphia: Fortress Press,1969), p. 359.

3. George A. Buttrick, John Knox, Herbert G. May, Samuel Terrien, and Emory S. Bucke (eds.), *The Interpreter's Dictionary of the Bible*, vol. 3 (Nashville, TN: Abingdon Press, 1962), p. 285.

4. Michael L. Satlow, *Jewish Marriage in Antiquity* (Princeton, NJ: Princeton University Press, 2001), p. 65

5. Tom Standage, *A History of the World in 6 Glasses* (New York: Walker & Company), p. 62.

6. Ibid., p. 43.

7. Patrick E. McGovern, *Ancient Wine: The Search for the Origins of Viniculture* (Princeton, NJ: Princeton University Press, 2003), p. 304.

8. Ibid., p. 238.

9. Grape juice remained nonalcoholic only for a very short period of time. Nonalcoholic grape juice is a modern phenomenon made possible by pasteurization. In 1869, Dr. Thomas B. Welch was the first to successfully pasteurize grape juice. A physician and dentist, he pasteurized the juice to make an *unfermented sacramental wine* for fellow church members.

10. Standage, *A History of the World in 6 Glasses*, p. 57.

11. Ibid.

12. Ibid. pp. 74–75.

Chapter 8

1. E. P. Sanders, *Judaism: Practice and Belief 63 BCE–66 CE* (London: SCM Press, 1992), p. 128.

2. There is mixed evidence as to whether some Jews who lived in foreign countries observed Passover away from the temple. Certainly Passover was observed at the home a thousand years earlier, before the temple was built. There is, however, no doubt that the vast majority of Jews waited to go to Jerusalem.

3. See Joachim Jeremias, *Jerusalem in the Time of Jesus* (Philadelphia: Fortress Press, 1969), pp. 83–84, esp. footnote 24 for an excellent discussion of the population of Jerusalem and attendance of the festivals at the time of Jesus. For a different perspective, Sanders, in *Judaism*, writes that the number of pilgrims for Passover might have been as many as 300,000 to 500,000, pp. 125–28.

4. Jeremias, *Jerusalem in the Time of Jesus*, pp. 60–61.

5. Sanders, *Judaism*, p. 138.

6. Pesahim 10:1–3, Jacob Neusner (trans.), *The Mishnah: A New Translation* (New Haven, CT: Yale University Press, 1988), p. 249. For another critical translation, see also Baruch M. Bokser, *The Origins of the Seder* (Berkeley: University of California Press, 1984), pp. 29–30.

7. Pesahim 10:5, Neusner, p. 250. See also Exodus: 13:8.

8. Bokser, *Origins of the Seder*, p. 32.

9. Were the Hallel psalms actually sung at the Passover feast? We know they were sung as part of the seder after the destruction of the temple in 70 CE, but there is a question as to whether they were sung before that time. We know that the men of the family had just heard them sung at the sacrifice by the temple choir and there may not have been a need to repeat them at home. Then again, we also know that the Hallel psalms were well known and that songs were sung at the Passover feast. Likely they were part of the celebration, but maybe not in as formal a way as later.

10. *Afikoman* literally means "that which comes after" or "dessert." Before 70 CE, the feast concluded with the taste of lamb, so typical first-century desserts (afikoman) such as nuts, pastries, and dried fruits were not served. In later centuries, with lamb absent from the menu, the unleavened bread ended the meal and became the afikoman, or "that which comes after."

Chapter 9

1. Winton Thomas, ed., *Documents from Old Testament Times* (New York: Harper & Row, Publishers, 1958), p. 201. See also, James B. Pritchard, ed., *The Ancient Near East, Vol. 1* (Princeton, NJ: Princeton University Press, 1958), p. 209.

2. Carey Ellen Walsh, *The Fruit of the Vine: Viticulture in Ancient Israel* (Winona Lake, IN: Eisenbrauns, 2000), p. 60.

3. This is often the way traditions develop. Over time, the practical roots of an action or tradition take on a religious or civil significance that was not connected to the original meaning. In the case of Booths, a harvest festival celebrated around the construction of a harvest booth became in part a celebration of the Exodus with the harvest booth used as a symbol of Israel's forty years in the wilderness. By the first century CE, the Festival of Booths contained elements of both a harvest and religious festival.

4. Sukkah 1:1, 3, Jacob Neusner (trans.), *The Mishnah: A New Translation* (New Haven, CT: Yale University Press, 1988), pp. 279–80.

5. Sukkah 4:9, ibid., p. 288. The Sadducees did not approve of the water rite because it was not prescribed in the Torah (first five books of the Old Testament).

They would purposefully make mistakes during the ritual, at least until one of them was pelted with citrons.

6. Sukkah 5:4, ibid., p. 289.

7. Sukkah 5:3, ibid.

8. Sukkah 5:1, ibid., p. 288.

9. A number of books have been published recently describing the role of cultivating grain with the advancement of civilization. For example, see Jared Diamond, *Guns, Germs, and Steel: The Fates of Human Societies* (New York: Norton, 1997) and Tom Standage, *An Edible History of Humanity* (New York: Walker, 2009).

10. Bulgur, cracked wheat, and pearled barley are available in health food stores and gourmet markets and many grocery stores. Cracked wheat is simply that, the wheat berry is cracked into several pieces. Pearled barley is a barley kernel with the bran removed.

Chapter 10

1. K. C. Hanson and Douglas E. Oakman, *Palestine in the Time of Jesus: Social Structures and Social Conflicts* (Minneapolis, MN: Fortress Press, 1998), pp. 142–43.

2. Doug first became intrigued by the Todah while in seminary, listening to the lectures of Dr. Larimore Holland on the subject. We are also especially indebted to authors Hartmut Gese and Dennis R. Lindsay for their exploration of the Todah and its possible influence on Christian theology and worship.

3. Hartmut Gese, "The Origin of the Lord's Supper," in *Essays on Biblical Theology* (Minneapolis, MN: Augsburg Publishing House, 1981), p. 128.

4. Ibid., p. 129.

5. Zebahim 5:6. Jacob Neusner (trans.), *The Mishnah: A New Translation* (New Haven, CT: Yale University Press, 1988), p. 708.

6. Psalm 116 is a Todah Song, a song of thanksgiving, likely written and used at a Todah sacrifice or meal. Other psalms of thanksgiving for deliverance include psalms 16, 30, 34, 40, 103, and 138.

7. See Jean Soler, "Biblical Reasons: The Dietary Rules of the Ancient Hebrews," in Albert Sonnenfeld, *Food: A Culinary History* (New York: Penguin Books, 1996), pp. 46–54.

Chapter 11

1. K. C. Hanson and Douglas E. Oakman, *Palestine in the Time of Jesus: Social Structures and Social Conflicts* (Minneapolis, MN: Fortress Press, 1998), p. 106. See also Matthew 9:9; Mark 2:15. Alternatively, some scholars believe that he might have worked as a tax collector for a major trade route that happened to skirt around the northern end of the Sea of Galilee within three miles of Capernaum.

2. Ibid., p. 109.

3. Underground economies continue to exist, even in the United States. A recent article in the *New York Times* describes an underground economy in New York City where one or two cigarettes at a time are sold on the street in clear violation of the law. The underground vendors are allowing customers to circumvent the current cost of $12.50 for a full pack of cigarettes that includes a number of taxes designed to force New Yorkers to quit smoking. Joseph Goldstein, "A Cigarette for 75 Cents, 2 for $1: The Brisk, Shady Sale of 'Loosies,'" *New York Times*, April 5, 2011, p. A1.

4. Hanson and Oakman, *Palestine in the Time of Jesus*, p. 110. See also Miriam Feinberg Vamosh, *Daily Life at the Time of Jesus* (Herzlia, Israel: Palphot, 2007), pp. 62–65.

5. The authors know from personal experience that a lake this size can become quite choppy with a strong wind. On a windy day, a lake near their home in Dallas that was three miles wide would be filled with white caps and would capsize any boat away from shore.

6. See also Matthew 4:19, Luke 5:10. The image of sending fishermen was also used by Jeremiah in 16:16.

7. See John Dominic Crossan, *The Historical Jesus: The Life of a Mediterranean Jewish Peasant* (San Francisco: HarperSanFrancisco, 1991), p. 410.

8. Shebiit 7:4, Jacob Neusner, *The Mishnah: A New Translation* (New Haven, CT: Yale University Press, 1988), p. 84. "Hunters of wild animals, fowl or fish who accidently caught unclean animals are permitted to sell such unclean animals."

9. Maguelonne Toussaint-Samat, *A History of Food* (New York: Three Rivers Press, 1988), p. 300.

10. Apicius contains an entire chapter on sauces for fish, though some food scholars believe the chapter was originally a Greek treatise that was translated for Apicius's cooks in the first century. Food historians agree that most Roman cooks preferred to leave nothing in its original state.

11. Toussaint-Samat, *History of Food*, p. 457.

12. To understand the significance of salt as a flavoring, try eating a small piece of cooked meat, such as a steak or hamburger, with absolutely no salt or other seasoning added, either before or after cooking. Then eat more, gradually adding more salt with each bite.

13. The Romans seemed to have ingested lead from a number of sources. For example, much of their drinking water was transported in lead pipes.

Chapter 12

1. The maternal side of Doug's family came from Missouri and always ate bread dressing with their thanksgiving dinner. The family experienced a degree of crisis when a brother-in-law from Kentucky introduced the family to his tradition of cornbread dressing!

Bibliography

Anderson, Bernhard W. *Understanding the Old Testament*, 3rd edition. Englewood Cliffs, NJ: Prentice-Hall, 1975.

Applebaum, S. "Economic Life in Palestine." In *The Jewish People in the First Century: Historical Geography, Political History, Social, Cultural and Religious Life and Institutions, vol. 2.* Edited by S. Safrai and M. Stern. Amsterdam: Van Gorcum, 1976.

Bahr, Gordon J. "The Seder of Passover and the Eucharistic Words." In *Essays in Greco-Roman and Related Talmudic Literature.* Edited by Harry M. Orlinsky. New York: KTAV, 1977.

Berlin, Andrea M. "What's for Dinner? The Answer is in the Pot." *Biblical Archaeology Review*, Nov/Dec 1999.

Bokser, Baruch M. *The Origins of the Seder: The Passover Rite and Early Rabbinic Judaism.* Berkley: University of California Press, 1984.

———. "Ritualizing the Seder." *Journal of the American Academy of Religion* 56, no. 3, Autumn, 1988.

Bradshaw, Paul F. *Eucharistic Origins.* London: Society for Promoting Christian Knowledge (SPCK), 2004.

Brown, Raymond. *An Introduction to the New Testament.* New York: Doubleday, 1997.

Buttrick, George Arthur, (ed.). *The Interpreter's Dictionary of the Bible: An Illustrated Encyclopedia* (*IDB*), 5 volumes. Nashville, TN: Abingdon, 1962.

Carroll, Ricki. *Home Cheese Making: Recipes for 75 Homemade Cheeses*, 3rd edition. North Adams, MA: Storey, 2002.

Capon, Robert Farrar. *The Supper of the Lamb: A Culinary Reflection.* New York: Smithmark Publishers, 1967, 1996.

Chiffolo, Anthony F., and Rayner W. Hesse Jr. *Cooking with the Bible: Biblical Food, Feasts, and Lore.* Westport, CT: Greenwood, 2006.

241

Counihan, Carole, and Penny Van Esterik (eds.). *Food and Culture: A Reader*. New York: Routledge, 1997.

Crossan, John Dominic. *The Historical Jesus: The Life of a Mediterranean Jewish Peasant*. San Francisco: HarperSanFrancisco, 1991.

Cullman, Oscar. *Early Christian Worship*. London: SCM Press, 1953.

Cuming, Geoffrey J. *Hippolytus: A Text for Students*. Bramcote, UK: Grove Books, 1976.

Diamond, Jared, *Guns, Germs, and Steel: The Fates of Human Societies*. New York: Norton, 1999.

Feely-Harnik, Gillian. "Religion and Food: An Anthropological Perspective." *Journal of the American Academy of Religion* 63, no. 3, Autumn, 1995.

Feely-Harnik, Gillian. *The Lord's Table: The Meaning of Food in Early Judaism and Christianity*. Washington, DC: Smithsonian Books, 1981.

Fredman, Ruth Gruber. *The Passover Seder: Afikoman in Exile*. Philadelphia: University of Pennsylvania Press, 1981.

Gese, Hartmut. "The Origin of the Lord's Supper." In *Essays on Biblical Theology*. Translated by Keith Crim. Minneapolis, MN: Augsburg, 1981.

Grant, Mark. *Roman Cookery: Ancient Recipes for Modern Kitchens*. London: Serif, 1999.

Greenspan, Dorie. *Baking with Julia*. New York: William Morrow, 1996.

Hanson, K. C., and Douglas E. Oakman. *Palestine in the Time of Jesus: Social Structures and Social Conflicts*. Minneapolis, MN: Fortress, 1998.

Jeremias, Joachim. *Jerusalem in the Time of Jesus: An Investigation into Economic and Social Conditions during the New Testament Period*. Philadelphia: Fortress, 1969.

———. *The Eucharistic Words of Jesus*. London: SCM Press, 1966.

Juengst, Sara Covin. *Breaking Bread: The Spiritual Significance of Food*. Louisville, KY: Westminster/John Knox Press, 1992.

Jungmann, Josef A. *The Early Liturgy: To the Time of Gregory the Great*. Notre Dame, IN: University of Notre Dame Press, 1959.

Kosofsky, Scott-Martin. *The Book of Customs: A Complete Handbook for the Jewish Year*. San Francisco: HarperSanFrancisco, 2004.

Kurlansky, Mark. *Salt: A World History*. New York: Walker and Company, 2002.

Lindsay, Dennis R. "Todah and Eucharist: The Celebration of the Lord's Supper as a 'Thank Offering' in the Early Church." *Restoration Quarterly* 39, no. 2, 1997.

McGovern, Patrick E. *Ancient Wine: The Search for the Origins of Viniculture*. Princeton, NJ: Princeton University Press, 2003.

Montanari, Massimo. *Food Is Culture*. Translated by Albert Sonnenfeld. New York: Columbia University Press, 2006.

Morse, Kitty. *A Biblical Feast: Foods from the Holy Land*. Berkeley, CA: Ten Speed, 1998.

Neusner, Jacob (trans.). *The Mishnah: A New Translation*. New Haven, CT: Yale University Press, 1988.

———. *Judaism in the Beginning of Christianity*. Philadelphia: Fortress, 1984.

Pritchard, James B. (ed.). *The Ancient Near East: An Anthology of Texts and Pictures*, *vol. 1*. Princeton, NJ: Princeton University Press, 1958.

Ranasinghe, Alex. "The Betrothal and Marriage Customs of the Hebrews during the Time of Christ." *Folklore* 81, no. 1, Spring, 1970.

Safrai, S. "Home and Family." In *The Jewish People in the First Century: Historical Geography, Political History, Social, Cultural and Religious Life and Institutions, vol. 2*. Edited by S. Safrai and M. Stern. Amsterdam: Van Gorcum, 1976.

——. "Religion in Everyday Life." In *The Jewish People in the First Century: Historical Geography, Political History, Social, Cultural and Religious Life and Institutions, vol. 2*. Edited by S. Safrai and M. Stern. Amsterdam: Van Gorcum, 1976.

——. "The Temple." In *The Jewish People in the First Century: Historical Geography, Political History, Social, Cultural and Religious Life and Institutions, vol. 2*. Edited by S. Safrai and M. Stern. Amsterdam: Van Gorcum, 1976.

Sanders, E. P. *Judaism: Practice & Belief 63 BCE–66 CE*. London: SCM Press, 1992.

Satlow, Michael L. *Jewish Marriage in Antiquity*. Princeton, NJ: Princeton University Press, 2001.

Seasoltz, R. Kevin (ed.). *Living Bread, Saving Cup: Readings of the Eucharist*. Collegeville, MN: The Liturgical Press, 1982.

Shepherd, Massey H. Jr. "Are Both the Synoptics and John Correct about the Date of Jesus' Death?" *Journal of Biblical Literature* 80, no. 2, June, 1961.

Smith, Jeff. *The Frugal Gourmet Keeps the Feast: Past, Present, and Future*. New York: William Morrow, 1995.

Smith, Dennis E. *From Symposium to Eucharist: The Banquet in the Early Christian World*. Minneapolis, MN: Fortress, 2003.

Sonnenfeld, Albert, *Food: A Culinary History from Antiquity to the Present*. New York: Penguin Books, 1999.

Stadd, Arlene. *Cooking with the Ancients: The Bible Food Book*. Aurora, CO: Glenbridge, 1997.

Standage, Tom. *A History of the World in 6 Glasses*. New York: Walker, 2005.

——. *An Edible History of Humanity*. New York: Walker, 2009.

Stein, S. "The Influence of Symposia Literature on the Literary Form of the Pesah Haggadah" (1957). In *Essays in Greco-Roman and Related Talmudic Literature*. Edited by Harry M. Orlinsky. New York: KTAV, 1977.

Strong, Roy. *Feast: A History of Grand Eating*. Orlando, FL: Harcourt, 2002.

Swenson, Allan A. *Foods Jesus Ate and How to Grow Them*. New York: Skyhorse, 2008.

Tannahill, Reay. *Food in History*. New York: Three Rivers, 1988.

Thomas, D. Winton (ed.). *Documents from Old Testament Times*. New York: Harper & Row, 1958.

Toussaint-Samat, Maguelonne. *A History of Food*. Translated by Anthea Bell. New York: Three Rivers, 1988.

Vamosh, Miriam Feinberg. *Daily Life at the Time of Jesus*. Herzilia, Israel: Palphot, 2007.

———. *Food at the Time of the Bible: From Adam's Apple to the Last Supper*. Herzilia, Israel: Palphot, 2007.

Vehling, Joseph Dommers (trans.). *Apicius: Cookery and Dining in Imperial Rome*. New York: Dover, 1977.

Walsh, Carey Ellen. *The Fruit of the Vine: Viticulture in Ancient Israel*. Harvard Semitic Monographs, edited by Peter Machinist. Winona Lake, IN: Eisenbrauns, 2000.

Walker, Winifred. *All the Plants of the Bible*. New York: Harper and Bros., 1957.

Werblowski, R. J. Zwi, and Geoffrey Wigoder (eds.). *The Oxford Dictionary of the Jewish Religion*. New York: Oxford University Press, 1997.

Whiston, William. (trans.). *The Works of Josephus*. Peabody, MA: Hendrickson, 1987.

Wolfert, Paula. *The Cooking of the Eastern Mediterranean: 215 Healthy, Vibrant, and Inspired Recipes*. New York: HarperCollins, 1994.

Wright, Clifford A. *Mediterranean Vegetables*. Boston: The Harvard Common Press, 2001.

Zerwick, Max, and Mary Grosvenor. *A Grammatical Analysis of the Greek New Testament, vol. 1*. Rome: Biblical Institute Press, 1974.

General Index

Aaronic blessing, 196
afikoman, 152, 237n10
altar. *See* temple, altar
Altar Dance, 181
amphora, amphorae, 59–60, 128–29,
    182, 213
animals, domesticated 99, 185, 201,
    203
Apicius, 7, 25, 109, 134, 239n10
Assyria, Assyrians, 4, 30
Athens, 13

Bacchus. *See* Dionysius
Baladi cow, 202
banquet, 2, 5, 7, 11, 16, 21, 25, 29, 40,
    56, 68, 80, 93–103, 105–8, 122–24,
    126, 130, 150, 154, 163, 176, 195,
    198, 204, 212, 227–28, 230–31;
    couch, couches, 95–98, 100, 150;
    entertainment at, 101–3; guests, 93–
    97, 99–102; Jesus, 95–97, 99, 102;
    room, 24, 56, 95, 96–101, 123, 198
beer, 14, 39, 42, 128, 228
bees, 18, 53, 84–85, 177
Bethsaida, 215

betrothal, 96, 119–20; feast, 96, 119
blood, 36, 141, 146, 148, 153, 166–67,
    193–94, 196–98, 200, 204–5;
    prohibited, 36, 204–205
Booths, Feast of (Tabernacles), 143,
    176, 181–84, 188, 237n3
brazier, 34
bread, unleavened, 37, 39–40, 141,
    143–45, 147–51, 161–65, 167–68
breakfast, 35, 211–12, 217
bride, 96, 115–17, 119–25, 131, 234n6
bridegroom, groom, 1, 96–97, 115–17,
    119–22, 124–26, 131; blessing, 119,
    121–22
bridesmaid, 120, 124

Cana, wedding at, 97, 126
Canaan, Canaanite, 39, 127, 235n1
Canaanite woman, 38, 118
Capernaum, 215–16, 238
Cato, 8, 138
cereal offering, 39
Columella, 8
cookware (pots, pans, bowls, kettles), 2,
    14, 21, 34, 81, 84, 203, 227, 230

Food Index

almond, almonds, 17, 19, 20, 47, 99,
105, 132–33, 145, 149, 157, 164;
dip, recipe for, 133

anise, 24

appetizer, 15, 17, 35, 71, 94, 96, 107,
131, 148–50, 164, 223

apricots, 18–20, 33, 59, 87, 90–91, 125,
157, 192; braised chicken with figs
and, recipe for, 90; poached, and
yogurt, recipe for, 91

artichokes, 17

asparagus, 16–17, 93, 108–109, 175

barbels, 218

barley, 13–15, 29, 32, 38, 43–44, 55,
59–60, 77, 103–4, 125, 128, 131–33,
135, 145, 151, 176–78, 181, 185–87,
189, 196, 201–2, 206, 228, 235,
238; and wheat bread, recipe for,
132; polenta, 18; stew, beef ribs and,
recipe for, 135

bay leaves, 8, 111–12, 138

beans. *See* legumes

beef, 9, 22, 99–100, 132, 135, 201–2,
228; short ribs and barley stew,
recipe for, 135

beer, 14, 39, 42, 128, 228

beets, 17

bitter herbs, 15–16, 145, 148–49, 152,
154, 156, 161, 164, 167–68. *See also*
individual herbs and lettuces

blackberries, 20

black coriander, (nutmeg flower,
fitches), 24

bread, 2, 6–10, 14, 25, 29–32, 34–46,
48, 53–55, 57, 62, 66, 68, 70–71,
79–83, 85–89, 98, 102–3, 105, 107–
8, 110, 117–18, 122–23, 125–26,
131, 132–33, 138–39, 141, 143–45,
147–56, 161–65, 167–68, 175–76,
178, 181–82, 185–86, 188–89, 193,
196–98, 200–1, 206–7, 212, 216–17,
222–23, 227–28, 230, 234n7,
235n7, 237n10; barley and wheat,
recipe for, 132–33; egg, recipe for,
87–88; flat (pita), recipe for, 188–89;

About the Authors

Douglas E. Neel is an Episcopal priest and currently serves a parish in Colorado. He also is a lecturer on ancient food and feasts. He previously owned a Dallas-based catering company, *Manna Catering*, which specialized in replicating first-century meals. He lives in Pagosa Springs, where he makes his own cheese, wine, and beer.

Joel A. Pugh is a CPA and president of a Texas-based research and development company. He is also an inventor with seventeen patents. He is a student of historical economics and the impact that food production and distribution have on historical events. He lives in Dallas, where he cooks, bakes bread, and brews beer.

CPSIA information can be obtained at www.ICGtesting.com
Printed in the USA
BVOW070408180612

292852BV00001B/10/P